DE CIVE

THOMAS HOBBES

Philosophicall Rudiments Concerning Government and Society. Or, A Dissertation Concerning Man in his severall habitudes and respects, as the Member of a Society, first Secular, and than Sacred.

Containing The Elements of Civill Politie in the Agreement which it hath both with Naturall and Divine Lawes.

In which is demonstrated, Both what the Origine of Justice is, and wherein the Essence of Christian Religion doth consist. Together with The Nature, Limits and Qualifications both of Regiment and Subjection.

By Thomas Hobbes.

London, Printed by J.C. for R. Royston, at the Angel in Ivie—Lane. 1651.

To the Right Honourable, William, Earle of Devonshire, My most honoured Lord May it please your Lordship,

It was the speech of the Roman people (to whom the name of King had been render'd odious, as well by the tyrannie of the Tarquins, as by the Genius and Decretals of that City) 'Twas the speech I say of the publick, however pronounced from a private mouth, (if yet Cato the Censor were no more than such) That all Kings are to be reckon'd amongst ravenous Beasts. But what a Beast of prey was the Roman people, whilst with its conquering Eagles it erected its proud Trophees so far and wide over the world, bringing the Africans, the Asiaticks, the Macedonians, and the Achaeans, with many other despoyled Nations, into a specious bondage, with the pretence of preferring them to be Denizens of Rome? So that if Cato's saying were a wise one, 'twas every whit as wise that of Pontius Telesinus; who flying about with open mouth through all the Companies of his Army, (in that famous encounter which he had with Sylla) cryed out, That Rome her selfe, as well as Sylla, was to be raz'd; for that there would alwayes be Wolves and Depraedatours of their Liberty, unlesse the Forrest that lodg'd them were grubb'd up by the roots. To speak impartially, both sayings are very true; That Man to Man is a kind of God; and that Man to Man is an arrant Wolfe. The first is true, if we compare Citizens amongst themselves; and the second, if we compare Cities. In the one, there's some analogie of similitude with the Deity, to wit, Justice and Charity, the twin—sisters of peace: But in the other, Good men must defend themselves by taking to them for a Sanctuary the two daughters of War, Deceipt and Violence: that is in plaine termes a meer brutall Rapacity: which although men object to one another as a reproach, by an inbred custome which they have of beholding their own actions in the persons of other men, wherein, as in a Mirroir, all things on the left side appeare to be on the right, all things on the right side to be as plainly on the left; yet the naturall right of preservation which we all receive from the uncontroulable Dictates of Necessity, will not admit it to be a Vice, though it confesse it to be an Unhappinesse. Now that with Cato himselfe, (a person of so great a renowne for wisdome) Animosity should so prevaile instead of Judgement, and partiality instead of Reason, that the very same thing which he thought equall in his popular State, he should censure as unjust in a Monarchical, other men perhaps may have leisure to admire. But I have been long since of this opinion, That there was never yet any more than vulgar prudence that had the luck of being acceptable to the Giddy people; but either it hath not been understood, or else having been so, hath been levell'd and cryed downe. The more eminent Actions and Apothegms both of the Greeks and Romans have been indebted for their Eulogies not so much to the Reason, as to the Greatnesse of them, and very many times to that prosperous usurpation (with which our Histories doe so mutually upbraid each other) which as a conquering Torrent carryes all before it, as well publick Agents as publick Actions, in the streame of Time.

Wisdome properly so call'd is nothing else but this, The perfect knowledge of the Truth in all matters whatsoever. Which being derived from the Registers and Records of Things, and that as 'twere through the Conduit of certain definite Appellations, cannot possibly be the work of a suddaine Acutenesse, but of a well−ballanc'd Reason, which by the Compendium of a word, we call philosophy. For by this it is, that a way is open'd to us, in which we travell from the contemplation of particular things to the Inference or result of universall Actions. Now look how many sorts of things there are which properly fall within the cognizance of humane reason, into so many branches does the tree of philosophy divide it selfe. And from the diversity of the matter about which they are conversant, there hath been given to those branches a diversity of Names too: For treating of Figures, tis call'd Geometry; of motion, physick; of naturall right, Moralls; put all together, and they make up philosophy. Just as the British, the Atlantick, and the Indian Seas, being diversly christen'd from the diversity of their shoares, doe notwithstanding all together make up The Ocean. And truly the Geometricians have very admirably perform'd their part. For whatsoever assistance doth accrew to the life of man, whether from the observation of the Heavens, or from the description of the Earth, from the notation of Times, or from the remotest Experiments of Navigation; Finally, whatsoever things they are in which this present Age doth differ from the rude simplenesse of Antiquity, we must acknowledge to be a debt which we owe meerly to Geometry. If the Morall philosophers had as happily discharg'd their duty, I know not what could have been added by humane Industry to the completion of that happinesse, which is consistent with humane life. For were the nature of humane Actions as distinctly knowne, as the nature of Quantity in Geometricall Figures, the strength of Avarice and Ambition, which is sustained by the erroneous opinions of the Vulgar, as touching the nature of Right and Wrong, would presently faint and languish; And Mankinde should enjoy such an Immortall peace, that (unlesse it were for habitation, on supposition that the Earth should grow too narrow for her Inhabitants) there would hardly be left any pretence for war. But now on the contrary, that neither the Sword nor the pen should be allowed any Cessation; That the knowledge of the Law of Nature should lose its growth, not advancing a whit beyond its antient stature; that there should still be such siding with the severall factions of philosophers, that the very same Action should bee decryed by some, and as much elevated by others; that the very same man should at severall times embrace his severall

opinions, and esteem his own Actions farre otherwise in himselfe than he does in others; These I say are so many signes, so many manifest Arguments, that what hath hitherto been written by Morall philosophers, hath not made any progress in the knowledge of the Truth; but yet have took with the world, not so much by giving any light to the understanding, as entertainment to the Affections, whilest by the successefull Rhetorications of their speech they have confirmed them in their rashly received opinions. So that this part of philosophy hath suffered the same destiny with the publick Wayes, which lye open to all passengers to traverse up and down or the same lot with high wayes and open streets; Some for divertisement, and some for businesse; so that what with the Impertinencies of some, and the Altercations of others, those wayes have never a seeds time, and therefore yield never a harvest. The onely reason of which unluckines should seem to be this; That amongst all the writers of that part of philosophy, there is not one that hath used an idoneous principle of Tractation: For we may not, as in a Circle, begin the handling of a Science from what point we please. There is a certain Clue of Reason, whose beginning is in the dark, but by the benefit of whose Conduct, wee are led as 'twere by the hand into the clearest light, so that the principle of Tractation is to be taken from

3

that Darknesse, and then the light to be carried thither for the irradiating its doubts. As often therefore as any writer, doth either weakly forsake that Clue, or wilfully cut it asunder, he describes the Footsteps, not of his progresse in Science, but of his wandrings from it. And upon this it was, that when I applyed my Thoughts to the Investigation of Naturall Justice, I was presently advertised from the very word Justice, (wich signifies a steady Will of giving every one his Owne) that my first enquiry was to be, from whence it proceeded, that any man should call any thing rather his Owne, than another man's. And when I found that this proceeded not from Nature, but Consent, (for what Nature at first laid forth in common, men did afterwards distribute into severall Impropriations, I was conducted from thence to another Inquiry, namely to what end, and upon what Impulsives, when all was equally every mans in common, men did rather think it fitting, that every man should have his Inclosure; And I found the reason was, that from a Community of Goods, there must needs arise Contention whose enjoyment should be greatest, and from that Contention all kind of Calamities must unavoydably ensue, which by the instinct of Nature, every man is taught to shun. Having therefore thus arrived at two maximes of humane Nature, the one arising from the concupiscible part, which desires to appropriate to it selfe the use of those things in which all others have a joynt interest, the other proceeding from the rationall, which teaches every man to fly a contre–naturall Dissolution, as the greatest mischiefe that can arrive to Nature; Which principles being laid down, I seem from them to have demonstrated by a most evident connexion, in this little work of mine, first the absolute necessity of Leagues and Contracts, and thence the rudiments both of morall and of civill prudence. That Appendage which is added concerning the Regiment of God, hath been done with this intent, that the Dictates of God Almighty in the Law of nature, might not seem repugnant to the written Law, revealed to us in his word. I have also been very wary in the whole tenour of my discourse, not to meddle with the civill Lawes of any particular nation whatsoever, That is to say, I have avoyded coming a shore, which those Times have so infested both with shelves, and Tempests. At what expence of time and industry I have beene in this scrutiny after Truth, I am not ignorant; but to what purpose, I know not. For being partiall Judges of our selves, we lay a partiall estimate upon our own productions. I therefore offer up this Book to your Lordships, not favour, but censure first, as having found by many experiments, that it is not the credit of the Author, nor the newnesse of the work, nor yet the ornament of the style, but only the weight of Reason, which recommends any Opinion to your Lordships Favour and Approbation. If it fortune to please, that is to say, if it be sound, if it be usefull, if it be not vulgar; I humbly offer it to your Lordship as both my Glory, and my protection; But if in any thing I have erred, your Lordship will yet accept it as a Testimony of my Gratitude, for that the means of study which I enjoyed by your Lordships Goodnesse, I have employed to the procurement of your Lordships Favour. The God of Heaven crown your Lordship with length of Dayes in this earthly Station, and in the heavenly Jerusalem, with a crown of Glory.

Your Honours most humble, and most devoted Servant, Tho. Hobbs.

THE AUTHOR'S PREFACE TO THE READER

Reader, I promise thee here such things, which ordinarily promised, doe seeme to challenge the greatest attention, and I lay them here before thine eyes, whether thou regard the dignity or profit of the matter treated of, or the right method of handling it, or the honest motive, and good advice to undertake it, or lastly the moderation of the Authour. In this Book thou shalt finde briefly described the duties of men, First as Men, then as Subjects, Lastly, as Christians; under which duties are contained not only the elements of the Lawes of Nature, and of Nations, together with the true originall, and power of Justice, but also the very essence of Christian Religion it selfe, so farre forth as the measure of this my purpose could well bear it.

Which kinde of doctrine (excepting what relates to Christian Religion) the most antient Sages did judge fittest to be delivered to posterity, either curiously adorned with Verse, or clouded with Allegories, as a most beautifull and hallowed mystery of Royall authority; lest by the disputations of private men, it might be defiled; Other philosophers in the mean time, to the advantage of mankinde, did contemplate the faces, and motions of things; others, without disadvantage, their natures, and causes. But in after times, Socrates is said to have been the first, who truly loved this civill Science, although hitherto not throughly understood, yet glimmering forth as through a cloud in the government of the Common weale, and that he set so great a value on this, that utterly abandoning, and despising all other parts of philosophy, he wholly embraced this, as judging it onely worthy the labour of his minde. After him comes Plato, Aristotle, Cicero, and other philosophers, as well Greeke, as Latine. And now at length all men of all Nations, not only philosophers, but even the vulgar, have, and doe still deale with this as a matter of ease, exposed and prostitute to every Mother−wit, and to be attained without any great care or study. And which makes mainly for its dignity, those who suppose themselves to have it, or are in such employment, as they ought to have it, doe so wonderfully please themselves in its Idaea, as they easily brooke the followers of other arts to be esteemed and styled ingenuous, learned, skilfull, what you will; except prudent: for this Name, in regard of civill knowledge, they presume to be due to themselves onely. Whether therefore the worth of arts is to be weighed by the worthinesse of the persons who entertain them, or by the number of those who have written of them, or by the judgement of the wisest; certainly this must carry it, which so neerly relates to princes, and others engaged in the government of mankinde, in whose adulterate Species also the most part of men doe delight themselves, and in which the most excellent wits of philosophers have been conversant. The benefit of it when rightly delivered (that is) when derived from true principles by evident connexion, we shall then best discerne, when we shall but well have considered the mischiefes that have befallen mankinde in its counterfeit and babling form; for in such matters as are speculated for the exercise of our wits, if any errour escape us, it is without hurt; neither is there any losse, but of time onely: but in those things which every man ought to meditate for the steerage of his life, it necessarily happens, that not onely from errours, but even from ignorance it selfe, there arise offences, contentions, nay even slaughter it selfe. Look now, how great a prejudice these are, such, and so great is the benefit arising from this doctrine of morality, truly declared.

How many Kings (and those good men too) hath this one errour, That a Tyrant King might lawfully be put to death, been the slaughter of? How many throats hath this false position cut, That a prince for some causes may by some certain men be deposed? And what blood−shed hath not this erroneous doctrine caused, That Kings are not superiours to, but administrators for the multitude? Lastly, how many rebellions hath this opinion been the cause of which teacheth that the knowledge whether the commands of Kings be just or unjust, belongs to private men, and that before they yeeld obedience, they not only may, but ought to dispute them? Besides, in the morall philosophy now commonly received, there are many things no lesse dangerous than those, which it matters not now to recite. I suppose those antients foresaw this, who rather chose to have the Science of justice wrapt up in fables, than openly exposed to disputations: for before such questions began to be moved, princes did not sue for, but already exercised the supreme power. They kept their Empire entire, not by arguments, but by punishing the wicked, and protecting the good; likewise Subjects did not measure what was just by the sayings and judgements of private men, but by the Lawes of the Realme; nor were they kept in peace by disputations, but by power and authority: yea they reverenced the supreme power, whether residing in one man or in a councell, as a certain visible divinity; therefore they little used as in our

dayes, to joyn themselves with ambitious, and hellish spirits, to the utter ruine of their State; for they could not entertain so strange a phansie as not to desire the preservation of that by which they were preserved; in truth, the simplicity of those times was not yet capable of so learned a piece of folly. Wherefore it was peace, and a golden age, which ended not before that Saturn being expelled, it was taught lawfull to take up arms against Kings. This I say, the Antients not only themselves saw, but in one of their fables, they seem very aptly to have signified it to us; for they say, that when Ixion was invited by Jupiter to a banquet, he fell in love, and began to court Juno her selfe; offering to embrace her, he clasp't a clowd, from whence the Centaures proceeded, by nature halfe men, halfe horses, a fierce, a fighting, and unquiet generation; which changing the names only, is as much as if they should have said, that private men being called to Counsels of State desired to prostitute justice, the onely sister and wife of the supreme, to their own judgements, and apprehensions, but embracing a false and empty shadow instead of it, they have begotten those hermaphrodite opinions of morall philosophers, partly right and comely, partly brutall and wilde, the causes of all contentions, and blood–sheds. Since therefore such opinions are daily seen to arise, if any man now shall dispell those clowds, and by most firm reasons demonstrate that there are no authenticall doctrines concerning right and wrong, good and evill, besides the constituted Lawes in each Realme, and government; and that the question whether any future action will prove just or unjust, good or ill, is to be demanded of none, but those to whom the supreme hath committed the interpretation of his Lawes; surely he will not only shew us the high way to peace, but will also teach us how to avoyd the close, darke, and dangerous by–paths of faction and sedition, than which I know not what can be thought more profitable.

Concerning my Method, I thought it not sufficient to use a plain and evident style in what I had to deliver, except I took my begining from the very matter of civill government, and thence proceeded to its generation, and form, and the first beginning of justice; for every thing is best understood by its constitutive causes; for as in a watch, or some such small engine, the matter, figure, and motion of the wheeles, cannot well be known, except it be taken in sunder, and viewed in parts; so to make a more curious search into the rights of States, and duties of Subjects, it is necessary, (I say not to take them in sunder, but yet that) they be so considered, as if they were dissolved, (i.e.) that wee rightly understand what the quality of humane nature is, in what matters it is, in what not fit to make up a civill government, and how men must be agreed among themselves, that intend to grow up into a well–grounded State. Having therefore followed this kind of Method; In the first place I set down for a principle by experience known to all men, and denied by none, to wit, that the dispositions of men are naturally such, that except they be restrained through feare of some coercive power, every man will distrust and dread each other, and as by naturall right he may, so by necessity he will be forced to make use of the strength hee hath, toward the preservation of himself You will object perhaps, that there are some who deny this; truly so it happens, that very many do deny it. But shall I therefore seem to fight against my self because I affirm that the same men confesse, and deny the same thing? In truth I do not, but they do, whose actions disavow what their discourses approve of. We see all countries though they be at peace with their neighbours, yet guarding their Frontiers with armed men, their Townes with Walls and ports, and keeping constant watches. To what purpose is all this, if there be no feare of the neighbouring power? Wee see even in well−governed States, where there are lawes and punishments appointed for offendors, yet particular men travell not without their Sword by their sides, for their defences, neither sleep they without shutting not only their doores against their fellow Subjects, but also their Trunks and Coffers for feare of domestiques. Can men give a clearer testimony of the distrust they have each of other, and all, of all? How since they doe thus, and even Countreyes as well as men, they publiquely professe their mutuall feare and diffidence; But in disputing they deny it, thats as much as to say, that out of a desire they have to contradict others, they gainsay themselves. Some object that this principle being admitted, it would needs follow, not onely that all men were wicked (which perhaps though it seeme hard, yet we must yeeld to, since it is so clearly declar'd by holy writ) but also wicked by nature (which cannot be granted without impiety). But this, that men are evill by nature, followes not from this principle; for though the wicked were fewer than the righteous, yet because we cannot distinguish them, there is a necessity of suspecting, heeding, anticipating, subjugating, selfe−defending, ever incident to the most honest, and fairest condition'd; much lesse do's it follow that those who are wicked are so by nature, for though from nature, that is from their first birth, as they are meerly sensible Creatures, they have this disposition, that immediately as much as in them lies, they desire and doe whatsoever is best pleasing to them, that either through feare they fly from, or through hardnesse repell those dangers which approach them, yet are they not for this reason to be accounted wicked; for the affections of the minde which arise onely from the lower parts of the soule are not wicked themselves, but the actions thence proceeding may be so sometimes, as when they are either offensive, or against duty. Unlesse you give Children all they aske for, they are peevish, and cry, I and strike their parents sometimes, and all this they have from nature, yet are they free from guilt, neither may we properly call them wicked; first, because they cannot hurt; next, because wanting the free use of reason they are exempted from all duty; these when they come to riper yeares having acquired power whereby they may doe hurt, if they shall continue to doe the same things, then truly they both begin to be, and are properly accounted wicked; In so much as a wicked man is almost the same thing with a childe growne strong and sturdy, or a man of a childish disposition; and malice the same with a defect of reason in that age, when nature ought to be better governed through good education and experience. Unlesse therefore we will say that men are naturally evill, because they receive not their education and use of reason from nature, we must needs acknowledge that men may derive desire, feare, anger, and other passions from nature, and yet not impute the evill effects of those unto nature. The foundation therefore which I have laid standing firme, I demonstrate in the first place, that the state of men without civill society (which state we may properly call the state of nature) is nothing else but a meere warre of all against all; and in that warre all men have equall right unto all things; Next, that all men as soone as they arrive to understanding of this hatefull condition, doe desire (even nature it selfe compelling them) to be freed from this misery. But that this cannot be done except by compact, they all quitt that right which they have unto all things. Furthermore I declare, and confirme what the nature of compacts is; how and by what meanes the right of one might be transfer'd unto another to make their compacts valid; also what rights, and to whom they must necessarily be granted for the establishing of peace, I meane what those dictates of reason are, which may properly be term'd the Lawes of nature; and all these are contain'd in that part of this booke which I entitle Liberty.

These grounds thus layd, I shew farther what civill government, and the supreme power in it, and the divers kinds of it are; by what meanes it becomes so, what rights particular men, who intend to constitute this civill government, must so necessarily transfer from themselves on the supreme power, whether it be one man, or an assembly of men, that except they doe so it will evidently appeare to be no civill government, but the rights which all men have to all things, that is the rights of warre will still remaine. Next, I distinguish the divers kindes of it, to wit, Monarchie, Aristocratie, Democratie, and paternall Dominion, and that of Masters over their Servants; I declare how they are constituted, and I compare their severall conveniences and inconveniences each with other. Furthermore, I unfold what those things are which destroy it, and what his or their duty is who rule in chiefe. Last of all, I explicate the natures of the Law, and of sinne, and I distinguish Law from Counsell, from compact, from that which I call Right; all which I comprehend under the title of Dominion.

In the last part of it which is entituled Religion, lest that right which by strong reason I had confirm'd the Soveraigne powers in the preceding discourse have over their Subjects, might seem to be repugnant to the sacred Scriptures, I shew in the first place how it repugns not the Divine right, for as much as God overrules all rulers by nature, (i.e.) by the Dictates of naturall reason. In the second, for as much as God himselfe had a peculiar dominion over the Jewes by vertue of that antient Covenant of Circumcision. In the third, because God doth now rule over us Christians by vertue of our Covenant of Baptisme; and therefore the authority of Rulers in chiefe, or of civill government, is not at all, we see, contrary to Religion.

In the last place I declare what duties are necessarily requir'd from us, to enter into the Kingdome of Heaven; and of those I plainly demonstrate, and conclude out of evident testimonies of holy writ, according to the interpretation made by all, that the obedience which I have affirm'd to be due from particular Christian Subjects unto their Christian princes cannot possibly in the least sort be repugnant unto Christian Religion.

You have seene my Method, receive now the reason which mov'd me to write this; I was studying philosophie for my minde sake, and I had gathered together its first Elements in all kinds, and having digested them into three Sections by degrees, I thought to have written them so as in the first I would have treated of a body, and its generall properties; in the second of man and his speciall faculties, and affections; in the third, of civill government and the duties of Subjects: therefore the first Section would have contained the first philosophie, and certaine elements of physick; in it we would have considered the reasons of Time, Place, Cause, Power, Relation, Proportion, Quantity, Figure, and motion. In the second we would have beene conversant about imagination, Memory, intellect, ratiocination, appetite, will, good and Evill, honest and dishonest, and the like. What this last Section handles, I have now already shewed you. Whilest I contrive, order, pensively and slowly compose these matters, for I onely doe reason, I dispute not, it so happen'd in the interim, that my Country some few yeares before the civill warres did rage, was boyling hot with questions concerning the rights of Dominion, and the obedience due from Subjects, the true forerunners of an approaching war. And was the cause which (all those other matters deferr'd) ripen'd, and pluckt from me this third part. Therefore it happens that what was last in order, is yet come forth first in time, and the rather, because I saw that grounded on its owne principles sufficiently knowne by experience it would not stand in need of the former Sections. I have not yet made it out of a desire of praise (although if I had, I might have defended my selfe with this faire excuse, that very few doe things laudably, who are not affected with commendation) but for your sakes Readers, who I perswaded my selfe, when you should rightly apprehend and throughly understand this Doctrine I here present you with, would rather chuse to brooke with patience some inconveniences under government (because humane affairs cannot possibly be without some) than selfe opiniatedly disturb the quiet of the publique; That, weighing the justice of those things you are about, not by the perswasion and advise of private men, but by the Lawes of the Realme, you will no longer suffer ambitious men through the streames of your blood to wade to their owne power; That you will esteeme it better to enjoy your selves in the present state though perhaps not the best, than by waging warre, indeavour to procure a reformation for other men in another age, your selves in the meane while either kill'd, or consumed with age; Farthermore, for those who will not acknowledge themselves subject to the civill Magistrate, and will be exempt from all publique burthens, and yet will live under his Jurisdiction, and look for protection from the violence and injuries of others, that you would not looke on them as fellow Subjects, but esteeme them for enemies, and spies, and that yee rashly admit not for Gods Word all which either openly or privately they shall pretend to bee so. I say more plainly, if any preacher, Confessor, or Casuist, shal but say that this doctrin is agreeable with Gods word, namely, That the chief ruler, nay any private man may lawfully be put to death without the chiefes command, or that Subjects may resist, conspire, or covenant against the supreme power, that ye by no means beleeve them, but instantly declare their names. He who approves of these reasons, will also like my intention in writing this book.

Last of al, I have propounded to my self this rule through this whole discourse; First, not to define ought which concerns the justice of single actions, but leave them to be determined by the laws. Next not to dispute the laws of any government in special, that is, not to point which are the laws of any country, but to declare what the laws of all countries are. Thirdly not to seem of opinion, that there is a lesse proportion of for obedience due to an Aristocraty or Democraty, than a Monarchy; though I have endeavoured by arguments in my tenth Chapter to gain a belief in men, that Monarchy is the most commodious government (which one thing alone I confesse in this whole book not to be demonstrated, but only probably stated) yet every where I expresly say, that in all kind of Government whatsoever, there ought to be a supreme and equall power.

Fourthly, not in any wise to dispute the positions of Divines, except those which strip Subjects of their obedience, and shake the foundations of civill government. Lastly, lest I might imprudently set forth somewhat of which there would be no need, what I had thus written, I would not presently expose to publique interest, wherefore I got some few copies privately disperst among some of my friends, that discrying the opinions of others, if any things appeared erroneous, hard, or obscure, I might correct, soften, and explain them.

These things I found most bitterly excepted against: that I had made the civill powers too large, but this by Ecclesiasticall persons; that I had utterly taken away liberty of conscience, but this by Sectaries; that I had set princes above the civil Laws, but this by Lawyers; wherefore I was not much moved by these mens reprehensions, (as who in doing this did but do their own business) except it were tye those knots so much faster.

But for their sakes who have a litle been staggered at the principles themselves, to wit the nature of men, the authority or right of nature, the nature of compacts and contracts, and the originall of civill government, because in finding fault they have not so much followed their passions, as their common sense, I have therefore in some places added some annotations whereby I presumed I might give some satisfaction to their differing thoughts; Lastly I have

9

endevoured to offend none beside those whose principles these contradict, and whose tender mindes are lightly offended by every difference of opinions.

Wherefore if ye shall meet with some things which have more of sharpnesse, and lesse of certainty than they ought to have, since they are not so much spoken for the maintenance of parties, as the establishment of peace, and by one whose just grief for the present calamities of his country, may very charitably be allowed some liberty, it is his only request to ye Readers, ye will deign to receive them with an equall mind.

De Cive

by Thomas Hobbes

Philosophicall Elements of a true Citizen. Liberty

CHAPTER I. OF THE STATE OF MEN WITHOUT CIVILL SOCIETY

I. The faculties of Humane nature may be reduc'd unto four kinds; Bodily strength, Experience, Reason, Passion. Taking the beginning of this following Doctrine from these, we will declare in the first place what manner of inclinations men who are endued with these faculties bare towards each other, and whether, and by what faculty, they are born apt for Society, and so preserve themselves against mutuall violence; then proceeding, we will shew what advice was necessary to be taken for this businesse, and what are the conditions of Society, or of Humane Peace; that is to say, (changing the words onely) what are the fundamentall Lawes of Nature.

II. The greatest part of those men who have written ought concerning Commonwealths, either suppose, or require us, or beg of us to believe, That Man is a Creature born fit [1] for Society: The Greeks call him Zoon politikon, and on this foundation they so build up the Doctrine of Civill Society, as if for the preservation of Peace, and the Government of Man-kind there were nothing else necessary, than that Men should agree to make certaine Covenants and Conditions together, which themselves should then call Lawes. Which Axiom, though received by most, is yet certainly False, and an Errour proceeding from our too slight contemplation of Humane Nature; for they who shall more narrowly look into the Causes for which Men come together, and delight in each others company, shall easily find that this happens not because naturally it could happen no otherwise, but by Accident: For if by nature one Man should Love another (that is) as Man, there could no reason be return'd why every Man should not equally Love every Man, as being equally Man, or why he should rather frequent those whose Society affords him Honour or Profit. We doe not therefore by nature seek Society for its own sake, but that we may receive some Honour or Profit from it; these we desire Primarily, that Secondarily: How by what advice Men doe meet, will be best known by observing those

things which they doe when they are met: For if they meet for Traffique, it's plaine every man regards not his Fellow, but his Businesse; if to discharge some Office, a certain Market-friendship is begotten, which hath more of Jealousie in it than True love, and whence Factions sometimes may arise, but Good will never; if for Pleasure, and Recreation of mind, every man is wont to please himself most with those things which stirre up laughter, whence he may (according to the nature of that which is Ridiculous) by comparison of another mans Defects and Infirmities, passe the more currant in his owne opinion; and although this be sometimes innocent, and without offence; yet it is manifest they are not so much delighted with the Society, as their own Vain glory. But for the most part, in these kind of meetings, we wound the absent; their whole life, sayings, actions are examin'd, judg'd, condemn'd; nay, it is very rare, but some present receive a fling before they part, so as his reason was not ill, who was wont alwayes at parting to goe out last. And these are indeed the true delights of Society, unto which we are carryed by nature, (i.e.) by those passions which are incident to all Creatures, untill either by sad experience, or good precepts, it so fall out (which in many never happens) that the Appetite, of present matters, be dul'd with the memory of things past, without which, the discourse of most quick and nimble men, on this subject, is but cold and hungry.

But if it so happen, that being met, they passe their time in relating some Stories, and one of them begins to tell one which concernes himselfe; instantly every one of the rest most greedily desires to speak of himself too; if one relate some wonder, the rest will tell you miracles, if they have them, if not, they'l fein them: Lastly, that I may say somewhat of them who pretend to be wiser than others; if they meet to talk of Philosophy, look how many men, so many would be esteem'd Masters, or else they not only love not their fellowes, but even persecute them with hatred: So clear is it by experience to all men who a little more narrowly consider Humane affaires, that all free congress ariseth either from mutual poverty, or from vain glory, whence the parties met, endeavour to carry with them either some benefit, or to leave behind them that same eudokimein, some esteem and honour with those, with whom they have been conversant: The same is also collected by reason out of the definitions themselves, of Will, Good, Honour, Profitable. For when we voluntarily contract Society, in all manner of Society we look after the object of the Will, i.e. that, which every one of those, who gather together, propounds to himselfe for good; now whatsoever seemes good, is pleasant, and relates either to the senses, or the mind, but all the mindes pleasure is either Glory, (or to have a good opinion of ones selfe) or referres to Glory in the end; the rest are Sensuall, or conducing to sensuality, which may be all comprehended under the word Conveniencies. All Society therefore is either for Gain, or for Glory; (i.e.) not so much for love of our Fellowes, as for love of our Selves: but no society can be great, or lasting, which begins from Vain Glory; because that Glory is like Honour, if all men have it, no man hath it, for they consist in comparison and precellence; neither doth the society of others advance any whit the cause of my glorying in my selfe; for every man must account himself, such as he can make himselfe, without the help of others. But though the benefits of this life may be much farthered by mutuall help, since yet those may be better attain'd to by Dominion, than by the society of others: I hope no body will doubt but that men would much more greedily be carryed by Nature, if all fear were removed, to obtain Dominion, than to gaine Society. We must therefore resolve, that the Originall of all great, and lasting Societies, consisted not in the mutuall good will men had towards each other, but in the mutuall fear [2] they had of each other.

III. The cause of mutuall fear consists partly in the naturall equality of men, partly in their mutuall will of hurting: whence it comes to passe that we can neither expect from others, nor promise to our selves the least security: For if we look on men fullgrown, and consider how brittle the frame of our humane body is, (which perishing, all its strength, vigour, and wisdome it selfe perisheth with it) and how easie a matter it is, even for the weakest man to kill the strongest, there is no reason why any man trusting to his own strength should conceive himself made by nature above others: they are equalls who can doe equall things one against the other; but they who can do the greatest things, (namely kill) can doe equall things. All men therefore among themselves are by nature equall; the inequality we now discern, hath its spring from the Civill Law.

IV. All men in the State of nature have a desire, and will to hurt, but not proceeding from the same cause, neither equally to be condemn'd; for one man according to that naturall equality which is among us, permits as much to others, as he assumes to himself (which is an argument of a temperate man, and one that rightly values his power); another, supposing himselfe above others, will have a License to doe what he lists, and challenges Respect, and Honour, as due to him before others, (which is an Argument of a fiery spirit:) This mans will to hurt ariseth from Vain glory, and the false esteeme he hath of his owne strength; the other's, from the necessity of defending himselfe, his liberty, and his goods against this mans violence.

V. Furthermore, since the combate of Wits is the fiercest, the greatest discords which are, must necessarily arise from this Contention; for in this case it is not only odious to contend against, but also not to consent; for not to approve of what a man saith is no lesse than tacitely to accuse him of an Errour in that thing which he speaketh; as in very many things to dissent, is as much as if you accounted him a fool whom you dissent from; which may appear hence, that there are no Warres so sharply wag'd as between Sects of the same Religion, and Factions of the same Commonweale, where the Contestation is Either concerning Doctrines, or Politique Prudence. And since all the pleasure, and jollity of the mind consists in this; even to get some, with whom comparing, it may find somewhat wherein to Tryumph, and Vaunt it self; its impossible but men must declare sometimes some mutuall scorn and contempt either by Laughter, or by Words, or by Gesture, or some signe or other; than which there is no greater vexation of mind; and than from which there cannot possibly arise a greater desire to doe hurt.

VI. But the most frequent reason why men desire to hurt each other, ariseth hence, that many men at the same time have an Appetite to the same thing; which yet very often they can neither enjoy in common, nor yet divide it; whence it followes that the strongest must have it, and who is strongest must be decided by the Sword.

VII. Among so many dangers therefore, as the naturall lusts of men do daily threaten each other withall, to have a care of ones selfe is not a matter so scornfully to be lookt upon, as if so be there had not been a power and will left in one to have done otherwise; for every man is desirous of what is good for him, and shuns what is evill, but chiefly the chiefest of naturall evills, which is Death; and this he doth, by a certain impulsion of nature, no lesse than that whereby a Stone moves downward: It is therefore neither absurd, nor reprehensible; neither against the dictates of true reason for a man to use all his endeavours to preserve and defend his Body, and the Members thereof from death and sorrowes; but that which is not contrary to right reason, that all men account to be done justly, and with right; Neither by the word Right is any thing else signified, than that liberty which every man hath to make use of his naturall faculties according to right reason: Therefore the first foundation of naturall Right is this, That every man as much as in him lies endeavour to protect his life and members.

VIII. But because it is in vaine for a man to have a Right to the end, if the Right to the necessary meanes be deny'd him; it followes, that since every man hath a Right to preserve himself, he must also be allowed a Right to use all the means, and do all the actions, without which He cannot Preserve himself.

IX. Now whether the means which he is about to use, and the action he is performing, be necessary to the preservation of his Life, and Members, or not, he Himself, by the right of nature, must be judg; for say another man, judg that it is contrary to right reason that I should judg of mine own perill: why now, because he judgeth of what concerns me, by the same reason, because we are equall by nature, will I judge also of things which doe belong to him; therefore it agrees with right reason (that is) it is the right of nature that I judge of his opinion, (i.e.) whether it conduce to my preservation, or not.

X. Nature hath given to every one a right to all. That is it was lawfull for every man in the bare state of nature, [3] or before such time as men had engag'd themselves by any Covenants, or Bonds, to doe what hee would, and against whom he thought fit, and to possesse, use, and enjoy all what he would, or could get. Now because whatsoever a man would, it therefore seems good to him because he wills it, and either it really doth, or at least seems to him to contribute toward his preservation, (but we have already allowed him to be judge in the foregoing Article whether it doth or not, in so much as we are to hold all for necessary whatsoever he shall esteeme so) and by the 7. Article it appeares that by the right of Nature those things may be done, and must be had, which necessarily conduce to the protection of life, and members, it followes, that

13

in the state of nature, To have all, and do all is lawfull for all. And this is that which is meant by that common saying, Nature hath given all to all, from whence we understand likewise, that in the state of nature, Profit is the measure of Right.

XI. But it was the least benefit for men thus to have a common Right to all things; for the effects of this Right are the same, almost, as if there had been no Right at all; for although any man might say of every thing, This is mine, yet could he not enjoy it, by reason of his Neighbour, who having equall Right, and equall power, would pretend the same thing to be his.

XII. If now to this naturall proclivity of men, to hurt each other, which they derive from their Passions, but chiefly from a vain esteeme of themselves: You adde, the right of all to all, wherewith one by right invades, the other by right resists, and whence arise perpetuall jealousies and suspicions on all hands, and how hard a thing it is to provide against an enemy invading us, with an intention to oppresse, and ruine, though he come with a small Number, and no great Provision; it cannot be deny'd but that the naturall state of men, before they entr'd into Society, was a meer War, and that not simply, but a War of all men, against all men; for what is WAR, but that same time in which the will of contesting by force, is fully declar'd either by Words, or Deeds? The time remaining, is termed PEACE.

XIII. But it is easily judg'd how disagreeable a thing to the preservation either of Man—kind, or of each single Man, a perpetuall War is: But it is perpetuall in its own nature, because in regard of the equality of those that strive, it cannot be ended by Victory; for in this state the Conquerour is subject to so much danger, as it were to be accounted a Miracle, if any, even the most strong should close up his life with many years, and old age. They of America are Examples hereof, even in this present Age: Other Nations have been in former Ages, which now indeed are become Civill, and Flourishing, but were then few, fierce, short—lived, poor, nasty, and destroy'd of all that Pleasure, and Beauty of life, which Peace and Society are wont to bring with them. Whosoever therefore holds, that it had been best to have continued in that state in which all things were lawfull for all men, he contradicts himself; for every man, by naturall necessity desires that which is good for him: nor is there any that esteemes a war of all against all, which necessarily adheres to such a State, to be good for him. And so it happens that through feare of each other we think it fit to rid our selves of this condition, and to get some fellowes; that if there needs must be war, it may not yet be against all men, nor without some helps.

XIV. Fellowes are gotten either by constraint, or by consent; By Constraint, when after fight the Conqueror makes the conquered serve him either through feare of death, or by laying fetters on him: By consent, when men enter into society to helpe each other, both parties consenting without any constraint. But the Conqueror may by right compell the Conquered, or the strongest the weaker, (as a man in health may one that is sick, or he that is of riper yeares a childe) unlesse he will choose to die, to give caution of his future obedience. For since the right of protecting our selves according to our owne wills proceeded from our danger, and our danger from our equality, its more consonant to reason, and more certaine for our conservation, using the present advantage to secure our selves by taking caution; then, when they shall be full growne and strong, and got out of our power, to endeavour to recover that power againe by doubtfull fight. And on the other side, nothing can be thought more absurd, than by discharging whom you already have weak in your power, to make him at once both an enemy, and a strong one. From whence we may understand likewise as a Corollarie in the naturall state of men, That a sure and irresistible Power confers the right of Dominion, and ruling over those who cannot resist; insomuch, as the right of all things, that can be done, adheres essentially, and immediately unto this omnipotence hence arising.

XV. Yet cannot men expect any lasting preservation continuing thus in the state of nature (i.e.) of War, by reason of that equality of power, and other humane faculties they are endued withall. Wherefore to seek Peace, where there is any hopes of obtaining it, and where there is none, to enquire out for Auxiliaries of War, is the dictate of right Reason; that is, the Law of Nature, as shall be shewed in the next Chapter.

1. Born fit. Since we now see actually a constituted Society among men, and none living out of it, since we discern all desirous of congresse, and mutuall correspondence, it may seeme a wonderfull kind of stupidity, to lay in the very threshold of this Doctrine, such a stumbling block before the Readers, as to deny Man to be born fit for Society: Therefore I must more plainly say, That it is true indeed, that to Man, by nature, or as Man, that is, as soone as he is born, Solitude is an enemy; for Infants have need of others to help them to live, and those of riper years to help them to live well, wherefore I deny not that men (even nature compelling) desire to come together. But civill Societies are not meer Meetings, but Bonds, to the making whereof, Faith and Compacts are necessary: The Vertue whereof to Children, and Fooles, and the profit whereof to those who have not yet tasted the miseries which accompany its defects, is altogether unknown; whence it happens, that those, because they know not what Society is, cannot enter into it; these, because ignorant of the benefit it brings, care not for it. Manifest therefore it is, that all men, because they are born in Infancy, are born unapt for Society. Many also (perhaps most men) either through defect of minde, or want of education remain unfit during the whole course of their lives; yet have Infants, as well as those of riper years, an humane nature; wherefore Man is made fit for Society not by Nature, but by Education: furthermore, although Man were born in such a condition as to desire it, it followes not, that he therefore were Born fit to enter into it; for it is one thing to desire, another to be in capacity fit for what we desire; for even they, who through their pride, will not stoop to equall conditions, without which there can be no Society, do yet desire it.

2. The mutuall fear. It is objected: It is so improbable that men should grow into civill Societies out of fear, that if they had been afraid, they would not have endur'd each others looks: They Presume, I believe, that to fear is nothing else than to be affrighted: I comprehend in this word Fear, a certain foresight of future evill; neither doe I conceive flight the sole property of fear, but to distrust, suspect, take heed, provide so that they may not fear, is also incident to the fearfull. They who go to Sleep, shut their Dores; they who Travell carry their Swords with them, because they fear Theives. Kingdomes guard their Coasts and Frontiers with Forts, and Castles; Cities are compact with Walls, and all for fear of neighbouring Kingdomes and Townes; even the strongest Armies, and most accomplisht for Fight, yet sometimes Parly for Peace, as fearing each others Power, and lest they might be overcome. It is through fear that men secure themselves, by flight indeed, and in corners, if they think they cannot escape otherwise, but for the most part by Armes, and Defensive Weapons; whence it happens, that daring to come forth, they know each others Spirits; but then, if they fight, Civill Society ariseth from the Victory, if they agree, from their Agreement.

3. In the bare state of Nature. This is thus to be understood: What any man does in the bare state of Nature is injurious to no man; not that in such a State he cannot offend God, or break the Lawes of Nature; for Injustice against men presupposeth Humane Lawes, such, as in the State of Nature there are none: Now the truth of this proposition thus conceived is

sufficiently demonstrated to the mindfull Reader in the Articles immediately foregoing; but because in certaine cases the difficulty of the conclusion makes us forget the premises, I will contract this Argument, and make it most evident to a single view; every man hath right to protect himself, as appears by the seventh Article. The same man therefore hath a right to use all the means which necessarily conduce to this end by the eight Article: But those are the necessary means which he shall judge to be such by the ninth Article. He therefore hath a right to make use, of and to doe all whatsoever he shall judge requisite for his preservation: wherefore by the judgement of him that doth it, the thing done is either right, or wrong; and therefore right. True it is therefore in the bare State of Nature, But if any man pretend somewhat to tend necessarily to his preservation, which yet he himself doth not confidently believe so, he may offend against the Lawes of Nature, as in the third Chapter of this Book is more at large declar'd.

It hath been objected by some: If a Sonne kill his Father, doth he him no injury? I have answered, That a Sonne cannot be understood to be at any time in the State of Nature, as being under the Power and command of them to whom he ownes his protection as soon as ever he is born, namely either his Fathers, or his Mothers, or his that nourisht him, as is demonstrated in the ninth Chapter.

CHAPTER II. OF THE LAW OF NATURE CONCERNING CONTRACTS

I. All Authors agree not concerning the definition of the Naturall Law, who notwithstanding doe very often make use of this terme in their Writings. The Method therefore, wherein we begin from definitions, and exclusion of all equivocation, is only proper to them who leave no place for contrary Disputes; for the rest, if any man say, that somwhat is done against the Law of Nature, one proves it hence, because it was done against the generall Agreement of all the most wise, and learned Nations: But this declares not who shall be the judg of the wisdome and learning of all Nations: Another hence, That it was done against the Generall consent of all Man-kind; which definition is by no means to be admitted; for then it were impossible for any but Children, and Fools, to offend against such a Law; for sure, under the notion of Man-kind, they comprehend all men actually endued with Reason. These therefore either doe Naught against it, or if they doe Ought, it is without their joint accord, and therefore ought to be excus'd; but to receive the Lawes of Nature from the Consents of them, who oftner Break, than Observe them, is in truth unreasonable: besides, Men condemne the same things in others, which they approve in themselves; on the other side, they publickly commend what they privately condemne; and they deliver their Opinions more by Hear-say, than any Speculation of their own; and they accord more through hatred of some object, through fear, hope, love, or some other perturbation of mind, than true Reason. And therefore it comes to passe, that whole Bodyes of people often doe those things by Generall accord, or Contention, which those Writers most willingly acknowledge to be against the Law of Nature. But since all doe grant that is done by RIGHT, which is not done against Reason, we ought to judg those Actions onely wrong, which are repugnant to right Reason, (i.e.) which contradict some certaine Truth collected by right reasoning from true Principles; but that Wrong which is done, we say it is done against some Law: therefore True Reason is a certaine Law, which (since it is no lesse a part of Humane nature, than any other faculty, or affection of the mind) is also termed naturall. Therefore the Law of Nature, that I may define it, is the Dictate of right Reason, [1] conversant about those things which are either to be done, or omitted for the constant preservation of Life, and Members, as much as in us lyes.

II. But the first and fundamentall Law of Nature is, That Peace is to be sought after where it may be found; and where not, there to provide our selves for helps of War: For we shewed in the last Article of the foregoing Chapter, that this precept is the dictate of right reason; but that the Dictates of right reason are naturall Lawes, that hath been newly prov'd above; But this is the first, because the rest are deriv'd from this, and they direct the wayes either to Peace, or self-defence.

III. But one of the Naturall Lawes deriv'd from this fundamentall one is this, That the right of all men, to all things, ought not to be retain'd, but that some certain rights ought to be transferr'd, or relinquisht: for if every one should retain his right to all things, it must necessarily follow, that some by right might invade; and others, by the same right, might defend themselves against them, (for every man, by naturall necessity, endeavours to defend his Body, and the things which he judgeth necessary towards the protection of his Body) therefore War would follow. He therefore acts against the reason of Peace, (i.e.) against the Law of Nature, whosoever he be, that doth not part with his Right to all things.

IV. But he is said to part with his right, who either absolutely renounceth it, or conveys it to another. He absolutely renounceth it, who by some sufficient Signe, or meet Tokens, declares that he is willing that it shall never be lawfull for him to doe that again, which before, by Right, he might have done; but he conveys

it to another, who by some sufficient Signe, or meet Tokens, declares to that other, that he is willing it should be unlawfull for him to resist him, in going about to do somewhat in the performance where he might before, with Right, have resisted him; but that the conveyance of Right consists meerly in not resisting, is understood by this, that before it was convey'd, he, to whom he convey'd it, had even then also a right to all, whence he could not give any new Right: But the resisting Right he had, before he gave it, by reason whereof the other could not freely enjoy his Rights, is utterly abolisht: Whosoever therefore acquires some Right in the naturall state of men, he onely procures himself security, and freedome from just molestation in the enjoyment of his Primitive Right: As for example, if any man shall sell, or give away a Farme, he utterly deprives himself only from all Right to this Farme, but he does not so from others also.

V. But in the conveyance of Right the will is requisite not onely of him that conveys, but of him also that accepts it. If either be wanting, the Right remaines: for if I would have given what was mine, to one who refus'd to accept of it, I have not therefore either simply renounc'd my Right, or convey'd it to any man; for the cause which mov'd me to part with it to this Man was in him onely, not in others too.

VI. But if there be no other Token extant of our will either to quit, or convey our Right, but onely Words; those words must either relate to the present, or time past; for if they be of the future onely, they convey nothing: for example, he that speaks thus of the time to come, I will give to morrow, declares openly that yet he hath not given it; so that all this day his right remaines, and abides to morrow too, unlesse in the interim he actually bestowes it: for what is mine, remains mine till I have parted with it. But if I shall speak of the time present, suppose thus; I doe give, or have given you this to be received to morrow, by these words is signified that I have already given it, and that his Right to receive it to morrow, is conveyed to him by me to day.

VII. Neverthelesse, although words alone are not sufficient tokens to declare the Will; if yet to words relating to the future, there shall some other signes be added, they may become as valid, as if they had been spoken of the present: If therefore, as by reason of those other signes, it appear, that he that speaks of the future, intends those words should be effectuall toward the perfect transferring of his Right, they ought to be valid; for the conveyance of right depends not on words, but (as hath been instanc'd in the 4. Article) on the declaration of the Will.

VIII. If any man conveigh some part of his right to another, and doth not this for some certain benefit received, or for some compact, a conveighance in this kind is called a Gift, or free Donation. But in free donation those words onely oblige us which signifie the present, or the time past; for if they respect the future, they oblige not as words, for the reason given in the foregoing Article: It must needs therefore be, that the Obligation arise from some other tokens of the Will: But, because whatsoever is voluntarily done, is done for some good to him that wils it; there can no other token be assigned of the Will to give it, except some benefit either already receiv'd, or to be acquir'd; but is suppos'd, that no such benefit is acquired, nor any compact in being; for if so, it would cease to be a free gift: It remains therefore, that a mutuall good turne without agreement be expected; but no signe can be given, that he, who us'd future words toward him who was in no sort engag'd to return a benefit, should desire to have his words so understood, as to oblige himselfe thereby. Nor is it suitable to Reason, that those who are easily enclined to doe well to others, should be oblig'd by every promise, testifying their present good affection: And for this cause, a promiser in this kind, must be understood to have time to deliberate, and power to change that affection as well as he to whom he made that promise, may alter his desert. But he that deliberates, is so farre forth free, nor can be said to have already given: But if he promise often, and yet give seldome, he ought to be condemn'd of levity, and be called not a Donour, but Doson.

IX. But the act of two, or more, mutually conveighing their Rights, is call'd a Contract. But in every Contract, either both parties instantly performe what they contract for, insomuch as there is no trust had from either to other; or the one performes, the other is trusted, or neither performe. Where both parties performe presently, there the Contract is ended, as soon as 'tis performed; but where there is credit given either to one, or both, there the party trusted promiseth after—performance; and this kind of promise is called a COVENANT.

X. But the Covenant made by the party trusted with him, who hath already performed, although the promise be made by words pointing at the future, doth no lesse transfer the right of future time, than if it had been made by words signifying the present, or time past: for the others performance is a most manifest signe that he so understood the speech of him whom he trusted, as that he would certainly make performance also at the appointed time; and by this signe the party trusted knew himselfe to be thus understood, which, because he hindred not, 'twas an evident token of his Will to performe. The promises therefore which are made for some benefit received (which are also Covenants) are Tokens of the Will; that is, (as in the foregoing Section hath been declared) of the last act of deliberating, whereby the liberty of non—performance is abolisht, and by consequence are obligatory; for where Liberty ceaseth, there beginneth Obligation.

XI. But the Covenants, which are made in contract of mutuall trust, neither party performing out of hand, if there arise [2] a just suspicion in either of them, are in the state of nature invalid: for he that first performes by reason of the wicked disposition of the greatest part of men studying their owne advantage, either by right, or wrong, exposeth himself to the perverse will of him with whom he hath Contracted; for it suites not with reason, that any man should performe first, if it be not likely that the other will make good his promise after; which, whether it be probable, or not, he that doubts it, must be judge of, as hath been shewed in the foregoing Chapter in the 9. Article. Thus, I say, things stand in the state of nature, but in a Civill State, when there is a power which can compell both parties, he that hath contracted to perform first, must first performe; because, that since the other may be compell'd, the cause which made him fear the others non—performance, ceaseth.

XII. But from this reason, that in all Free—gifts, and Compacts, there is an acceptance of the conveighance of Right required: it followes, that no man can Compact with him who doth not declare his acceptance; and therefore we cannot compact with Beasts, neither can we give, or take from them any manner of Right, by reason of their want of speech, and understanding, Neither can any man Covenant with God, or be oblig'd to him by Vow, except so far forth as it appeares to him by Holy Scriptures, that he hath substituted certaine men who have authority to accept of such like Vowes and Covenants, as being in Gods stead.

19

XIII. Those therefore doe vow in vain, who are in the state of nature, where they are not tyed by any Civill Law, (except by most certain Revelation the Will of God to accept their Vow, or Pact, be made known to them) for if what they Vow, be contrary to the Law of Nature, they are not tyed by their Vow, for no man is tyed to perform an unlawfull act; but if what is vowed, be commanded by some Law of nature, it is not their Vow, but the Law it self which ties them; but if he were free before his vow, either to doe it, or not doe it, his liberty remaines, because that the openly declar'd Will of the obliger is requisite to make an obligation by Vow, which in the case propounded is suppos'd not to be: Now I call him the Obliger to whom any one is tyed, and the Obliged him who is tyed.

XIV. Covenants are made of such things onely as fall under our deliberation, for it can be no Covenant without the Will of the Contractor, but the Will is the last act of him who deliberates; therefore they onely concerne things possible, and to come; no man therefore, by his Compact, obligeth himself to an impossibility. But yet, though we often Covenant to doe such things as then seem' d possible when we promis'd them, which yet afterward appear to be impossible, are we therefore freed from all obligation? The reason whereof is, that he who promiseth a future incertainty receives a present benefit; on condition, that he return another for it: for his Will, who performes the present benefit hath simply before it, for its object, a certain good [equally] valuable with the thing promised; but the thing it selfe not simply, but with condition if it could be done; but if it should so happen, that even this should prove impossible, why then he must perform as much as he can. Covenants therefore oblige us not to perform just the thing it selfe covenanted for, but our utmost endeavour; for this onely is, the things themselves are not in our power.

XV. We are freed from Covenants two wayes, either by performing, or by being forgiven: By performing, for beyond that we oblig'd not our selves. By being forgiven, because he whom we oblig'd our selves to by forgiving, is conceiv'd to return us that Right which we past over to him; for, forgiving, implies giving: that is, by the fourth Article of this Chapter, a conveyance of Right to him to whom the gift is made.

XVI. Its an usuall question, Whether Compacts extorted from us, through fear, do oblige, or not: For example, If to redeeme my life, from the power of a Robber, I promise to pay him 100 l. next day; and that I will doe no act whereby to apprehend, and bring him to Justice, whether I am tyed to keep promise, or not? But though such a Promise must sometimes be judged to be of no effect, yet it is not to be accounted so, because it proceeded from fear, for then it would follow that those promises which reduc'd men to a civill life, and by which Lawes were made, might likewise be of none effect, (for it proceeds from fear of mutuall slaughter, that one man submits himselfe to the Dominion of another:) And he should play the fool finely, who should trust his captive covenanting with the price of his redemption. It holds universally true, that promises doe oblige when there is some benefit received; and that to promisee and the thing promised, be lawfull: But it is lawfull, for the redemption of my life, both to promise, and to give what I will of mine owne to any man, even to a Thief. We are oblig'd therefore, by promises proceeding from fear, except the Civill Law forbid them, by vertue whereof, that which is promised becomes unlawfull.

XVII. Whosoever shall contract with one to doe, or omit somewhat, and shall after Covenant the contrary with another; he maketh not the former, but the latter Contract unlawfull: for, he hath no longer Right to doe, or to omit ought, who by former Contracts hath conveyed it to another; wherefore he can conveigh no Right by latter Contracts, and what is promised, is promis'd without Right: He is therefore tyed onely to his first Contract; to break which is unlawfull.

XVIII. No man is oblig'd by any Contracts whatsoever not to resist him who shall offer to kill, wound, or any other way hurt his Body; for there is in every man a certain high degree of feare through which he apprehends that evill which is done to him to be the greatest, and therefore by naturall necessity he shuns it all he can, and 'tis suppos'd he can doe no otherwise: When a man is arrived to this degree of fear, we cannot expect but he will provide for himself either by flight, or fight. Since therefore no man is tyed to impossibilities, they who are threatned either with deathe (which is the greatest evill to nature) or wounds, or some other bodily hurts, and are not stout enough to bear them, are not obliged to endure them. Farthermore, he that is tyed by Contract is trusted, (for Faith only is the Bond of Contracts) but they who are brought to punishment, either Capitall, or more gentle, are fettered, or strongly guarded, which is a most certain signe that they seem'd not sufficiently bound from non resistance by their Contracts. Its one thing if I promise thus: If I doe it not at the day appointed, kill me. Another thing if thus: If I doe it not, though you should offer to kill me, I will not resist: All men, if need be, contract the first way; but there is need sometimes. This second way, none, neither is it ever needfull; for in the meer state of nature, if you have a mind to kill, that state it selfe affords you a Right; insomuch as you need not first trust him, if for breach of trust you will afterward kill him. But in a Civill State, where the Right of life, and death, and of all corporall punishment is with the Supreme; that same Right of killing cannot be granted to any private person. Neither need the Supreme himselfe contract with any man patiently to yeeld to his punishment, but onely this, that no man offer to defend others from him. If in the state of nature, as between two Cities, there should a Contract be made, on condition of killing, if it were not perform'd, we must presuppose another Contract of not killing before the appointed day. Wherefore on that day, if there be no performance, the right of Warre returnes; that is, an hostile state, in which all things are lawfull, and therefore resistance also. Lastly, by the contract of not resisting, we are oblig'd of two Evills to make choice of that which seemes the greater; for certaine Death is a greater evill than Fighting; but of two Evills it is impossible not to chuse the least: By such a Compact therefore we should be tyed to impossibilities, which is contrary to the very nature of compacts.

XIX. Likewise no man is tyed by any Compacts whatsoever to accuse himself, or any other, by whose dammage he is like to procure himselfe a bitter life; wherefore neither is a Father oblig'd to bear witnesse against his Sonne, nor a Husband against his Wife, nor a Sonne against his Father; nor any man against any one, by whose meanes he hath his subsistance; for in vain is that testimony which is presum'd to be corrupted from nature; but although no man be tyed to accuse himself by any compact, yet in a publique tryall he may, by torture, be forc'd to make answer; but such answers are no testimony of the fact, but helps for the searching out of truth; insomuch as whether the party tortur'd his answer be true, or false, or whether he answer not at all, whatsoever he doth, he doth it by Right.

XX. Swearing is a speech joyned to a promise, whereby the promiser declares his renouncing of Gods mercy, unlesse he perform his word; which definition is contained in the words themselves, which have in them the very essence of an Oath, to wit, so God help me, or other equivalent, as with the Romans, Doe thou Jupiter so destroy the deceiver, as I slay this same Beast: neither is this any let, but that an Oath may as well sometimes be affirmatory, as promissory; for he that confirmes his affirmation with an Oath, promiseth that he speaks truth. But though in some places it was the fashion for Subjects to Swear by their Kings; that custome took its Originall hence, That those Kings took upon them Divine Honour; for Oathes were therefore introduc'd that by Religion, and consideration of the Divine Power men might have a greater dread of breaking their Faiths, than that wherewith they fear men, from whose eyes their actions may lie hid.

XXI. Whence it followes, that an Oath must be conceived in that forme which he useth, who takes it; for in vain is any man brought to Swear by a God whom he beleeves not, and therefore neither feares him. For though by the light of nature it may be known that there is a God, yet no man thinks he is to Swear by him in any other fashion, or by any other name than what is contain'd in the precepts of his own proper, that is, (as he who Swears imagines) the true Religion.

XXII. By the definition of an Oath we may understand, that a bare Contract obligeth no lesse, than that to which we are Sworn; for it is the contract which binds us, the Oath relates to the Divine punishment, which it could not provoke, if the breach of contract were not in its selfe unlawfull; but it could not be unlawfull if the Contract were not obligatory. Furthermore, he that renounceth the mercy of God obligeth himselfe not to any punishment, because it is ever lawfull to deprecate the punishment howsoever provok'd, and to enjoy Gods Pardon if it be granted. The onely effect therefore of an Oath is this, To cause men who are naturally inclin'd to break all manner of faith, through fear of punishment, to make the more Conscience of their words and actions.

XXIII. To exact an Oath, where the breach of contract, if any be made, cannot but be known, and where the party compacted, withall wants not power to punish, is to do somewhat more than is necessary unto self–defence, and shewes a mind desirous not so much to benefit it selfe, as to prejudice another. For an Oath, out of the very form of swearing, is taken in order to the provocation of Gods anger, that is to say, of him that is Omnipotent against those who therefore violate their Faith, because they think that by their own strength they can escape the punishment of men; and of him that is Omniscient against those, who therefore usually break their trust, because they hope that no man shall see them.

1. Right Reason. By Right Reason in the naturall state of men, I understand not, as many doe, an infallible faculty, but the act of reasoning, that is, the peculiar and true ratiocination of every man concerning those actions of his which may either redound to the dammage, or benefit of his neighbours. I call it Peculiar, because although in a Civill Government the reason of the Supreme (i.e. the Civill Law) is to be received by each single subject for the right; yet being without this Civill Government, (in which state no man can know right reason from false, but by comparing it with His owne) every mans owne reason is to be accounted not onely the rule of His owne actions which are done at His owne perill, but also for the measure of another mans reason, in such things as doe concerne him. I call it True; that is, concluding from true principles rightly fram'd, because that the whole breach of the Lawes of Nature consists in the false reasoning, or rather folly of

those men who see not those duties they are necessarily to performe toward others in order to their owne conservation; but the Principles of Right reasoning about such like duties are those which are explained in the 2, 3, 4, 5, 6, and 7. articles of the first Chapter.

2. Arise. For, except there appear some new cause of fear, either from somewhat done, or some other token of the will not to performe from the other part, it cannot be judg'd to be a just fear; for the cause which was not sufficient to keep him from making Compact, must not suffice to authorize the breach of it, being made.

CHAPTER III. OF THE OTHER LAWES OF NATURE.

I. Another of the Lawes of Nature is, to performe Contracts, or to keep trust; for it hath been shewed in the foregoing Chapter that the Law of Nature commands every man, as a thing necessary, to obtain Peace; to conveigh certain rights from each to other, and that this (as often as it shall happen to be done) is called a Contract: But this is so farre forth onely conducible to peace, as we shall performe Our selves, what we contract with others, shall be done, or omitted; and in vaine would Contracts be made, unlesse we stood to them. Because therefore, to stand to our Covenants, Or to keep faith, is a thing necessary for the obtaining of peace, it will prove by the second Article of the second Chapter to be a precept of the naturall Law.

II. Neither is there in this matter, any exception of the persons, with whom we Contract, as if they keep no faith with others; Or hold, that none ought to be kept, or are guilty of any other kind of vice: for he that Contracts, in that he doth contract, denies that action to be in vaine, and it is against reason for a knowing man to doe a thing in vain; and if he think himself not bound to keep it, in thinking so, he affirms the Contract to be made in vain: He therefore, who Contracts with one with whom he thinks he is not bound to keep faith, he doth at once think a Contract to be a thing done in vaine, and not in vaine, which is absurd. Either therefore we must hold trust with all men, or else not bargain with them; that is, either there must be a declared Warre, Or a sure and faithfull Peace.

III. The breaking of a Bargain, as also the taking back of a gift, (which ever consists in some action, Or omission) is called an INJURY: But that action, or omission, is called unjust, insomuch as an injury, and an unjust action, or omission, signifie the same thing, and both are the same with breach of Contract and trust: And it seemes the word Injury came to be given to any action, or omission, because they were without Right. He that acted, or omitted, having before conveyed his Right to some other. And there is some likenesse between that, which in the common course of life we call Injury; and that, which in the Schools is usually called absurd. For even as he, who by Arguments is driven to deny the Assertion which he first maintain'd, is said to be brought to an absurdity; in like manner, he who through weaknesse of mind does, or omits that which before he had by Contract promis'd not to doe, or omit, commits an Injury, and falls into no lesse contradiction, than he, who in the Schools is reduc'd to an Absurdity. For by contracting for some future action, he wills it done; by not doing it, he wills it not done, which is to will a thing done, and not done at the same time, which is a contradiction. An Injury therefore is a kind of absurdity in conversation, as an absurdity is a kind of injury in disputation.

IV. From these grounds it followes, that an injury can be done to no man [1] but him with whom we enter Covenant, or to whom somewhat is made over by deed of gift, or to whom somwhat is promis'd by way of bargain. And therefore damaging and injuring are often disjoyn'd: for if a Master command his Servant, who hath promis'd to obey him, to pay a summe of money, or carry some present to a third man; the Servant, if he doe it not, hath indeed damag'd this third party, but he injur'd his Master onely. So also in a civill government, if any man offend another, with whom he hath made no Contract, he damages him to whom the evill is done, but he injures none but him to whom the power of government belongs: for if he, who receives the hurt, should expostulate the mischief; and he that did it, should answer thus, What art thou to me? Why should I rather doe according to yours, than mine owne will, since I do not hinder, but you may do your own, and not my mind? In which speech, where there hath no manner of pre—contract past, I see not, I confesse, what is reprehensible.

V. These words just, and unjust, as also justice, and injustice, are equivocall; for they signifie one thing when they are attributed to Persons, another when to actions: When they are attributed to Actions, Just signifies as much as what's done with Right, and unjust, as what's done with injury: he who hath done some just thing is not therefore said to be a just Person, but guiltlesse, and he that hath done some unjust thing, we doe not therefore say he is an unjust, but guilty man. But when the words are applyed to Persons; to be just, signifies as much as to be delighted in just dealing, to study how to doe righteousnesse, or to indeavour in all things to doe that which is just; and to be unjust, is to neglect righteous dealing, or to think it is to be measured not according to my contract, but some present benefit; so as the justice or injustice of the mind, the intention, or the man, is one thing; that of an action, or omission, another; and innumerable actions of a just man may be unjust, and of an unjust man, just: But that man is to be accounted just, who doth just things because the Law commands it, unjust things only by reason of his infirmity; and he is properly said to be unjust who doth righteousness for fear of the punishment annext unto the Law, and unrighteousnesse by reason of the iniquity of his mind.

VI. The justice of actions is commonly distinguisht into two kinds; Commutative, and Distributive, the former whereof they say consists in Arithmeticall, the latter in Geometricall proportion: and that is conversant in exchanging, in buying, selling, borrowing, lending, location, and conduction, and other acts whatsoever belonging to Contracters, where, if there be an equall return made, hence they say springs a commutative justice: But this is busied about the dignity, and merits of men; so as if there be rendred to every man kata pen axian more to him who is more worthy, and lesse to him that deserves lesse, and that proportionably, hence they say ariseth distributive justice: I acknowledge here some certaine distinction of equality; to wit, that one is an equality simply so called, as when two things of equall value are compar'd together, as a pound of silver with twelve ounces of the same silver; the other is an equality, secundum quod; as when a 1000 pound is to be divided to an hundred men, 600 pounds are given to 60 men, and 400 to 40 where there is no equality between 600 and 400. But when it happens, that there is the same inequality in the number of them to whom it is distributed, every one of them shall take an equall part, whence it is called an equall distribution: But such like equality is the same thing with Geometricall proportion. But what is all this to Justice? for neither, if I sell my goods for as much as I can get for them, doe I injure the buyer, who sought, and desir'd them of me? neither if I divide more of what is mine to him who deserves lesse, so long as I give the other what I have agreed for, do I wrong to either? which truth our Saviour himself, being God, testifies in the Gospell. This therefore is no distinction of Justice, but of equality; yet perhaps it cannot be deny'd, but that Justice is a certain equality, as consisting in this onely; that since we are all equall by nature, one should not arrogate more Right to himselfe, than he grants to another, unlesse he have fairly gotten it by Compact. And let this suffice to be spoken against this distinction of Justice, although now almost generally receiv'd by all, lest any man should conceive an injury to be somewhat else, than the breach of Faith, or Contract, as hath been defin'd above.

VII. It is an old saying, Volenti non fit iniuria (the willing man receives no injury) yet the truth of it may be deriv'd from our Principles. For grant, that a man be willing that that should be done, which he conceives to be an injury. to him; why then that is done by his will, which by Contract was not lawfull to be done; but he being willing that should be done, which was not lawfull by Contract, the Contract it self (by the 15. Article of the foregoing Chapter) becomes void: The Right therefore of doing it returnes, therefore it is done by Right; wherefore it is no injury.

VIII. The third precept of the Naturall Law, is, That you suffer not him to be the worse for you, who out of the confidence he had in you, first did you a good turn; or that you accept not a gift, but with a mind to endeavour, that the giver shall have no just occasion to repent him of his gift. For without this he should act

without reason that would conferre a benefit where he sees it would be lost; and by this meanes all beneficence, and trust, together with all kind of benevolence would be taken from among men, neither would there be ought of mutuall assistance among them, nor any commencement of gaining grace and favour; by reason whereof the state of Warre would necessarily remain, contrary to the fundamentall Law of Nature: But because the breach of this Law is not a breach of trust, or contract, (for we suppose no Contracts to have pass'd among them) therefore is it not usually termed an injury, but because good turns and thankes have a mutuall eye to each other, it is called INGRATITUDE.

IX. The fourth precept of Nature, is, That every man render himself usefull unto others: which, that we may rightly understand, we must remember that there is in men, a diversity of dispositions to enter into society, arising from the diversity of their affections, not unlike that which is found in stones, brought together in the Building, by reason of the diversity of their matter, and figure. For as a stone, which in regard of its sharp and angular form takes up more room from other stones than it fils up it selfe, neither because of the hardnesse of its matter cannot well be prest together, or easily cut, and would hinder the building from being fitly compacted, is cast away, as not fit for use: so a man, who for the harshness of his disposition in retaining superfluities for himself, and detaining of necessaries from others, and being incorrigible, by reason of the stubbornnesse of his affections, is commonly said to be uselesse, and troublesome unto others. Now, because each one not by Right onely, but even by naturall necessity is suppos'd, with all his main might, to intend the procurement of those things which are necessary to his own preservation; if any man will contend on the other side for superfluities, by his default there will arise a Warre, because that on him alone there lay no necessity of contending, he therefore acts against the fundamentall Law of Nature: Whence it followes (which wee were to shew) that it is a precept of nature; That every man accommodate himselfe to others. But he who breaks this Law may be called uselesse, and troublesome. Yet Cicero opposeth inhumanity to this usefulnesse, as having regard to this very Law.

X. The fifth precept of the Law of nature is: That we must forgive him who repents, and asketh pardon for what is past; having first taken caution for the time to come. The pardon of what is past, or the remission of an offence, is nothing else but the granting of Peace to him that asketh it, after he hath warr'd against us, now is become penitent. But Peace granted to him that repents not, that is, to him that retains an hostile mind, or that gives not caution for the future; that is, seeks not Peace, but oportunity, is not properly Peace but feare, and therefore is not commanded by nature. Now to him that will not pardon the penitent, and that gives future caution, peace it selfe it seems is not pleasing; which is contrary to the naturall Law.

XI. The sixth precept of the naturall Law is, That in revenge and punishments we must have our eye not at the evill past, but the future good. That is: It is not lawfull to inflict punishment for any other end, but that the offender may be corrected, or that others warned by his punishment may become better. But this is confirmed chiefly from hence, that each man is bound by the law of nature to forgive one another, provided he give caution for the future, as hath been shewed in the foregoing Article. Furthermore, because revenge, if the time past be onely considered, is nothing else but a certain triumph, and glory of minde, which points at no end, (for it contemplates onely what is past; but the end is a thing to come) but that which is directed to no end is vain; That revenge therefore which regards not the future, proceeds from vaine glory, and therefore without reason. But to hurt another without reason introduces a warre, and is contrary to the fundamentall Law of Nature; It is therefore a precept of the Law of nature, that in revenge wee look not backwards but forward. Now the breach of this Law, is commonly called CRUELTY.

XII. But because all signes of hatred, and contempt provoke most of all to brawling and fighting, insomuch as most men would rather lose their lives, (that I say not their Peace) than suffer reproach; it followes in the seventh place, That it is prescribed by the Law of nature, that no man either by deeds, or words, countenance, or laughter, doe declare himselfe to hate, or scorne another. The breach of which Law is called Reproach. But although nothing be more frequent than the scoffes and jeers of the powerfull against the weak, and namely of Judges against guilty persons, which neither relate to the offence of the guilty, nor the duty of the Judges, yet these kind of men do act against the Law of nature, and are to be esteemed for contumelious.

XIII. The question whether of two men be the more worthy, belongs not to the naturall, but civill state; for it hath been shewed before, Chap. I. Art. 3. that all men by nature are equall, and therefore the inequality which now is, suppose from riches, power, nobility of kindred, is come from the civill Law. I know that Aristotle in his first book of Politiques affirmes as a foundation of the whole politicall science, that some men by nature are made worthy to command, others onely to serve; as if Lord and Master were distinguished not by consent of men, but by an aptnesse, that is, a certain kind of naturall knowledge, or ignorance; which foundation is not onely against reason (as but now hath been shewed) but also against experience: for neither almost is any man so dull of understanding as not to judge it better to be ruled by himselfe, than to yeeld himselfe to the government of another; neither if the wiser and stronger doe contest, have these ever, or often the upper hand of those. Whether therefore men be equall by nature, the equality is to be acknowledged, or whether unequall, because they are like to contest for dominion, its necessary for the obtaining of Peace, that they be esteemed as equall; and therefore it is in the eight place a precept of the Law of nature, That every man be accounted by nature equall to another, the contrary to which Law is PRIDE.

XIV. As it was necessary to the conservation of each man, that he should part with some of his Rights, so it is no lesse necessary to the same conservation, that he retain some others, to wit the Right of bodily protection, of free enjoyment of ayre, water, and all necessaries for life. Since therefore many common Rights are retained by those who enter into a peaceable state, and that many peculiar ones are also acquired, hence ariseth this ninth dictate of the naturall Law, to wit, That what Rights soever any man challenges to himselfe, he also grant the same as due to all the rest: otherwise he frustrates the equality acknowledged in the former Article. For what is it else to acknowledge an equality of persons in the making up of society, but to attribute equall Right and Power to those whom no reason would else engage to enter into society? But to ascribe equall things to equalls, is the same with giving things proportionall to proportionals. The observation of this Law is called MEEKNES, the violation pleonexia, the breakers by the Latines are styled Immodici et immodesti.

XV. In the tenth place it is commanded by the Law of nature, That every man in dividing Right to others, shew himselfe equall to either party. By the foregoing Law we are forbidden to assume more Right by nature to our selves, than we grant to others. We may take lesse if we will, for that sometimes is an argument of modesty. But if at any time matter of Right be to be divided by us unto others, we are forbidden by this Law to favour one more or lesse than another. For he that by favouring one before another, observes not this naturall equality, reproaches him whom he thus undervalues: but it is declared above, that a reproach is against the Lawes of Nature. The observance of this Precept is called EQUITY; the breach, Respect of Persons. The Greeks in one word term it prosopolepsia.

XVI. From the foregoing Law is collected this eleventh, Those things which cannot be divided, must be used in common, (if they can) and (that the quantity of the matter permit) every man as much as he lists, but if the quantity permit not, then with limitation, and proportionally to the number of the users: for otherwise that equality can by no means be observed, which we have shewed in the forgoing Article to be commanded by the Law of Nature.

XVII. Also what cannot be divided, nor had in common, it is provided by the Law of nature (which may be the twelfth Precept) that the use of that thing be either by turns, or adjudged to one onely by lot, and that in the using it by turns, it be also decided by lot who shall have the first use of it; For here also regard is to be had unto equality: but no other can be found, but that of lot.

XVIII. But all lot is twofold; arbitrary, or naturall; Arbitrary is that which is cast by the consent of the Contenders, and it consists in meer chance (as they say) or fortune. Naturall is primogeniture (in Greek klironomia, as it were given by lot) or first possession. Therefore the things which can neither be divided, nor

had in common, must be granted to the first possessour, as also those things which belonged to the Father are due to the Sonne, unlesse the Father himselfe have formerly conveighed away that Right to some other. Let this therefore stand for the thirteenth Law of Nature.

XIX. The 14. Precept of the Law of nature is; That safety must be assured to the mediators for Peace. For the reason which commands the end, commands also the means necessary to the end. But the first dictate of Reason is Peace. All the rest are means to obtain it, and without which Peace cannot be had. But neither can Peace be had without mediation, nor mediation without safety; it is therefore a dictate of Reason, that is, a Law of nature, That we must give all security to the Mediators for Peace.

XX. Furthermore, because, although men should agree to make all these, and whatsoever other Lawes of Nature, and should endeavour to keep them, yet doubts, and controversies would daily arise concerning the application of them unto their actions, to wit, whether what was done, were against the Law, or not, (which we call, the question of Right) whence will follow a fight between Parties, either sides supposing themselves wronged; it is therefore necessary to the preservation of Peace (because in this case no other fit remedy can possibly be thought on) that both the disagreeing Parties refer the matter unto some third, and oblige themselves by mutuall compacts to stand to his judgement in deciding the controversie. And he to whom they thus refer themselves is called an Arbiter. It is therefore the 15. Precept of the naturall Law, That both parties disputing concerning the matter of right submit themselves unto the opinion and judgement of some third.

XXI. But from this ground, that an Arbiter or Judge is chosen by the differing Parties to determine the controversie, we gather, that the Arbiter must not be one of the Parties: for every man is presumed to seek what is good for himselfe naturally, and what is just, onely for Peaces sake, and accidentally; and therefore cannot observe that same equality commanded by the Law of nature so exactly as a third man would do: It is therefore in the sixteenth place contained in the Law of nature, That no man must be Judge or Arbiter in his own cause.

XXII. From the same ground followes in the seventeenth place, That no man must be Judge who propounds unto himself any hope of profit, or glory, from the victory of either part: for the like reason swayes here, as in the foregoing Law.

XXIII. But when there is some controversie of the fact it selfe, to wit, whether that bee done or not, which is said to bee done, the naturall Law wills, that the Arbiter trust both Parties alike, that is, (because they affirm contradictories) that hee believe neither: He must therefore give credit to a third, or a third and fourth, or more, that he may be able to give judgement of the fact, as often as by other signes he cannot come to the knowledge of it. The 18. Law of nature therefore injoynes Arbiters, and Judges of fact, That where firm and certain signes of the fact appear not, there they rule their sentence by such witnesses, as seem to be indifferent to both Parts.

XXIV. From the above declared definition of an Arbiter may be furthermore understood, That no contract or promise must Passe between him and the parties whose Judge he is appointed, by vertue whereof he may be engaged to speak in favour of either part, nay, or be oblig'd to judge according to equity, or to pronounce such sentence as he shall truly judge to be equall. The Judge is indeed bound to give such sentence as he shall judge to be equall by the Law of Nature recounted in the 15. Article. To the obligation of which Law nothing can be added by way of Compact. Such compact therefore would be in vain. Besides, if giving wrong judgement, he should contend for the equity of it, except such Compact be of no force, the Controversie would remain after Judgement given, which is contrary to the constitution of an Arbiter, who is so chosen, as both parties have oblig'd themselves to stand to the judgement which he should pronounce. The Law of Nature therefore commands the Judge to be disengaged, which is its 19. precept.

XXV. Farthermore, forasmuch as the Lawes of Nature are nought else but the dictates of Reason, so as, unlesse a man endeavour to preserve the faculty of right reasoning, he cannot observe the Lawes of Nature, it is manifest, that he, who knowingly, or willingly, doth ought, whereby the rationall faculty may be destroyed, or weakned, he knowingly, and willingly, breaks the Law of nature: For there is no difference between a man who performes not his Duty, and him who does such things willingly, as make it impossible for him to doe it. But they destroy and weaken the reasoning faculty, who doe that which disturbs the mind from its naturall state; that which most manifestly happens to Drunkards and Gluttons; we therefore sin in the 20. place against the Law of Nature by Drunkennesse.

XXVI. Perhaps some man, who sees all these precepts of Nature deriv'd by a certain artifice from the single dictate of Reason advising us to look to the preservation, and safegard of our selves, will say, That the deduction of these Lawes is so hard, that it is not to be expected they will be vulgarly known, and therefore neither will they prove obliging: for Lawes, if they be not known, oblige not, nay, indeed are not Lawes. To this I answer, it's true, That hope, fear, anger, ambition, covetousnesse, vain glory, and other perturbations of mind, doe hinder a man so, as he cannot attaine to the knowledge of these Lawes, whilst those passions prevail in him: But there is no man who is not sometimes in a quiet mind; At that time therefore there is nothing easier for him to know, though he be never so rude and unlearn'd, than this only Rule, That when he doubts, whether what he is now doing to another, may be done by the Law of Nature, or not, he conceive himselfe to be in that others stead. Here instantly those perturbations which perswaded him to the fact, being now cast into the other scale, disswade him as much: And this Rule is not onely easie, but is Anciently celebrated in these words, Quod tibi fieri non vis, alteri ne feceris: Do not that to others, you would not have done to your self.

XXVII. But because most men, by reason of their perverse desire of present profit, are very unapt to observe these Lawes, although acknowledg'd by them, if perhaps some others more humble than the rest should exercise that equity and usefulnesse which Reason dictates, those not practising the same, surely they would not follow Reason in so doing; nor would they hereby procure themselves peace, but a more certain quick destruction, and the keepers of the Law become a meer prey to the breakers of it. It is not therefore to be imagin'd, that by Nature, (that is, by Reason) men are oblig'd to the exercise of all these Lawes [2] in that state of men wherein they are not practis'd by others. We are oblig'd yet in the interim to a readinesse of mind to observe them whensoever their observation shall seeme to conduce to the end for which they were ordain'd. We must therefore conclude, that the Law of Nature doth alwayes, and every where oblige in the internall Court, or that of Conscience, but not alwayes in the externall Court, but then onely when it may be done with safety.

XXVIII. But the Lawes which oblige Conscience, may be broken by an act, not onely contrary to them, but also agreeable with them, if so be that he who does it be of another opinion: for though the act it self be answerable to the Lawes, yet his Conscience is against them.

XXIX. The Lawes of Nature are immutable, and eternall; What they forbid, can never be lawfull; what they command, can never be unlawfull: For pride, ingratitude, breach of Contracts (or injury), inhumanity, contumely, will never be lawfull; nor the contrary vertues to these ever unlawfull, as we take them for dispositions of the mind, that is, as they are considered in the Court of Conscience, where onely they oblige, and are Lawes. Yet actions may be so diversified by circumstances, and the Civill Law, that what's done with equity at one time, is guilty of iniquity at another; and what suits with reason at one time, is contrary to it another. Yet Reason is still the same, and changeth not her end, which is Peace, and Defence; nor of the minde which the meanes to attaine them, to wit, those vertues we have declar'd above, and which cannot be abrogated by any Custome, or Law whatsoever.

XXX. It's evident by what hath hitherto been said, how easily the Lawes of Nature are to be observ'd, because they require the endeavour onely, (but that must be true and constant) which who so shall performe, we may rightly call him JUST. For he who tends to this with his whole might, namely, that his actions be squar'd according to the precepts of Nature, he shewes clearly that he hath a minde to fulfill all those Lawes, which is all we are oblig'd to by rationall nature. Now he that hath done all he is oblig'd to, is a Just Man.

XXXI. All Writers doe agree that the Naturall Law is the same with the Morall. Let us see wherefore this is true. We must know therefore, that Good and Evill are names given to things to signifie the inclination, or aversion of them by whom they were given. But the inclinations of men are diverse, according to their diverse Constitutions, Customes, Opinions; as we may see in those things we apprehend by sense, as by tasting, touching, smelling; but much more in those which pertain to the common actions of life, where what this man commends, (that is to say, calls Good) the other undervalues, as being Evil; Nay, very often the same man at diverse times, praises, and dispraises the same thing. Whilst thus they doe, necessary it is there should be discord, and strife: They are therefore so long in the state of War, as by reason of the diversity of the present appetites, they mete Good and Evill by diverse measures. All men easily acknowledge this state, as long as they are in it, to be evill, and by consequence that Peace is good. They therefore who could not agree concerning a present, doe agree concerning a future Good, which indeed is a work of Reason; for things present are obvious to the sense, things to come to our Reason only. Reason declaring Peace to be good, it followes by the same reason, that all the necessary means to Peace be good also, and therefore, that Modesty, Equity, Trust, Humanity, Mercy (which we have demonstrated to be necessary to Peace) are good Manners, or habits, (that is) Vertues. The Law therefore, in the means to Peace, commands also Good Manners, or the practise of Vertue: And therefore it is call'd Morall.

XXXII. But because men cannot put off this same irrationall appetite, whereby they greedily prefer the present good (to which, by strict consequence, many unforeseen evills doe adhere) before the future, it happens, that though all men doe agree in the commendation of the foresaid vertues, yet they disagree still concerning their Nature, to wit, in what each of them doth consist; for as oft as anothers good action displeaseth any man, that action hath the name given of some neighbouring vice; likewise the bad actions, which please them, are ever entituled to some Vertue; whence it comes to passe that the same Action is prais'd by these, and call'd Vertue, and dispraised by those, and termed vice. Neither is there as yet any remedy found by Philosophers for this matter; for since they could not observe the goodnesse of actions to consist in this, that it was in order to Peace, and the evill in this, that it related to discord, they built a morall Philosophy wholly estranged from the morall Law, and unconstant to it self; for they would have the nature of vertues seated in a certain kind of mediocrity betweene two extremes, and the vices in the extremes themselves; which is apparently false: For to dare is commended, and under the name of fortitude is taken for a vertue, although it be an extreme, if the cause be approved. Also the quantity of a thing given, whether it be great, or little, or between both, makes not liberality, but the cause of giving it. Neither is it injustice, if I give any man more, of what is mine own, than I owe him. The Lawes of Nature therefore are the summe of Morall Philosophy, whereof I have onely delivered such precepts in this place, as appertain to the preservation of our selves against those dangers which arise from discord. But there are other precepts of rationall nature, from whence spring other vertues: for temperance also is a precept of Reason, because intemperance tends to sicknesse, and death. And so fortitude too, (that is) that same faculty of resisting stoutly in present dangers, (and which are more hardly declined than overcome) because it is a means tending to the preservation of him that resists.

XXXIII. But those which we call the Lawes of nature (since they are nothing else but certain conclusions understood by Reason, of things to be done, and omitted; but a Law to speak properly and accurately, is the speech of him who by Right commands somewhat to others to be done, or omitted) are not (in propriety of speech) Lawes, as they proceed from nature; yet as they are delivered by God in holy Scriptures, (as we shall see in the Chapter following) they are most properly called by the name of Lawes: for the sacred Scripture is the speech of God commanding over all things by greatest Right.

1. Injury can be done to no man. The word injustice relates to some Law: Injury to some Person, as well as some Law. For what's unjust, is unjust to all; but there may an injury be done, and yet not against me, nor thee, but some other; and sometimes against no private Person, but the Magistrate only; sometimes also neither against the Magistrate, nor any private man, but onely against God; for through Contract, and conveighance of Right, we say, that an injury is done against this, or that man. Hence it is (which we see in all kind of Government) that what private men contract between themselves by word, or writing, is releast againe at the will of the Obliger. But those mischiefes which are done against the Lawes of the Land, as theft, homicide, and the like, are punisht not as he wills, to whom the hurt is done, but according to the will of the Magistrate; that is, the constituted Lawes.

2. The exercise of all these Lawes. Nay among these Lawes some things there are, the omission whereof (provided it be done for Peace, or Self−preservation) seemes rather to be the fulfilling, than breach of the Naturall Law; for he that doth all things against those that doe all things, and plunders plunderers, doth equity; but on the other side, to doe that which in Peace is an handsome action, and becomming an honest man, is dejectednesse, and Poornesse of spirit, and a betraying of ones self in the time of War, But there are certain naturall Lawes, whose exercise ceaseth not even in the time of War it self; for I cannot understand what drunkennesse, or cruelty (that is, Revenge which respects not the future good) can advance toward Peace, or the preservation of any man. Briefly, in the state of nature, what's just, and unjust, is not to be esteem'd by the Actions, but by the Counsell, and Conscience of the Actor. That which is done out of necessity, out of endeavour for Peace, for the preservation of our selves, is done with Right; otherwise every damage done to a man would be a breach of the naturall Law, and an injury against God.

CHAPTER IV. THAT THE LAW OF NATURE IS A DIVINE LAW.

I. The same Law which is Naturall, and Morall, is also wont to be called Divine, nor undeservedly, as well because Reason, which is the law of Nature, is given by God to every man for the rule of his actions; as because the precepts of living which are thence derived, are the same with those which have been delivered from the divine Majesty, for the LAWES of his heavenly Kingdome, by our Lord Jesus Christ, and his holy Prophets and Apostles. What therefore by reasoning we have understood above concerning the law of nature, we will endeavour to confirme the same in this Chapter by holy writ.

II. But first we will shew those places in which it is declared, that the Divine Law is seated in right reason. Psalm 37:30,31. The mouth of the righteous will be exercised in wisdome, and his tongue will be talking of Judgement: The law of God is in his heart. Jerem. 31:33. I will put my law in their inward parts, and write it in their hearts. Psal. 19:7. The law of the Lord is an undefiled law, converting the soule. ver. 8. The Commandement of the Lord is Pure, and giveth light unto the eyes. Deuteron. 30:11. This Commandement which I command thee this day, it is not hidden from thee, neither is it far off, vers. 14. But the word is very nigh unto thee, in thy mouth, and in thine heart; that thou maist doe it. Psal. 119:34. Give me understanding, and I shall keep thy law. vers. 105. Thy word is a lamp unto my feet, and a light unto my paths. Proverbs 9:10. The knowledge of the holy is understanding. Christ the Law−giver himselfe is called (John 1:1.) the word. The same Christ is called (vers. 9.) the true light that lighteth every man that cometh in the world. All which are descriptions of right reason, whose dictates, we have shewed before, are the lawes of nature.

III. But that which wee set downe for the fundamentall law of nature, namely, that Peace was to be sought for, is also the summe of the divine law, will be manifest by these places. Rom. 3:17. Righteousnesse, (which is the summe of the law) is called the way of Peace Psal. 85:10. Righteousnesse and Peace have kissed each other. Matth. v. 9. Blessed are the Peace−makers, for they shall be called the children of God. And after Saint Paul in his 6. Chapter to the Hebrewes, and the last verse had called Christ (the Legislator of that law we treat of) an High−Priest for ever after the order of Melchizedeck; he addes in the following Chapter, the first verse,

This Melchizedeck was King of Salem, Priest of the most high God, vers. 2. First being by interpretation King of Righteousnesse, and after that also King of Salem, which is, King of peace. Whence it is cleare, that Christ the King in his Kingdome placeth Righteousnesse and Peace together. Psal. 34. Eschue evill and doe good, seek Peace and pursue it. Isaiah 9:6,7. Unto us a child is born, unto us a Sonne is given, and the government shall be upon his shoulder, and his name shall be called Wonderfull, Counsellour, the mighty God, the everlasting Father, the Prince of peace. Isaiah 52:7. How beautifull upon the mountaines are the feet of him that bringeth good tidings, that publisheth Peace, that bringeth good tidings of good, that publisheth salvation, that saith unto Sion, thy God reigneth! Luke 2:14. In the Nativity of Christ, the voice of them that praised God saying, Glory be to God on high, and in earth Peace, good will towards men. And Isaiah 53:5.

The Gospell is called the chastisement of our Peace. Isaiah 59:8. Righteousnesse is called the way of Peace. The way of Peace they know not, and there is no judgement in their goings.

Micah 5:4,5. speaking of the Messias, he saith thus, He shall stand and feed in the strength of the Lord, in the Majesty of the name of the Lord his God, and they shall abide, for now shall he be great unto the end of the earth; And this man shall be your Peace, Prov. 3:1,2. My sonne forget not my law, but let thine heart keep my Commandements, for length of dayes, and long life, and Peace, shall they adde to thee.

IV. What appertains to the first law of abolishing the community of all things, or concerning the introduction of meum tuum, We perceive in the first place how great an adversary this same Community is to Peace, by those words of Abraham to Lot, Gen. 13:8,9. Let there be no strife I Pray thee, between thee and me, and between thy heard−men, and my heard−men, for we be brethren. Is not the whole land before thee? Separate thy selfe I Pray thee from me. And all those places of Scripture by which we are forbidden to trespasse upon our neighbours, as, Thou shalt not kill, thou shalt not commit adultery, thou shalt not steal, doe confirm the law of distinction between Mine, and Thine. for they suppose the right of all men to all things to be taken away.

V. The same precepts establish the second law of nature of keeping trust: for what doth, Thou shalt not invade anothers right, import, but this? Thou shalt not take possession of that, which by thy contract ceaseth to be thine; but expressely set down, Psal. 15: vers. 1. To him that asked, Lord who shall dwell in thy Tabernacle? It is answered, vers. 4: He that sweareth unto his neighbour, and disappointeth him not; and Prov. 6:1,2. My sonne if thou be surety for thy friend, if thou have stricken thy hand with a stranger, Thou art snared with the words of thy mouth.

VI. The third Law concerning gratitude is proved by these places, Deut. 25:4. Thou shalt not muzzle the Oxe when he treadeth out the corn; which Saint Paul I. Cor. 9:9. interprets to be spoken of men, not Oxen onely. Prov. 17:13. Who so rewardeth evill for good, evill shall not depart from his house. And Deut. 20:10,11. When thou comest nigh unto a city to fight against it, then proclaim Peace unto it. And it shall be if it make thee answer of Peace, and open unto thee, then it shall be that all the people that is found therein, shall be tributaries unto thee, and they shall serve thee. Proverbs 3:29. Devise not evill against thy neighbour, seeing he dwelleth securely by thee.

VII. To the fourth Law of accommodating our selves, these precepts are conformable, Exod. 23:4,5. If thou meet thine enemies Oxe, or his Asse going astray, thou shalt surely bring it back to him again; if thou see the Asse of him that hateth thee lying under his burden, and wouldest forbear to help him, thou shalt surely help with him. Also, vers. 9. Thou shalt not oppresse a stranger. Prov. 3:30. Strive not with a man without a cause, if he have done thee no harme. Prov. 15:18. A wrathfull man stirreth up strife, but he that is slow to anger, appeaseth strife. Prov. 18:24. There is a friend that sticketh closer than a brother. The same is confirmed, Luke 10, by the Parable of the Samaritan, who had compassion on the Jew that was wounded by theeves, and by Christs precept, Matth. v. 39. But I say unto you, that ye resist not evill, but whosoever shall smite thee on the right cheek, turn to him the other also,

VIII. Among infinite other places which prove the fifth law, these are some. Matth. 6:14,15. If you forgive men their trespasses, your heavenly Father will also forgive you: but if you forgive not men their trespasses, neither will your Father forgive your trespasses. Matth. 18:21, 22. Lord how oft shall my Brother sinne against me, and I forgive him? till seven times? Jesus saith unto him, I say not till seven times, but till seventy times seven times: that is, toties quoties.

IX. For the confirmation of the sixth law, all those places are pertinent which command us to shew mercy; such as Mat. v. 7. Blessed are the mercifull, for they shall obtain mercy. Levit. 19:18. Thou shalt not avenge, nor bear any grudge against the children of thy people. But there are, who not onely think this law is not proved by Scripture, but plainly disproved from hence, that there is an eternall punishment reserved for the wicked after death, where there is no place either for amendment, or example. Some resolve this objection by answering, That God, whom no law restrains, refers all to his glory, but that man must not doe so; as if God sought his glory, (that is to say) pleased himselfe in the death of a sinner. It is more rightly answered, that the institution of eternall punishment was before sin, and had regard to this onely, that men might dread to commit sinne for the time to come.

X. The words of Christ prove this seventh, Matth. v. 22. But I say unto you, That whosoever is angry with his brother without a cause, shall be in danger of the judgement, and whosoever shall say unto his Brother Racha, shall be in danger of the Counsell, but whosoever shall say, thou foole, shall be in danger of hell fire. Prov. 10:18. Hee that uttereth a slander is a foole. Prov. 14:21. Hee that despiseth his neighbour, sinneth. Prov. 15:1. Grievous words stir up anger. Prov. 22:10. Cast out the scorner, and contention shall goe out, and reproach shall cease.

XI. The eighth law of acknowledging equality of nature, that is, of humility, is established by these places. Mat. 5:3. Blessed are the Poor in spirit, for theirs is the Kingdom of heaven. Prov. 6:16–19. These six things doth the Lord hate, yea seven are an abomination unto him: A proud look, Prov. 16:5. Every one that is proud is an abomination unto the Lord, though hand joyne in hand, he shall not be unpunished. Prov. 11:2. When pride cometh, then cometh shame, but with the lowly, is wisdome. Thus Isaiah 40:3. (where the comming of the Messias is shewed forth, for preparation towards his Kingdome) The voyce of him that cryed in the wildernesse, was this: Prepare ye the way of the Lord, make strait in the desart a high way for our God. Every valley shall be exalted, and every mountain, and hill, shall be made low; which doubtlesse is spoken to men, and not to mountaines.

XII. But that same Equity which we proved in the ninth place to be a Law of Nature, which commands every man to allow the same Rights to others they would be allowed themselves, and which containes in it all the other Lawes besides, is the same which Moses sets down, Levit. 19:18. Thou shalt love thy neighbour as thy self; and our Saviour calls it the summe of the morall Law, Mat. 22:36–40. Master, which is the great Commandement in the Law? Jesus said unto him, Thou shalt love the Lord thy God with all thine heart, and with all thy soul, and with all thy mind; this is the first and great Commandement, and the second is like unto it, Thou shalt love thy neighbour as thy self. On these two Commandements hang all the Law and the Prophets. But to love our neighbor as our selves, is nothing else, but to grant him all we desire to have granted to our selves.

XIII. By the tenth Law respect of Persons is forbid; as also by these places following, Mat. v. 45. That ye may be children of your Father which is in Heaven; for he maketh the sun to rise on the Evill, and on the Good, Collos. 3:11. There is neither Greek, nor Jew, circumcision, nor uncircumcision, Barbarian, or Scythian, bond, or free, but Christ is all, in all. Acts 10:34. Of a truth, I perceive, that God is no respecter of Persons. 2 Chron. 19:7. There is no iniquity with the Lord our God, nor respect of Persons, nor taking of gifts. Eccles. 35:12. The Lord is Judge, and with him is no respect of Persons. Rom. 2:11. For there is no respect of Persons with God.

XIV. The eleventh Law, which commands those things to be held in common which cannot be divided, I know not whether there be any expresse place in Scripture for it, or not; but the practise appears every where in the common use of Wels, Wayes, Rivers, sacred things, for else men could not live.

XV. We said in the twelfth place, that it was a Law of Nature, That where things could neither be divided, nor possess'd in common, they should be dispos'd by lot, which is confirmed as by the example of Moses, who by Gods command, Numb. 26:55. divided the severall parts of the land of promise unto the Tribes by Lot: So Acts 1:24. by the example of the Apostles, who receiv'd Matthias, before Justus, into their number, by casting Lots, and saying, Thou Lord, who knowest the hearts of all men, shew whether of these two thou hast chosen, Prov. 16:33. The lot is cast into the lappe, but the whole disposing thereof is of the Lord. And which is the thirteenth Law, the Succession was due unto Esau, as being the First—born of Isaac, if himself had not sold it, (Gen. 25:30.) or that the Father had not otherwise appointed.

XVI. Saint Paul writing to the Corinthians, 1 Epist. 6, reprehends the Corinthians of that City for going to Law one with another before infidell Judges who were their enemies, calling it a fault, that they would not rather take wrong, and suffer themselves to be defrauded; for that is against that Law, whereby we are commanded to be helpful to each other. But if it happen the Controversie be concerning things necessary, what is to be done? Therefore the Apostle, Ver. 5. speaks thus, I speak to your shame. Is it so that there is not one wise man among you, no, not one that shall be able to judge between his brethren? He therefore, by those words confirmes that Law of Nature which we call'd the fifteenth, to wit, Where Controversies cannot be avoided, there by the consent of Parties to appoint some Arbiter, and him some third man; so as (which is the 16 Law) neither of the Parties may be judge in his own Cause.

XVII. But that the Judge, or Arbiter, must receive no reward for his Sentence, (which is the 17. Law) appears, Exod. 23:8. Thou shalt take no gift; for the gift blindeth the wise, and perverteth the words of the righteous. Eccles. 20:29. Presents and gifts blind the eyes of the wise. Whence it followes, that he must not be more oblig'd to one part than the other, which is the 19. Law, and is also confirm'd, Deut. 1:17. Ye shall not respect Persons in Judgment, ye shall hear the small as well as the great; and in all those places which are brought against respect of Persons.

XVIII. That in the judgement of Fact, witnesses must be had, (which is the 18. Law) the Scripture not only confirmes, but requires more than one, Deut. 17:6. At the mouth of two witnesses, or three witnesses, shall he that is worthy of death be put to death. The same is repeated, Deut. 19:15.

XIX. Drunkennesse, which we have therefore in the last place numbred among the breaches of the Naturall Law, because it hinders the use of right Reason, is also forbid in sacred Scripture for the same reason. Prov. 20:1. Wine is a mocker, strong drink is raging, whosoever is deceived thereby is not wise. And Prov. 31:4,5. It is not for Kings to drink wine, lest they drink, and forget the Law, and pervert the judgement of any of the afflicted: but that we might know that the malice of this vice consisted not formally in the quantity of the drink, but in that it destroyes Judgement and Reason, it followes in the next Verse, Give strong drink to him that is ready to perish, and wine to those that be heavy of heart. Let him drink, and forget his poverty, and remember his misery no more. Christ useth the same reason in prohibiting drunkenesse, Luk. 21:34. Take heed to your selves, lest at any time your hearts be overcharg'd with surfetting and drunkennesse.

XX. That we said in the foregoing Chapter, The Law of Nature is eternall, is also prov'd out of Matth. 5:18. Verily I say unto you, till Heaven and Earth Passe, one jot, or one tittle, shall in no wise Passe from the Law, and Psal. 119:160. Every one of thy righteous judgements endureth for ever.

XXI. We also said, That the Lawes of Nature had regard chiefly unto Conscience; that is, that he is just, who by all possible endeavour strives to fulfill them. And although a man should order all his actions (so much as belongs to externall obedience) just as the Law commands, but not for the Lawes sake, but by reason of some

punishment annext unto it, or out of Vain glory, yet he is unjust. Both these are proved by the Holy Scriptures. The first, Isaiah 60:7. Let the wicked forsake his way, and unrighteous man his thoughts, and let him return unto the Lord, and he wil have mercy upon him, and to our God, for he will abundantly pardon. Ezek. 18:31. Cast away from you all your transgressions whereby you have transgressed, make you a new heart, and a new spirit; for why will you die O house of Israel? By which, and the like places, we may sufficiently understand that God will not punish their deeds whose heart is right. The second out of Isaiah 29:13,14. The Lord said, Forasmuch as this people draw near me with their mouth, and with their lips doe honour me, but have removed their heart far from me, therefore I will proceed, Mat. 5:20. Except your righteousnesse shall exceed the righteousnesse of the Scribes and Pharisees ye shall in no case enter into the Kingdom of Heaven; and in the following verses our Saviour explains to them how that the commands of God are broken, not by Deeds only, but also by the Will; for the Scribes and Pharises did in outward act observe the Law most exactly, but for Glories sake onely; else they would as readily have broken it. There are innumerable places of Scripture in which is most manifestly declar'd that God accepts the Will for the Deed, and that as well in good, as in evill actions.

XXII. That the Law of Nature is easily kept, Christ himself declares in Matthew 11:28–30. Come unto me, Take my yoke upon you, and learn of me, for my yoke is easie, and my burthen light.

XXIII. Lastly, the Rule by which I said any man might know whether what he was doing, were contrary to the Law, or not, to wit, what thou wouldst not be done to, doe not that to another, is almost in the self same words delivered by our Saviour, Mat. 7:12. Therefore all things whatsoever ye would that men should do unto you, do you even so to them.

XXIV. As the law of nature is all of it Divine, so the Law of Christ by conversion, (which is wholly explain'd in the 5. 6. and 7. Chapter of S. Matthewes Gospell) is all of it also (except that one Commandement of not marrying her who is put away for adultery, which Christ brought for explication of the divine positive Law, against the Jewes, who did not rightly interpret the Mosaicall Law) the doctrine of Nature: I say the whole Law of Christ is explain'd in the fore–named Chapters, not the whole Doctrine of Christ; for Faith is a part of Christian Doctrine, which is not comprehended under the title of a Law; for Lawes are made, and given, in reference to such actions as follow our will, not in order to our Opinions, and, Belief which being out of our power, follow not the Will.

Dominion

CHAPTER V. OF THE CAUSES, AND FIRST BEGINING OF CIVILL GOVERNMENT

I. It is of it selfe manifest, that the actions of men proceed from the will, and the will from hope, and feare, insomuch as when they shall see a greater good, or lesse evill, likely to happen to them by the breach, than observation of the Lawes, they'l wittingly violate them. The hope therefore which each man hath of his security, and self−preservation, consists in this, that by force or craft he may disappoint his neighbour, either openly, or by stratagem. Whence we may understand, that the naturall lawes, though well understood, doe not instantly secure any man in their practise, and consequently, that as long as there is no caution had from the invasion of others, there remains to every man that same primitive Right of selfe−defence, by such means as either he can or will make use of (that is) a Right to all things, or the Right of warre; and it is sufficient for the fulfiling of the naturall law, that a man be prepared in mind to embrace Peace when it may be had.

II. It is an old saying, That all lawes are silent in the time of warre, and it is a true one, not onely if we speak of the civill, but also of the naturall lawes, provided they be referr'd not to the mind, but to the actions of men, by the third Chapter, Art. 29. And we mean such a war as is of all men against all men; such as is the meer state of nature; although in the warre of nation against nation a certain mean was wont to be observed. And therefore in old time there was a manner of living, and as it were a certain oeconomy, which they called leotrikon, living by Rapine, which was neither against the law of nature, (things then so standing) nor voyd of glory to those who exercised it with valour, not with cruelty. Their custome was, taking away the rest, to spare life, and abstain from Oxen fit for plough, and every instrument serviceable to husbandry, which yet is not so to be taken, as if they were bound to doe thus by the law of nature, but that they had regard to their own glory herein, lest by too much cruelty, they might be suspected guilty of feare.

III. Since therefore the exercise of the naturall law is necessary for the preservation of Peace, and that for the exercise of the naturall law security is no lesse necessary, it is worth the considering what that is which affords such a security: for this matter nothing else can be imagined, but that each man provide himselfe of such meet helps, as the invasion of one on the other may bee rendered so dangerous, as either of them may think it better to refrain, than to meddle. But first it is plain, that the consent of two or three cannot make good such a security; because that the addition but of one, or some few on the other side, is sufficient to make the victory undoubtedly sure, and hartens the enemy to attacque us. It is therefore necessary, to the end the security sought for may be obtained, that the number of them who conspire in a mutuall assistance be so great, that the accession of some few to the enemies party may not prove to them a matter of moment sufficient to assure the victory.

IV. Farthermore, how great soever the number of them is who meet on selfe−defence, if yet they agree not among themselves of some excellent means whereby to compasse this, but every man after his own manner shall make use of his endeavours, nothing will be done; because that divided in their opinions they will be an hinderance to each other, or if they agree well enough to some one action through hope of victory, spoyle, or revenge, yet afterward through diversity of wits, and Counsels, or emulation, and envy, with which men naturally contend, they will be so torne and rent, as they will neither give mutuall help, nor desire peace, except they be constrained to it by some common feare. Whence it followes, that the consent of many, (which

37

consists in this onely, as we have already defined in the foregoing section, that they direct all their actions to the same end, and the common good) that is to say, that the society proceeding from mutuall help onely, yeelds not that security which they seek for, who meet, and agree in the exercise of the above—named lawes of nature; but that somewhat else must be done, that those who have once consented for the common good, to peace and mutuall help, may by fear be restrained, lest afterward they again dissent, when their private Interest shall appear discrepant from the common good.

V. Aristotle reckons among those animals which he calls Politique, not man only, but divers others; as the Ant, the Bee, which though they be destitute of reason, by which they may contract, and submit to government, notwithstanding by consenting, (that is to say) ensuing, or eschewing the same things, they so direct their actions to a common end, that their meetings are not obnoxious unto any seditions. Yet is not their gathering together a civill government, and therefore those animals not to be termed politicall, because their government is onely a consent, or many wills concurring in one object, not (as is necessary in civill government) one will. It is very true that in those creatures, living only by sense and appetite, their consent of minds is so durable, as there is no need of any thing more to secure it, and (by consequence) to preserve peace among them, than barely their naturall inclination. But among men the case is otherwise. For first among them there is a contestation of honour and preferment; among beasts there is none: whence hatred and envy, out of which arise sedition and warre, is among men; among beasts no such matter. Next, the naturall appetite of Bees, and the like creatures, is conformable, and they desire the common good which among them differs not from their private; but man scarce esteems any thing good which hath not somewhat of eminence in the enjoyment, more than that which others doe possesse. Thirdly, those creatures which are voyd of reason, see no defect, or think they see none, in the administration of their Common—weales; but in a multitude of men there are many who supposing themselves wiser than others, endeavour to innovate, and divers Innovators innovate divers wayes, which is a meer distraction, and civill warre. Fourthly, these brute creatures, howsoever they may have the use of their voyce to signify their affections to each other, yet want they that same art of words which is necessarily required to those motions in the mind, whereby good is represented to it as being better, and evill as worse than in truth it is; But the tongue of man is a trumpet of warre, and sedition; and it is reported of Pericles, that he sometimes by his elegant speeches thundered, and lightened, and confounded whole Greece it selfe. Fiftly, they cannot distinguish between injury and harme; Thence it happens that as long as it is well with them, they blame not their fellowes: But those men are of most trouble to the Republique, who have most leasure to be idle; for they use not to contend for publique places before they have gotten the victory over hunger, and cold. Last of all, the consent of those brutall creatures is naturall, that of men by compact onely, (that is to say) artificiall; it is therefore no matter of wonder if somewhat more be needfull for men to the end they may live in peace. Wherefore consent, or contracted society, without some common power whereby particular men may be ruled through feare of punishment, doth not suffice to make up that security which is requisite to the exercise of naturall justice.

VI. Since therefore the conspiring of many wills to the same end doth not suffice to preserve peace, and to make a lasting defence, it is requisite that in those necessary matters which concern Peace and selfe—defence, there be but one will of all men. But this cannot be done, unlesse every man will so subject his will to some other one, to wit, either Man or Counsell, that whatsoever his will is in those things which are necessary to the common peace, it be received for the wills of all men in generall, and of every one in particular. Now the gathering together of many men who deliberate of what is to be done, or not to be done, for the common good of all men, is that which I call a COUNSELL.

VII. This submission of the wils of all those men to the will of one man, or one Counsell, is then made, when each one of them obligeth himself by contract to every one of the rest, not to resist the will of that one man, or counsell, to which he hath submitted himselfe; that is, that he refuse him not the use of his wealth, and strength, against any others whatsoever (for he is supposed still to retain a Right of defending himselfe against violence) and this is called UNION. But we understand that to be the will of the counsell, which is the will of the major part of those men of whom the Counsell consists.

VIII. But though the will it self be not voluntary, but only the beginning of voluntary actions (for we will not to will, but to act) and therefore falls least of all under deliberation, and compact; yet he who submits his will to the will of an other, conveighs to that other the Right of his strength, and faculties; insomuch as when the rest have done the same, he to whom they have submitted hath so much power, as by the terrour of it hee can conforme the wills of particular men unto unity, and concord.

IX. Now union thus made is called a City, or civill society, and also a civill Person; for when there is one will of all men, it is to be esteemed for one Person, and by the word (one) it is to be knowne, and distinguished from all particular men, as having its own Rights and properties; insomuch as neither any one Citizen, nor all of them together (if we except him whose will stands for the will of all) is to be accounted the City. A CITY therefore (that we may define it) is one Person, whose will, by the compact of many men, is to be received for the will of them all; so as he may use all the power and faculties of each particular person, to the maintenance of peace, and for common defence.

X. But although every City be a civill Person, yet every civill Person is not a City; for it may happen that many Citizens, by the permission of the City, may joyne together in one Person, for the doing of certain things. These now will be civill Persons, as the companies of Merchants, and many other Convents; but Cities they are not, because they have not submitted themselves to the will of the company simply, and in all things, but in certain things onely determined by the City; and on such termes as it is lawfull for any one of them to contend in judgement against the body it selfe of the sodality; which is by no means allowable to a Citizen against the City; such like societies therefore are civill Persons subordinate to the City.

XI. In every city, That Man, or Counsell, to whose will each particular man hath subjected his will (so as hath been declared) is said to have the SUPREME POWER, or CHIEFE COMMAND, or DOMINION; which

Power, and Right of commanding, consists in this, that each Citizen hath conveighed all his strength and power to that man, or Counsell; which to have done (because no man can transferre his power in a naturall manner) is nothing else than to have parted with his Right of resisting. Each Citizen, as also every subordinate civill Person, is called the SUBJECT of him who hath the chiefe command.

XII. By what hath been sayed, it is sufficiently shewed, in what manner, and by what degrees many naturall Persons, through desire of preserving themselves, and by mutuall feare, have growne together into a civill Person, whom we have called a City. But they who submit themselves to another for feare, either submit to him whom they feare, or some other whom they confide in for protection; They act according to the first manner who are vanquished in warre, that they may not be slain; they according to the second, who are not yet overcome, that they may not be overcome. The first manner receives its beginning from naturall Power, and may be called the naturall beginning of a City; the latter from the Counsell, and constitution of those who meet together, which is a beginning by institution. Hence it is, that there are two kinds of Cities, the one naturall, such as is the paternall, and despoticall; the other institutive, which may be also called politicall. In the first the Lord acquires to himselfe such Citizens as he will; in the other the Citizens by their own wills appoint a Lord over themselves, whether he be one man, or one company of men endued with the command in chiefe. But we will speak in the first place of a City politicall or by institution, and next of a City naturall.

CHAPTER VI. OF THE RIGHT OF HIM, WHETHER COUNSELL, OR ONE MAN ONELY, WHO HATH THE SUPREME POWER IN THE CITY

I. We must consider first of all what a multitude [1] of men (gathering themselves of their owne free wills into society) is, namely, that it is not any one body, but many men, whereof each one hath his owne will, and his peculiar judgment concerning all things that may be propos'd. And though by particular Contracts each single man may have his own Right, and Propriety, so as one may say This is mine, the other, That is his; yet will there not be any thing of which the whole multitude, as a Person distinct from a single man, can rightly say, This is mine, more than anothers. Neither must we ascribe any action to the multitude, as it's one, but (if all, or more of them doe agree) it will not be an Action, but as many actions, as Men. For although in some great Sedition, it's commonly said, That the People of that City have taken up Armes; yet is it true of those onely who are in Armes, or who consent to them. For the City, which is one Person, cannot take up Armes against it selfe. Whatsoever therefore is done by the multitude, must be understood to be done by every one of those by whom it is made up; and that he, who being in the Multitude, and yet consented not, nor gave any helps to the things that were done by it, must be judg'd to have done nothing. Besides, in a multitude not yet reduc'd into one Person, in that manner as hath been said, there remaines that same state of nature in which all things belong to all men and there is no place for Meum Tuum, which is call'd Dominion, and Propriety, by reason that that security is not yet extant which we have declar'd above to be necessarily requisite for the practise of the Naturall Laws.

II. Next, we must consider that every one of the Multitude (by whose meanes there may be a beginning to make up the City) must agree with the rest, that in those matters which shall be propounded by any one in the Assembly, that be received for the will of all which the major part shall approve of; for otherwise there will be no will at all of a Multitude of Men, whose Wills and Votes differ so variously. Now if any one will not consent, the rest notwithstanding shall among themselves constitute the City without him: Whence it will come to passe, that the City retaines its primitive Right against the Dissentour, that is, the Right of war, as against an Enemy.

III. But because we said in the foregoing Chapter, the sixth Article, That there was requir'd to the security of men, not onely their Consent, but also the Subjection of their wills in such things as were necessary to Peace and Defence; and that in that Union, and Subjection, the nature of a City consisted; We must discerne now in this place, out of those things which may be propounded, discuss'd, and stated in an Assembly of men, (all whose wills are contain'd in the will of the major part) what things are necessary to Peace, and common defence: But first of all, it is necessary to Peace, that a man be so farre forth protected against the violence of others, that he may live securely, that is, that he may have no just cause to fear others, so long as he doth them no injury. Indeed, to make men altogether safe from mutuall harmes, so as they cannot be hurt, or injuriously kill'd, is impossible, and therefore comes not within deliberation. But care may be had there be no just cause of fear; for security is the end wherefore men submit themselves to others, which if it be not had, no man is suppos'd to have submitted himselfe to ought, or to have quitted his Right to all things, before that there was a care had of his security.

IV. It is not enough to obtain this security, that every one of those who are now growing up into a City, doe covenant with the rest, either by words, or writing, Not to steal, not to kill, and to observe the like Lawes; for the pravity of humane disposition is manifest to all, and by experience too well known how little (removing the punishment) men are kept to their duties, through conscience of their promises. We must therefore provide for our security, not by Compacts, but by Punishments; and there is then sufficient provision made, when there are so great punishments appointed for every injury, as apparently it prove a greater evill to have done it, than not to have done it: for all men, by a necessity of nature, chuse that which to them appears to be the lesse evill.

V. Now the right of punishing is then understood to be given to any one, when every man Contracts not to assist him who is to be punished. But I will call this Right, The Sword of Justice. But these kind of contracts men observe well enough, for the most part, till either themselves, or their near friends are to suffer.

VI. Because therefore for the security of particular men, and, by consequence for the common peace, it is necessary that the right of using the Sword for punishment, be transferred to some Man or Counsell, that Man or Counsell is necessarily understood by Right to have the supreme Power in the City. For he that by Right punisheth at his own discretion, by Right compells all men to all things which he himselfe wills; than which a greater command cannot be imagined.

VII. But in vain doe they worship peace at home, who cannot defend themselves against forrainers; neither is it possible for them to protect themselves against forrainers, whose forces are not united; and therefore it is necessary for the preservation of particulars, that there be some one Counsell, or one man, who hath the Right to arm, to gather together, to unite so many Citizens in all dangers, and on all occasions, as shall be needfull for common defence against the certain number, and strength of the enemy; and again, (as often as he shall finde it expedient) to make peace with them. We must understand therefore, that particular Citizens have conveighed their whole Right of Warre, and Peace, unto some one Man or Counsell; And that this right (which we may call the Sword of Warre) belongs to the same Man, or Counsell, to whom the Sword of Justice belongs; for no Man can by Right compell Citizens to take up armes, and be at the expences of Warre, but he who by Right can punish him who doth not obey. Both Swords therefore, as well this of War, as that of Justice, even by the constitution it selfe of a City, and essentially, doe belong to the chiefe command.

VIII. But because the right of the Sword is nothing else but to have power by right to use the sword at his own will, it followes, that the judgement of its right use pertaines to the same party: for if the Power of judging were in one, and the power of executing in another, nothing would be done. For in vain would he give judgement, who could not execute his commands; or if he executed them by the power of another, he himselfe is not said to have the Power of the Sword, but that other, to whom he is onely an Officer. All judgement therefore in a City belongs to him who hath the swords, (i.e.) to him, who hath the supreme authority.

IX. Furthermore, since it no lesse, nay it much more conduceth to Peace to prevent brawles from arising, than to appease them being risen; and that all controversies are bred from hence, that the opinions of men differ

concerning Meum Tuum, just and unjust, profitable and unprofitable, good and evill, honest and dishonest, and the like, which every man esteems according to his own judgement; it belongs to the same chiefe power to make some common Rules for all men, and to declare them publiquely, by which every man may know what may be called his, what anothers, what just, what unjust, what honest, what dishonest, what good, what evill, that is summarily, what is to be done, what to be avoyded in our common course of life. But those Rules and measures are usually called the civill Lawes, or the Lawes of the City, as being the Commands of him who hath the supreme power in the City. And the CIVILL LAWES (that we may define them) are nothing else but the commands of him who hath the chiefe authority in the City, for direction of the future actions of his Citizens.

X. Furthermore, since the affaires of the City, both those of Warre, and Peace, cannot possibly be all administred by one man, or one Counsell, without Officers and subordinate Magistrates, and that it appertains to Peace, and common defence, that they to whom it belongs justly to judge of controversies, to search into neighbouring counsels, prudently to wage war, and on all hands warily to attend the benefit of the City, should also rightly exercise their offices; it is consonant to reason, that they depend on, and be chosen by him who hath the chiefe command both in War, and in Peace.

XI. It is also manifest, that all voluntary actions have their beginning from, and necessarily depend on the will, and that the will of doing, or omitting ought, depends on the opinion of the good and evill of the reward, or punishment, which a man conceives he shall receive by the act, or omission; so as the actions of all men are ruled by the opinions of each; wherefore by evident and necessary inference, we may understand that it very much concerns the interest of Peace, that no opinions or doctrines be delivered to Citizens, by which they may imagine, that either by Right they may not obey the Lawes of the City, that is, the commands of that man, or Counsell, to whom the supreme power is committed, or that it is lawfull for to resist him, or that a lesse punishment remaines for him that denies, than him that yeelds obedience. For if one command somewhat to be done under penalty of naturall death, another forbids it under pain of eternall death, and both by their own Right, it will follow that the Citizens, although innocent, are not onely by Right punishable, but that the City it selfe is altogether dissolved; for no man can serve two Masters: nor is he lesse, but rather more, a Master, whom we believe we are to obey for feare of damnation, than he whom we obey for feare of temporall death. It followes therefore, that this one, whether Man, or Court, to whom the City hath committed the supreme Power, have also this Right, That he both judge what opinions [2] and doctrines are enemies unto peace, and also that he forbid them to be taught.

XII. Last of all, from this consideration, that each Citizen hath submitted his Will to his who hath the Supreme Command in the City, so as he may not employ his strength against him; it followes manifestly, that whatsoever shall be done by him who commands, must not be punisht; for as he who hath not power enough, cannot punish him naturally; so neither can he punish him by Right, who by Right hath not sufficient power.

XIII. It is most manifest by what hath been said, That in every perfect City (that is, where no Citizen hath Right to use his faculties, at his owne discretion, for the preservation of himselfe, or where the Right of the private Sword is excluded) there is a Supreme Power in some one, greater than which cannot by Right be conferr'd by men, or greater than which no mortall man can have over himself. But that power, greater than which cannot by men, be conveigh'd on a man, we call ABSOLUTE: [3] for whosoever hath so submitted his will to the will of the City, That he can, unpunisht, doe any thing, make Lawes, judge Controversies, set Penalties, make use, at his own pleasure, of the strength, and wealth of men, and all this by Right, truly he hath given him the greatest dominion that can be granted. This same may be confirm'd by experience in all the Cities which are, or ever have beene; for though it be sometimes in doubt, what Man, or Counsell, hath the Chief Command, yet ever there is such a Command, and alwayes exercis'd, except in the time of Sedition, and Civill War, and then there are two Chiefe Commands made out of one: Now those seditious persons who dispute against absolute Authority, doe not so much care to destroy it, as to conveigh it on others; for removing this power, they together take away Civill Society, and a confusion of all things returnes. There is so much obedience joyn'd to this absolute Right of the Chief Ruler, as is necessarily requir'd for the Government of the City, that is to say, so much as that Right of his may not be granted in vaine. Now this kind of obedience, although for some reasons it may sometimes, by Right, be deny'd, yet because a greater cannot be perform'd, we will call it SIMPLE. But the obligation to performe this growes not immediately from that Contract by which we have conveigh'd all our Right on the City, but mediately from hence, That, without obedience, the Cities Right would be frustrate, and by consequence there would be no City constituted. For it is one thing if I say, I give you Right to Command what you will; another, if I say, I will doe whatsoever you Command; and the Command may be such, as I would rather die than doe it; forasmuch therefore as no man can be bound to will being kill'd, much lesse is he tyed to that, which to him is worse than death: if therefore I be commanded to kill my self, I am not bound to doe it; for though I deny to doe it, yet the Right of dominion is not frustrated, since others may be found, who being commanded, will not refuse to doe it; neither doe I refuse to doe that which I have contracted to doe. In like manner, if the Chief Ruler command any man to kill him, he is not tyed to doe it, because it cannot be conceiv'd that he made any such Covenant; nor if he command to execute a Parent, whether he be innocent, or guilty, and condemned by the Law, since there are others, who, being commanded, will doe that, and a Son will rather die, than live infamous, and hated of all the world. There are many other cases, in which, since the Commands are shamefull to be done by some, and not by others, Obedience may, by Right, be perform'd by these, and refus'd by those; and this, without breach of that absolute Right which was given to the Chief Ruler. For in no case is the Right taken away from him, of slaying those who shall refuse to obey him. But they who thus kill men, although by Right given them from him that hath it, yet if they use that Right otherwise than right Reason requires, they sin against the Lawes of Nature, (that is) against God.

XIV. Neither can any man give somewhat to himselfe; for he is already suppos'd to have what he can give himself; nor can he be oblig'd to himselfe, for the same party being both the obliged, and the Obliger, and the Obliger having power to release the obliged, it were meerly in vain for a man to be obliged to himselfe, because he can release himself at his own pleasure; and he that can doe this, is already actually free. Whence its plaine, that the City is not tyed to the Civill Lawes; for the Civill Lawes are the Lawes of the City, by which, if she were engag'd, she should be engag'd to her selfe. Neither can the City be oblig'd to her Citizen, because, if he will, he can free her from her obligation; and he will, as oft as she wills, (for the will of every Citizen is in all things comprehended in the will of the City); the City therefore is free when she pleaseth, that is, she is now actually free; but the will of a Councell, or one who hath the Supreme Authority given him, is the will of the City; he therefore containes the wills of all particular Citizens: Therefore neither is he bound to the Civill Lawes (for this is to be bound to himself) nor to any of his Citizens.

XV. Now because (as hath been shewn above) before the constitution of a City all things belong'd to all men, nor is there that thing which any man can so call his, as any other may not, by the same Right, claime as his own, (for where all things are common, there can be nothing proper to any man) it followes, that propriety receiv'd its beginning [4] when Cities receiv'd theirs,

44

and that that onely is proper to each man which he can keep by the Lawes, and the power of the whole City, (that is) of him on whom its chief command is conferr'd. Whence we understand, that each particular Citizen hath a propriety, to which none of his fellow–Citizens hath Right, because they are tyed to the same Lawes; but he hath no propriety in which the Chief Ruler (whose Commands are the Lawes, whose will contains the will of each man, and who, by every single person, is constituted the Supreme Judge) hath not a Right. But although there be many things which the City permits to its Citizens, and therefore they may sometimes goe to Law against their Chief; yet is not that action belonging to Civill Right, but to Naturall Equity; neither is it concerning what by Right he may doe [5] who hath the Supreme power, but what he hath been willing should be done, and therefore he shall be judge himself, as though (the equity of the cause being well understood) he could not give wrong judgment.

XVI. Theft, Murther, Adultery, and all injuries are forbid by the Lawes of nature; but what is to be called Theft, what Murther, what Adultery, what injury in a Citizen, this is not to be determined by the naturall, but by the civill Law: for not every taking away of the thing which another possesseth, but onely another mans goods is theft; but what is ours, and what anothers, is a question belonging to the civill Law. In like manner, not every killing of a man is murther, but onely that which the civill Law forbids; neither is all encounter with women Adultery, but onely that which the civill Law prohibits. Lastly, all breach of promise is an injury, where the promise it selfe is lawfull, but where there is no Right to make any compact, there can be no conveighance of it, and therefore there can no injury follow, as hath been said in the second Chapter, Artic.

17. Now what we may contract for, and what not, depends wholly upon the civill Lawes. The City of Lacedoemon therefore rightly ordered that those young men who could so take away certaine goods from others as not to be caught, should goe unpunisht; for it was nothing else, but to make a Law that what was so acquired should be their own, and not anothers. Rightly also is that man every where slain, whom we kill in warre, or by the necessity of selfe–defence. So also that copulation which in one City is Matrimony, in another will be judged Adultery. Also those contracts which make up Marriage in one Citizen, doe not so in another, although of the same City; because that he who is forbidden by the City (that is by that one man, or Councell, whose the supreme power is) to contract ought, hath no Right to make any contract, and therefore having made any, it is not valid, and by consequence, no Marriage. But his contract which received no prohibition, was therefore of force, and so was Matrimony: neither addes it any force to any unlawfull contracts, that they were made by an Oath, or Sacrament, [6] for those adde nothing to the strengthning of the contract, as hath been said above Chap. 2. Artic. 22. What therefore Theft, what Murther, what Adultery, and in generall what injury is, must be known by the civill Lawes, that is, the commands of him who hath the supreme authority.

XVII. This same supreme command, and absolute power, seems so harsh to the greatest part of men, as they hate the very naming of them; which happens chiefly through want of knowledge, what humane nature, and the civill Lawes are, and partly also through their default, who when they are invested with so great authority, abuse their power to their own lust. That they may therefore avoyd this kind of supreme authority, some of them will have a City well enough constituted, if they who shall be the Citizens convening, doe agree concerning certaine Articles propounded, and in that convent agitated and approved; and doe command them to be observed, and punishments prescribed to be inflicted on them who shall break them: to which purpose, and also to the repelling of a forraign enemy, they appoint a certain and limited return, with this condition, that if that suffice not, they may call a new convention of estates. Who sees

45

not in a City thus constituted, that the Assembly who prescribed those things had an absolute power? If therefore the assembly continue, or from time to time have a certain day, and place of meeting, that power will be perpetuall. But if they wholly dissolve, either the City dissolves with them, and so all is returned to the state of War, or else there is somewhere a power left to punish those who shall transgresse the Lawes, whosoever, or how many soever they be that have it, which cannot possibly be without an absolute power: for he that by right hath this might given, by punishments to restrain what Citizens he pleaseth, hath such a power, as a greater cannot possibly be given by any Citizens.

XVIII. It is therefore manifest, that in every City there is some one man, or Councell, or Court, who by Right hath as great a power over each single Citizen, as each man hath over himselfe considered out of that civill state, that is, supreme and absolute, to be limited onely by the strength and forces of the City it selfe, and by nothing else in the world: for if his power were limited, that limitation must necessarily proceed from some greater power; For he that prescribes limits, must have a greater power than he who is confin'd by them; now that confining power is either without limit, or is again restrained by some other greater than it selfe, and so we shall at length arrive to a power which hath no other limit, but that which is the terminus ultimus of the forces of all the Citizens together. That same is called the supreme command, and if it bee committed to a councell, a supreme councell, but if to one man, the supreme Lord of the City. Now the notes of supreme command are these, To make and abrogate Lawes. To determine War and peace, to know, and judge of all controversies, either by himselfe, or by Judges appointed by him; to elect all Magistrates; Ministers, and Counsellors. Lastly, if there be any man who by Right can doe some one action which is not lawfull for any Citizen or Citizens to doe beside himselfe, that man hath obtained the supreme power: For those things which by Right may not be done by any one or many Citizens, the City it selfe can onely doe: He therefore that doth those things useth the Cities Right, which is the supreme power.

XIX. They who compare a City and its Citizens, with a man and his members, almost all say, that he who hath the supreme power in the City, is in relation to the whole City, such as the head is to the whole man; But it appeares by what hath been already said, that he who is endued with such a power, (whether it be a man, or a Court) hath a relation to the City, not as that of the head, but of the soule to the body. For it is the soule by which a man hath a will, that is, can either will, or nill; so by him who hath the supreme power, and no otherwise, the City hath a will, and can either will or nill. A Court of Counsellors is rather to be compared with the head, or one Counsellor, whose only Counsell (if of any one alone) the chief Ruler makes use of in matters of greatest moment: for the office of the head is to counsell, as the soules is to command.

XX. Forasmuch as the supreme command is constituted by vertue of the compacts which each single Citizen, or subject, mutually makes with the other; but all contracts, as they receive their force from the contractors, so by their consent they lose it again, and are broken; perhaps some may inferre hence, that by the consent of all the subjects together, the supreme authority may be wholly taken away. Which inference if it were true, I cannot discerne what danger would thence by Right arise to the supreme Commanders. For since it is supposed, that each one hath obliged himselfe to each other, if any one of them shall refuse, whatsoever the rest shall agree to doe, he is bound notwithstanding; neither can any man without injury to me, doe that which by contract made with me, he hath obliged himselfe not to doe. But it is not to be imagined that ever it will happen, that all the subjects together, not so much as one excepted, will combine against the supreme power; wherefore there is no feare for Rulers in chiefe, that by any Right they can be despoyled of their authority. If notwithstanding it were granted, that their Right depended onely on that contract which each man makes with his fellow–citizen, it might very easily happen, that they might be robbed of that Dominion under pretence of Right; for subjects being called either by the command of the City, or seditiously flocking together, most men think that the consents of all are contained in the votes of the greater part. Which in truth is false; for it is not from nature that the consent of the major part should be received for the consent of all, neither is it true in tumults, but it proceeds from civill institution, and is then onely true, when that Man or Court which hath the supreme power, assembling his subjects, by reason of the greatnesse of their number, allowes those that are elected a power of speaking for those who elected them, and will have the major part of voyces, in such matters as are by him propounded to be discust, to be as effectuall as the whole. But we cannot imagine that he who is chiefe, ever convened his subjects with intention that they should dispute his Right, unlesse, weary of the burthen of his charge, he declared in plain termes, that he renounces and abandons his government. Now because most men through ignorance esteem not the consent of the major part of Citizens only, but even of a very few, provided they be of their opinion, for the consent of the whole City, it may very well seem to them, that the supreme authority may by right be abrogated, so it be done in some great Assembly of Citizens by the votes of the greater number; But though a government be constituted by the contracts of particular men with particulars, yet its Right depends not on that obligation onely; there is another tye also toward him who commands; for each Citizen compacting with his fellow, sayes thus, I conveigh my Right on this party, upon condition, that you passe yours to the same; by which means, that Right which every man had before to use his faculties to his own advantage, is now wholly translated on some certain man, or Councell, for the common benefit; wherefore what by the mutuall contracts each one hath made with the other, what by the donation of Right which every man is bound to ratifie to him that commands, the government is upheld by a double obligation from the Citizens, first that which is due to their fellow citizens, next that which they owe to their prince. Wherefore no subjects how many soever they be, can with any Right despoyle him who bears the chiefe Rule, of his authority, even without his own consent.

1. Multitude, The Doctrine of the Power of a City over it's Citizens, almost wholly depends on the understanding of the difference which is between a multitude of men ruling, and a multitude ruled: For such is the nature of a City, That a multitude, or company of Citizens, not onely may have command, but may also be subject to command, but in diverse senses; which difference I did beleeve was clearly enough explained in this first Article; but by the objections of many against those things which follow, I discern otherwise; wherefore it seemed good to me, to the end I might make a fuller explication, to adde these few things.

By Multitude, because it is a collective word, we understand more than one, so as a multitude of men is the same with many men; The same word, because it is of the singular number, signifies one thing, namely, one multitude; but in neither sense can a multitude be understood to have one will given to it by nature, but to either a severall; and therefore neither is any one action whatsoever to be attributed to it: therefore a Multitude cannot promise, contract, acquire Right, conveigh Right, act, have, Possesse, and the like, unlesse it be every one apart, and Man by Man; so as there must be as many promises, compacts, rights, and actions, as Men. Wherefore a Multitude is no naturall Person; but if the same Multitude doe Contract one with another, that the will of one man, or the agreeing wills of the major part of them, shall be received for the will of all, then it becomes one Person; for it is endu'd with a will, and therefore can doe voluntary actions, such as are Commanding, making Lawes, acquiring and transferring of Right, and so forth; and it is oftner call'd the People, than the Multitude. We must therefore distinguish thus. When we say the People, or Multitude, wills, commands, or doth any thing, it is understood that the City which Commands, wills and Acts by the will of one, or the concurring wills of more, which cannot be done, but in an Assembly; But as oft as any thing is said to be done by a Multitude of Men, whether great, or small, without the will of that man, or assembly of men, that's understood to be done by a subjected People, that is, by many single Citizens together, and not proceeding from one will, but from diverse wills of diverse men, who are Citizens, and Subjects, but not a City.

2. Judge what opinions, There is scarce any Principle, neither in the worship of God, nor humane sciences, from whence there may not spring dissentions, discords, reproaches, and by degrees war it selfe; neither doth this happen by reason of the falshood of the Principle, but of the disposition of men, who seeming wise to themselves, will needs appear such to all others: But though such dissentions cannot be hindered from arising, yet may they be restrained by the exercise of the supreme Power, that they Prove no hinderance to the publique peace. Of these kind of opinions therefore I have not spoken of in this place. There are certain doctrines wherewith Subjects being tainted, they verily believe that obedience may be refused to the City, and that by Right they may, nay ought, to oppose, and fight against chiefe Princes, and dignities. Such are those, which whether directly, and openly, or more obscurely, and by consequence require obedience to be given to others beside them to whom the supreme authority is committed. I deny not, but this reflects on that Power which many living under other government, ascribe to the chiefe head of the Church of Rome, and also on that, which elsewhere out of that Church, Bishops require in theirs, to be given to them; and last of all, on that liberty which the lower sort of Citizens under pretence of Religion doe challenge to themselves; for what civill war was there ever in the Christian world, which did not either grow from, or was nourisht by this Root? The judgement therefore of doctrines, whether they be repugnant to civill obedience or not, and if they be repugnant, the Power of prohibiting them to be taught, I doe here attribute to the civill authority; for since there is no man who grants not to the City the judgement of those things which belong to its Peace, and defence, and it is manifest, that the opinions which I have already recited do relate to its Peace, it followes necessarily, that the examination of those opinions, whether they be such, or not, must be referred to the City, that is, to him who hath the supreme authority.

3. Absolute. A popular state openly challengeth absolute dominion, and the Citizens oppose it not, for in the gathering together of many men, they acknowledge the face of a City; and even the unskilfull understand, that matters there are rul'd by Counsell. Yet monarchy is no lesse a City, than Democraty, and absolute Kings have their Counsellours, from whom they will take advice, and suffer their Power, in matters of greater consequence, to be guided, but not recall'd. But it appears not to most men how a City is contain'd in the person of a King; and therefore they object against Absolute Command: First, that if any man had such a Right, the condition of the Citizens would be miserable: For thus they think, he will take all, spoil all, kill all; and every man counts it his onely happinesse that he is not already spoil'd and kill'd. But why should he doe thus? Not because he can; for unlesse he have a mind to it, he will not doe it. Will he, to please one, or some few, spoil all the rest? First, though by Right, that is, without injury to them, he may doe it, yet can he not doe it justly, that is, without breach of the Naturall Lawes, and injury against God. And therefore there is some security for Subjects in the Oaths which princes take. Next, if he could justly doe it, or that he made no account of his Oath, yet appeares there no reason why he should desire it, since he findes no good in it. But it cannot be deny'd but a prince may sometimes have an inclination to doe wickedly; but grant then that thou hadst given him a power which were not absolute, but so much onely as suffic'd to defend thee from

the injuries of others, which, if thou wilt be safe, is necessary for thee to give; are not all the same things to be feared? For he that hath strength enough to protect all, wants not sufficiency to oppresse all. Here is no other difficulty then, but that humane affaires cannot be without some inconvenience. And this inconvenience it self is in the Citizens, not in the Government; for if men could rule themselves, every man by his own command, that's to say, could they live according to the Lawes of Nature, there would be no need at all of a City, nor of a common coercive power. Secondly, they object, That there is no Dominion in the Christian world Absolute; which indeed is not true, for all Monarchies, and all other States, are so; for although they, who have the chief Command, doe not all those things they would, and what they know profitable to the City, the reason of that is not the defect of Right in them, but the consideration of their Citizens, who busied about their private interest, and carelesse of what tends to the publique, cannot sometimes be drawn to performe their duties without the hazard of the City. Wherefore princes sometimes forbear the exercise of their Right, and prudently remit somewhat of the act, but nothing of their Right.

4. *Propriety receiv'd its beginning,* What's objected by some, That the propriety of goods, even before the constitution of Cities, was found in Fathers of Families, that objection is vaine, because I have already declar'd, That a Family is a little City. For the Sonnes of a Family have a propriety of their goods granted them by their Father, distinguisht indeed from the rest of the Sons of the same Family, but not from the propriety of the Father himself; but the Fathers of diverse Families, who are subject neither to any common Father, nor Lord, have a common Right in all things.

5. *What by Right he may doe,* As often as a Citizen is granted to have an action of Law against the Supreme, i.e. against the City, the question is not in that action, whether the City may, by Right, keep possession of the thing in controversie, but whether by the Lawes formerly made she would keep it; for the Law is the declared will of the Supreme: since then the City may raise money from the Citizens under two Titles, either as Tribute, or as Debt, in the former case there is no action of Law allowed; for there can be no question whether the City have Right to require Tribute: in the latter it is allowed, because the City will take nothing from its Citizens by fraud, or cunning, and yet if need require, all they have, openly; and therefore he that condemnes this place, saying, That by this doctrine it is easie for princes to free themselves from their Debts, he does it impertinently.

6. *That they were made by an Oath or Sacrament,* Whether Matrimony bee a Sacrament (in which sense that word is used by some Divines) or not, it is not my purpose to dispute: Onely I say, that the legitimate contract of a man and woman to live together, i.e. granted by the civill Law, whether it be a Sacrament, or not, is surely a legitimate Marriage; but that copulation which the City hath prohibited is no marriage, since it is of the essence of Marriage to be a legitimate contract. There were legitimate marriages in many places, as among the Jewes, the Grecians, the Romans, which yet might be dissolved. But with those who permit no such contracts, but by a Law that they shall never be broke, Wedlock cannot be dissolved; and the reason is, because the City hath commanded it to be indissoluble, not because Matrimony is a Sacrament. Wherefore the ceremonies which at weddings are to be performed in the Temple, to blesse, or (if I may say so) to consecrate the husband and wife, will perhaps belong only to the office of Clergy—men; all the rest, namely who, when, and by what contracts Marriages may be made, pertains to the Lawes of the City.

CHAPTER VII. OF THE THREE KINDES OF GOVERNMENT, DEMOCRACY, ARISTOCRACY, MONARCHIE

I. We have already spoken of a City by institution in its Genus; we will now say somewhat of its species. As for the difference of Cities, it is taken from the difference of the Persons, to whom the Supreme Power is committed; this Power is committed either to one Man, or Councell, or some one Court consisting of many men. Furthermore, a Councell of many men, consists either of all the Citizens, (insomuch as every man of them hath a Right to Vote, and an interest in the ordering of the greatest affaires, if he will himselfe) or of a part onely; from whence there arise three sorts of Government: The one, when the Power is in a Councell, where every Citizen hath a right to Vote, and it is call'd a DEMOCRATY. The other, when it is in a Councell, where not all, but some part onely have their suffrages, and we call it an ARISTOCRATY. The third is that, when the Supreme Authority rests onely in one, and it is stiled a MONARCHY. In the first, he that governes is called demos, The PEOPLE. In the second, the NOBLES. In the third, the MONARCH.

II. Now, although Ancient Writers of Politiques have introduc'd three other kindes of Government opposite to these, to wit, Anarchy or confusion to Democraty, Oligarchy, that is, the command of some few, to Aristocraty, and Tyranny to Monarchy, yet are not these three distinct formes of Government, but three diverse Titles given by those who were either displeas'd with that present Government, or those that bare Rule. For men, by giving names, doe usually, not onely signifie the things themselves, but also their own affections, as love, hatred, anger, and the like, whence it happens that what one man calls a Democraty, another calls an Anarchy; what one counts an Aristocraty, another esteemes an Oligarchie; and whom one titles a King, another stiles him a Tyrant; so as we see these names betoken not a diverse kinde of Government, but the diverse opinions of the Subjects concerning him who hath the Supreme Power. For first, who sees not that Anarchy is equally opposite to all the forenam'd Formes? For that word signifies that there is no Government at all, that is, not any City. But how is it possible that no City should be the species of a City? Farthermore, what difference is there between an Oligarchie, which signifies the Command of a few, or Grandees, or an Aristocraty, which is that of the Prime, or Chief Heads, more than that men differ so among themselves, that the same things seeme not good to all men? Whence it happens, that those persons, who by some are look'd on as the best, are by others esteem'd to be the worst of all men.

III. But men, by reason of their passions, will very hardly be perswaded that a Kingdome, and Tyranny, are not diverse kindes of Cities, who though they would rather have the City subject to one, than many, yet doe they not beleeve it to be well govern'd unlesse it accord with their judgements: But we must discover by Reason, and not by Passion, what the difference is between a King, and a Tyrant: but first, they differ not in this, That a Tyrant hath the greater Power, for greater than the Supreme cannot be granted; nor in this, That one hath a limited power, the other not; for he, whose authority is limited, is no King, but his Subject that limits him. Lastly, neither differ they in their manner of acquisition; for if in a Democraticall, or Aristocraticall Government some one Citizen should, by force, possesse himself of the Supreme Power, if he gain the consent of all the Citizens, he becomes a legitimate Monarch; if not, he is an Enemy, not a Tyrant. They differ therefore in the sole exercise of their command, insomuch as he is said to be a King, who governs wel, and he a Tyrant that doth otherwise. The case therefore is brought to this passe,

That a King legitimately constituted in his Government, if he seeme to his Subjects to Rule well, and to their liking, they afford him the appellation of a King, if not, they count him a Tyrant. Wherefore we see a Kingdome, and Tyranny, are not diverse Formes of Government, but one and the self–same Monarch hath the name of a King given him in point of Honour, and Reverence to him, and of a Tyrant in way of contumely, and reproach. But what we frequently finde in bookes said against Tyrants, took its originall from Greek, and Roman Writers, whose Government was partly Democraticall, and partly Aristocraticall, and therefore not Tyrants onely, but even Kings were odious to them.

IV. There are, who indeed doe think it necessary, That a Supreme Command should be somewhere extant in a City; but if it should be in any one, either Man, or Councell, it would follow (they say) that all the Citizens must be slaves. Avoiding this condition, they imagine that there may be a certaine Form of Government compounded of those three kinds we have spoken of, yet different from each particular, which they call a mixt Monarchie, or mixt Aristocraty, or mixt Democraty, according as any one of these three sorts shall be more eminent than the rest: For example, if the naming of Magistrates, and the arbitration of War, and Peace, should belong to the King, Judicature to the Lords, and contribution of Monies to the People, and the power of making Lawes too altogether, this kind of State would they call a mixt Monarchie forsooth. But if it were possible that there could be such a State, it would no whit advantage the liberty of the subject; for as long as they all agree, each single Citizen is as much subject as possibly he can be; but if they disagree, the State returns to a Civill War, and the Right of the private Sword, which certainly is much worse than any subjection whatsoever: But that there can be no such kind of Government [1] hath been sufficiently demonstrated in the foregoing Chapter, Artic: 6–12.

V. Let us see a little now in the constituting of each Form of Government, what the constitutours doe. Those who met together with intention to erect a City, were almost in the very act of meeting a Democraty; for in that they willingly met, they are suppos'd oblig'd to the observation of what shall be determin'd by the major part: which, while that convent lasts, or is adjourn'd to some certain dayes, and places, is a clear Democraty; for that convent, whose will is the will of all the Citizens, hath the Supreme Authority; and because in this Convent every man is suppos'd to have a Right to give his voice, it followes, that it is a Democraty by the definition given in the first Article of this Chap. But if they depart, and break up the Convent, and appoint no time, or place, where, and when they shall meet again, the publick weal returns to Anarchy, and the same state it stood in before their meeting, that is, to the state of all men warring against all. The People therefore retains the supreme power no longer than there is a certain day and place publiquely appointed, and known, to which whosoever will, may resort. For except that be known and determined, they may either meet at divers times, and places, that is in factions, or not at all; and then it is no longer demos, the People, but a dissolute multitude, to whom we can neither attribute any Action, or Right: Two things therefore frame a Democratie, whereof one (to wit the perpetuall prescription of Convents) makes demos, the People, the other (which is a plurality of voyces) to kratos or the power.

VI. Furthermore, it will not be sufficient for the People, so as to maintain its supremacy, to have some certain known times, and places of meeting, unless that either the intervals of the times be of lesse distance, than that any thing may in the mean time happen whereby (by reason of the defect of power) the City may be brought into some danger, or at least that the exercise of the supreme authority be, during the intervall, granted to some one man, or Councell. For unless this be done, there is not that wary care, and heed taken for the defence and Peace of single men which ought to be, and therefore will not deserve the name of a City, because that in it for want of security, every mans Right of defending himselfe at his own pleasure, returns to him again.

VII. Democraty is not framed by contract of particular persons with the People, but by mutuall compacts of single men each with other. But hence it appears in the first place, that the Persons contracting, must be in being before the contract it selfe. But the People is not in being before the constitution of government, as not being any Person, but a multitude of single Persons; wherefore there could then no contract passe between the People and the Subject. Now, if after that government is framed, the subject make any contract with the People, it is in vain, because the People contains within its will, the will of that subject to whom it is supposed to be obliged; and therefore may at its own will and pleasure disengage it selfe, and by consequence is now actually free. But in the second place, that single Persons doe contract each with other may be inferred from hence, that in vain sure would the City have been constituted, if the Citizens had been engaged by no contracts to doe, or omit what the City should command to be done or omitted. Because therefore such kind of compacts must be understood to passe as necessary to the making up of a City, but none can be made (as is already shewed) between the Subject and the People; it followes, that they must be made between single Citizens, namely that each man contract to submit his will to the will of the major part, on condition that the rest also doe the like, as if every one should say thus, I give up my Right unto the People for your sake, on condition, that you also deliver up yours, for mine.

VIII. An Aristocraty, or Councell of Nobles endued with supreme authoritie, receives its originall from a Democraty, which gives up its Right unto it; where we must understand that certain men distinguisht from others, either by eminence of title, blood, or some other Character, are propounded to the People, and by plurality of voyces are elected; and being elected, the whole Right of the People, or City, is conveighed on them, insomuch as whatsoever the People might doe before, the same by Right may this Court of elected Nobles now doe. Which being done, it is clear that the People, considered as one Person, (its supreme authority being already transferred on these) is no longer now in being.

IX. As in Democraty the People, so in an Aristocraty the Court of Nobles is free from all manner of obligation; for seeing subjects not contracting with the People, but by mutuall compacts among themselves, were tyed to all that the People did, hence also they were tyed to that act of the People in resigning up its Right of government into the hands of Nobles. Neither could this Court, although elected by the People, be by it obliged to any thing; for being erected, the People is at once dissolved, as was declared above, and the authority it had as being a Person utterly vanisheth. Wherefore the obligation which was due to the Person must also vanish, and perish together with it.

X. Aristocraty hath these considerations, together with Democraty; First, that without an appointment of some certain times, and places, at which the Court of Nobles may meet, it is no longer a Court, or one Person, but a dissolute multitude without any supreme power; Secondly, that the times of their assembling cannot be disjoyned by long intervalls, without prejudice to the supreme power, unless its administration be transferred to some one man: Now the reasons why this happens, are the same which we set down in the fifth Article.

XI. As an Aristocratie, so also a monarchy is derived from the Power of the People, transferring its Right, (that is) its Authoritie on one man: Here also we must understand, that some one man, either by name, or some other token, is propounded to be taken notice of above all the rest, and that by a plurality of voyces the whole Right of the People is conveighed on him, insomuch as whatsoever the People could doe before he were elected, the same in every Respect may he by Right now doe, being elected; which being done, the People is no longer one Person, but a rude multitude, as being only one before by vertue of the supreme command, whereof they now have made a conveyance from themselves on this one Man.

XII. And therefore neither doth the Monarch oblige himselfe to any for the command he receives, for he receives it from the People; but as hath been shewed above, the People, as soon as that act is done, ceaseth to be a Person; but the Person vanishing, all obligation to the Person vanisheth. The subjects therefore are tyed to perform obedience to the Monarch, by those compacts only by which they mutually obliged themselves to the observation of all that the People should command them, (that is) to obey that Monarch, if he were made by the People.

XIII. But a Monarchy differs as well from an Aristocraty, as a Democratie, in this chiefly, that in those there must be certain set times and places for deliberation, and consultation of affaires, that is, for the actuall exercise of it in all times, and places; For the People, or the Nobles not being one naturall Person must necessarily have their meetings. The Monarch who is one by nature, is alwayes in a present capacity to execute his authority.

XIV. Because we have declared above in the 7. 9. and 12. Articles, that they who have gotten the supreme command are by no compacts obliged to any man, it necessarily followes, that they can doe no injury to the subjects; for injury according to the definition made in the third Article of the third Chapter, is nothing else but a breach of contract: and therefore where no contracts have part, there can be no injury. Yet the People, the Nobles, and the Monarch may diverse wayes transgresse against the other Lawes of nature, as by cruelty, iniquity, contumely, and other like vices, which come not under this strict, and exact notion of injury. But if the subject yeeld not obedience to the supreme, he will in propriety of speech be said to be injurious as well to his fellow subjects, because each man hath compacted with the other to obey, as to his chief Ruler, in resuming that Right, which he hath given him, without his consent. And in a Democraty, or Aristocraty, if any thing be decreed against any Law of nature, the City it selfe (i.e.) the civill Person sinnes not, but those subjects only by whose votes it was decreed; for sinne is a consequence of the naturall expresse will, not of the politicall, which is artificiall; for if it were otherwise, they would be guilty, by whom the decree was absolutely disliked: But in a Monarchie, if the Monarch make any decree against the Lawes of nature, he sins himselfe, because in him the civill will and the naturall are all one.

XV. The people who are about to make a Monarch, may give him the supremacy either simply without limitation of time, or for a certaine season; and time determined; if simply, we must understand that he who receives it, hath the selfe−same power which they had, who gave it, on the same grounds: therefore that the People by Right could make him a Monarch, may he make another Monarch: insomuch as the Monarch to whom the command is simply given, receives a Right not of possession onely, but of succession also, so as he may declare whom hee pleaseth for his successor.

XVI. But if the power be given for a time limited, we must have regard to somewhat more than the bare gift onely: First, whether the People conveighing its authority, left it selfe any Right to meet at certain times, and places, or not. Next, if it have reserved this power, whether it were done, so as they might meet before that time were expired, which they prescribed to the

Monarch. Thirdly, whether they were contented to meet onely at the will of that temporary Monarch and not otherwise. Suppose now the People had delivered up its Power to some one man for term of life onely; which being done, let us suppose in the first place, that every man departed from the Counsell without making any order at all concerning the place where (after his death) they should meet again to make a new election. In this case it is manifest by the fifth Article of this Chapter, that the People ceaseth to be a Person, and is become a dissolute multitude, every one whereof hath an equall, to wit, a naturall Right to meet with whom he lists at divers times, and in what places shall best please him; nay, and if he can, engrosse the supreme power to himselfe, and settle it on his own head. What Monarch soever therefore hath a command in such a condition, he is bound by the Law of nature (set down in the [8.] Article of the third Chapter of not returning evill for good) prudently to provide, that by his death the City suffer not a dissolution, either by appointing a certain day place, in which those subjects of his who have a mind to it may assemble themselves, or else by nominating a successor: whether of these shall to him seem most conducible to their common benefit. He therefore who on this foresaid manner hath received his command during life, hath an absolute Power, and may at his discretion dispose of the succession. In the next place, if we grant that the people departed not from the election of the temporary Monarch, before they decreed a certain time and place of meeting after his death, then the Monarch being dead, the authority is confirmed in the people, not by any new acts of the subjects, but by vertue of the former Right; for all the supreme command (as Dominion) was in the People, but the use, and exercise of it was only in the temporary Monarch, as in one that takes the benefit, but hath not the Right. But if the People after the election of a temporary Monarch, depart not from the Court before they have appointed certain times, and places to convene, during the time prescribed him (as the Dictators in ancient times were made by the People of Rome) such an one is not to be accounted a Monarch, but the Prime Officer of the People; and if it shall seem good, the People may deprive him of his office even before that time, as the People of Rome did, when they conferred an equall power on Minutius, Master of the horse, with Quintus Fabius Maximus, whom before they had made Dictator. The reason whereof is, that it is not to be imagined, that, whether Man or Counsell who hath the readiest, and most immediate power to act, should hold his command on such termes as not to be able actually to execute it; for command is nothing else but a Right of commanding, as oft as nature allowes it possible. Lastly, if the People having declared a temporary Monarch, depart from the Court on such termes, as it shall not be lawfull for them to meet without the command of the Monarch, we must understand the People to be immediately dissolved, and that his authority who is thus declared, is absolute; forasmuch as it is not in the power of all the subjects to frame the City anew, unless he give consent who hath now alone the authority. Nor matters it, that he hath perhaps made any promise to assemble his Subjects on some certain times, since there remains no Person now in being, but at his discretion, to whom the promise was made.

What we have spoken of these four cases of a People electing a Temporary Monarch will be more clearly explain'd by comparing them with an absolute Monarch, who hath no heir apparent; for the People is Lord of the subject in such a manner as there can be no Heir but whom it self doth appoint. Besides, the spaces between the times of the subjects meeting may be fitly compar'd to those times wherein the Monarch sleepes, for in either the Acts of commanding ceases, the Power remaines: Farthermore, to dissolve the convent, so as it cannot meet againe, is the death of the People; just as sleeping, so as he can never wake more, is the death of a man: As therefore a King, who hath no Heir, going to his rest, so as never to rise again, (i.e.) dying, if he commit the exercise of his Regall Authority to any one till he awake, does by consequence give him the Succession; the People also electing a Temporary Monarch, and

54

not reserving a power to convene, delivers up to him the whole Dominion of the Country: Furthermore, as a King going to sleep for some season, entrusts the administration of his Kingdome to some other, and waking takes it again; so the people having elected a Temporary Monarch, and withall retaining a right to meet at a certain day, and place, at that day receives its supremacy again. And as a King who hath committed the execution of his Authority to another, himself in the mean while waking, can recall this commission againe when he pleaseth; so the People, who during the time prescribed to the Temporary Monarch, doth by Right convene, may if they please, deprive the Monarch of his Authority. Lastly, the King, who commits his Authority to another while himself sleeps, not being able to wake againe till he whom he entrusted, give consent, loses at once both his power, and his life; so the people, who hath given the Supreme Power to a temporary Monarch in such sort as they cannot assemble without his command is absolutely dissolv'd, and the power remaines with him whom they have chosen.

XVII. If the Monarch promise ought to any one, or many subjects together, by consequence whereof the exercise of his power may suffer prejudice, that Promise or Compact whether made by Oath, or without it, is null: for all Compact is a conveyance of Right, which by what hath been said in the fourth Article of the second Chapter, requires meet, and proper signes of the Will in the conveyer. But he who sufficiently signifies his will of retaining the end, doth also sufficiently declare that he quits not his Right to the means necessary to that end. Now he who hath promis'd to part with somewhat necessary to the Supreme Power, and yet retaines the Power it selfe, gives sufficient tokens, That he no otherwise promis'd it then so farre forth as the power might be retain'd without it. Whensoever therefore it shall appear that what is promis'd cannot be perform'd without prejudice to the Power, the promise must be valued as not made, (i.e.) of no effect.

XVIII. We have seen how Subjects, nature dictating, have oblig'd themselves by mutuall Compacts to obey the Supreme Power. We will see now by what meanes it comes to passe that they are releas'd from these bonds of obedience. And first of all this happens by rejection, namely, if a man cast off, or forsake, but conveigh not the Right of his Command on some other; for what is thus rejected, is openly expos'd to all alike, catch who catch can; whence again, by the Right of nature, every subject may heed the preservation of himselfe according to his own judgement. In the second place, If the Kingdome fall into the power of the enemy, so as there can no more opposition be made against them, we must understand that he, who before had the Supreme Authority, hath now lost it: For when the Subjects have done their full indeavour to prevent their falling into the enemies hands, they have fulfill'd those Contracts of obedience which they made each with other, and what, being conquer'd, they promise afterwards, to avoid death, they must, with no lesse endeavour, labour to performe. Thirdly, in a Monarchy, (for a Democraty, and Aristocraty cannot fail) if there be no successour, all the subjects are discharg'd from their obligations; for no man is suppos'd to be tyed he knows not to whom, for in such a case it were impossible to perform ought. And by these three wayes all subjects are restor'd from their civill subjection to that liberty, which all men have to all things, to wit, naturall, and salvage, (for the naturall state hath the same proportion to the Civill, I mean liberty to subjection, which Passion hath to Reason, or a Beast to a Man:) Furthermore, each subject may lawfully be freed from his subjection by the will of him who hath the Supreme Power, namely, if he change his soile, which may be done two wayes, either by permission, as he, who gets license to dwell in another Country; or Command, as he, who is Banisht: In both cases he is free from the Lawes of his former Country, because he is tyed to observe those of the latter.

55

1. But that there can be no such kinde of Government. Most men grant, That a Government ought not to be divided, but they would have it moderated, and bounded by some limits. Truly it is very reasonable it should be so; but if these men, when they speak of moderating, and limiting, do understand dividing it, they make a very fond distinction. Truly, for my part, I wish that not onely Kings, but all other Persons endued with Supreme Authority would so temper themselves as to commit no wrong, and onely minding their charges contain themselves within the limits of the naturall, and divine Lawes: But they who distinguish thus, they would have the chief Power bounded, and restrain'd by others; which, because it cannot be done, but that they who doe set the limits, must needs have some part of the Power, whereby they may be enabled to doe it, the Government is properly divided, not moderated.

CHAPTER VIII. OF THE RIGHTS OF LORDS OVER THEIR SERVANT

I. In the two fore−going Chapters we have treated of an institutive, or fram'd Government, as being that which receives its originall from the consent of many, who by Contract and Faith mutually given, have oblig'd each other. Now followes, what may be said, concerning a naturall Government, which may also be call'd, Acquired, because it is that which is gotten by power, and naturall force. But we must know in the first place by what means the Right of Dominion may be gotten over the Persons of men. Where such a Right is gotten, there is a kind of a little Kingdome; for to be a King, is nothing else but to have Dominion over many Persons; and thus a Great Family is a Kingdom, a Little Kingdome a Family. Let us return again to the state of nature, and consider men as if but even now sprung out of the earth, and suddainly (like Mushromes) come to full maturity without all kind of engagement to each other: There are but three wayes only whereby one can have the Dominion over the Person of another; whereof the first is, if by mutuall Contract made between themselves (for Peace, self−defences sake) they have willingly given up themselves to the Power and Authority of some man, or Councel of Men, of this we have already spoken. The 2d is, If a man taken Prisoner in the Wars, or overcome; or else distrusting his own forces, (to avoid Death) promises the Conquerour, or the stronger Party, his Service, i.e. to do all whatsoever he shall command him; in which Contract the good which the vanquisht, or inferiour, in strength doth receive, is the grant of his life, which by the Right of War in the naturall state of men he might have depriv'd him of, but the good which he promises, is his service and obedience. By vertue therefore of this promise, there is as absolute service and obedience due from the vanquisht, to the vanquisher, as possibly can be, excepting what repugns the Divine Lawes; for he who is oblig'd to obey the Commands of any man before he knowes what he will command him, is simply, and without any restriction tyed to the performance of all Commands whatsoever. Now he that is thus tyed, is call'd a SERVANT, he to whom he is tyed, a LORD. Thirdly, there is a Right acquir'd over the Person of a Man, by Generation; of which kind of acquisition somewhat shall be spoken in the following Chapter.

II. Every one that is taken in the War, and hath his life spar'd him, is not suppos'd to have Contracted with his Lord; for every one is not trusted with so much of his naturall liberty, as to be able, if he desir'd it, either to flie away, or quit his service, or contrive any mischief to his Lord. And these serve indeed but within Prisons, or bound within Irons, and therefore they were call'd not by the common name of Servant onely, but by the peculiar name of Slave, even as now at this day un serviteur, and un serf or un esclave have diverse significations.

III. The obligation therefore of a Servant to his Lord ariseth not from a simple grant of his life, but from hence rather, That he keeps him not bound, or imprison'd, for all obligation derives from Contract; but where's no trust, there can be no Contract, as appears by the 2. Chap. Artic. 9. where a Compact is defin'd to be the promise of him who is trusted. There is therefore a confidence and trust which accompanies the benefit of pardon'd life, whereby the Lord affords him his corporall liberty; so that if no obligation, nor bonds of Contract had happen'd, he might not onely have made his escape, but also have kill'd his Lord, who was the preserver of his life.

IV. Wherefore such kind of Servants as are restrain'd by imprisonment, or bonds, are not comprehended in that definition of Servants given above, because those serve not for the Contracts sake, but to the end they may not suffer; and therefore if they flie, or kill their Lord, they offend not against the Lawes of Nature, for to bind any man is a plain signe, that the binder supposes him that is bound not to be sufficiently tyed by any other obligation.

V. The Lord therefore hath no less Dominion over a Servant that is not, than over one that is bound, for he hath a Supreme Power over both, and may say of his Servant no lesse than of another thing, whether animate, or inanimate, This is mine; whence it followes, that whatsoever the Servant had before his servitude, that afterwards becomes the Lords; and whatsoever he hath gotten, it was gotten for his Lord: for he that can by Right dispose of the Person of a man, may surely dispose of all those things which that Person could dispose of. There is therefore nothing which the Servant may retaine as his own against the will of his Lord; yet hath he, by his Lords distribution, a propriety, and Dominion over his own goods, insomuch as one Servant may keep, and defend them against the invasion of his fellow Servant, in the same manner as hath been shewed before, that a subject hath nothing properly his owne against the will of the Supreme Authority, but every subject hath a propriety against his fellow subject.

VI. Since therefore both the Servant himself, and all that belongs to him are his Lords, and by the Right of Nature every man may dispose of his owne in what manner he pleases; the Lord may either sell, lay to pledge, or by Testament conveigh the Dominion he hath over his Servant, according to his own will and pleasure.

VII. Farthermore, what hath before been demonstrated concerning subjects in an institutive Government, namely, that he who hath the Supreme Power can doe his subject no injury; is true also concerning Servants, because they have subjected their will to the will of the Lord; wherefore, whatsoever he doth, it is done with their wills, but no injury can be done to him that willeth it.

VIII. But if it happen that the Lord, either by captivity or voluntary subjection, doth become a Servant or Subject to another, that other shall not onely be Lord of him, but also of his Servants; Supreme Lord over these, immediate Lord over him. Now because not the Servant only, but also all he hath are his Lords; therefore his Servants now belong to this man, neither can the mediate Lord dispose otherwise of them than shall seeme good to the Supreme. And therefore, if sometime in civill Governments, the Lord have an absolute power over his Servants, that's suppos'd to be deriv'd from the Right of Nature, and not constituted, but slightly pass'd over by the Civill Law.

IX. A servant is by the same manner freed from his servitude, that a Subject in an institutive government, is freed from his subjection; First, if his Lord enfranchize him, for the Right which the servant transferred to his Lord over himselfe, the same may the Lord restore to the servant again. And this manner of bestowing of liberty is called MANUMISSION; which is just as if a City should permit a Citizen to conveigh himselfe under the jurisdiction of some other City. Secondly, if the Lord cast off his servant from him, which in a City is banishment; neither differs it from Manumission in effect, but in manner onely: for there, liberty is granted as a favour, here, as a punishment: In both, the Dominion is renounced. Thirdly, if the servant be taken prisoner, the old servitude is abolished by the new; for as all other things, so servants also are acquired by warre, whom in equity the Lord must protect, if he will have them to be his. Fourthly, the servant is freed for want of knowledge of a successour, the Lord dying (suppose) without any Testament, or Heire, for no man is understood to be obliged, unlesse he know to whom he is to perform the obligation. Lastly, the servant that is put in bonds, or by any other means deprived of his corporall liberty, is freed from that other obligation of contract, for there can be no contract where there is no trust, nor can that faith be broken which is not given. But the Lord who himselfe serves another, cannot so free his servants, but that they must still continue under the power of the supreme, for, as hath been shewed before, such servants are not his, but the supreme Lords.

X. We get a right over irrationall Creatures in the same manner, that we doe over the Persons of men, to wit, by force and naturall strength; for if in the state of nature it is lawfull for every one, by reason of that warre which is of all against all, to subdue, and also to kill men as oft as it shall seem to conduce unto their good, much more will the same be lawfull against Brutes; namely at their own discretion, to reduce those to servitude which by art may be tamed, and fitted for use, and to persecute and destroy the rest by a perpetuall warre, as dangerous and noxious. Our Dominion therefore over beasts, hath its originall from the right of nature, not from divine positive Right: for if such a Right had not been before the publishing of the sacred Scriptures, no man by right might have killed a beast for his food, but he to whom the divine pleasure was made manifest by holy Writ; a most hard condition for men indeed whom the beasts might devoure without injury, and yet they might not destroy them: Forasmuch therefore as it proceeds from the right of nature, that a beast may kill a man; it is also by the same Right, that a man may slay a beast.

CHAPTER IX. OF THE RIGHT OF PARENTS OVER THEIR CHILDREN AND OF HEREDITARY GOVERNMENT

I. Socrates is a man, and therefore a living creature, is a right reasoning, and that most evident, because there is nothing needfull to the acknowledging of the truth of the consequence, but that the word Man be understood, because a living creature is in the definition it selfe of a Man, and every one makes up the proposition which was desired, namely this, Man is a living Creature; And this, Sophroniscus is Socrates his Father, and therefore his Lord, is perhaps a true inference, but not evident, because the word Lord is not in the definition of a Father: wherefore it is necessary to make it more evident, that the connexion of Father and Lord be somewhat unfolded. Those that have hitherto endeavoured to prove the Dominion of a Parent over his children, have brought no other argument than that of generation, as if it were of it selfe evident, that what is begotten by me, is mine; just as if a man should think, that because there is a triangle, it appeares presently without any farther discourse, that its angles are equall to two Rights. Besides, since Dominion (that is) supreme Power is indivisible, insomuch as no man can serve two Masters, but two Persons male and female, must concurre in the act of generation, its impossible that Dominion should at all be acquired by generation onely. Wherefore we will with the more diligence in this place, enquire into the original of paternal Government.

II. Wee must therefore returne to the state of nature, in which, by reason of the equality of nature all men of riper yeares are to be accounted equall; There by right of nature the Conqueror is Lord of the conquered: by the Right therefore of nature, the Dominion over the Infant first belongs to him who first hath him in his power'd but it's manifest that he who is newly born is in the Mothers power before any others, insomuch as she may rightly, and at her own wil, either breed him up, or adventure him to fortune.

III. If therefore she breed him (because the state of nature is the state of warre) she is supposed to bring him up on this condition, that being grown to full age he become not her enemy; (which is) that he obey her. For since by naturall necessity we all desire that which appears good unto us, it cannot be understood that any man hath on such termes afforded life to another, that he might both get strength by his years, and at once become an enemy; but each man is an enemy to that other whom he neither obeys nor commands. And thus in the state of nature, every woman that bears children, becomes both a Mother, and a Lord. But what some say, that in this case, the Father by reason of the preeminence of sexe, and not the Mother, becomes Lord, signifies nothing. For both reason shewes the contrary, because the inequality of their naturall forces is not so great, that the man could get the Dominion over the woman without warre. And custome also contradicts not; for women, namely Amazons, have in former times waged war against their adversaries, and disposed of their children at their own wils, and at this day in divers places, women are invested with the principall authority. Neither doe their husbands dispose of their children, but themselves; which in truth they do by the right of nature; forasmuch as they who have the supreme power, are not tyed at all (as hath bin shewed) to the civill lawes. Adde also that in the state of nature it cannot be known who is the Father but by the testimony of the Mother; the child therefore is his whose the Mother will have it, and therefore hers; Wherefore originall Dominion over children belongs to the Mother, and among men no lesse than other creatures: The birth followes the belly.

IV. The Dominion passes from the Mother to others, divers wayes; first, if she quit and forsake her Right by exposing the child. He therefore that shall bring up the childe thus exposed, shall have the same Dominion over it, which the Mother had. For that life which the Mother had given it (not by getting, but nourishing it) she now by exposing, takes from it; Wherefore the obligation also which arose from the benefit of life, is by this exposition made voyd. Now the preserved, oweth all to the preserver, whether in regard of his education as to a Mother, or of his service, as to a Lord; for although the Mother in the state of nature, where all men have a right to all things, may recover her sonne again (namely by the same Right that any body else might doe it) yet may not the Sonne rightly transferre himselfe again unto his Mother.

V. Secondly, if the Mother be taken prisoner, her Sonne is his that took her, because that he who hath Dominion over the Person, hath also Dominion over all belonging to the Person; Wherefore over the Sonne also, as hath been shewed in the foregoing Chapter, in the fifth Article. Thirdly, if the Mother be a subject under what government soever, he that hath the supreme authority in that government, will also have the Dominion over him that is born of her. for he is Lord also of the Mother, who is bound to obey him, in all things. Fourthly, if a woman for societie sake give her selfe to a man on this condition; that he shall bear the sway; he that receives his being from the contribution of both Parties, is the Fathers, in regard of the command he hath over the Mother; but if a woman bearing rule shall have children by a Subject, the children are the Mothers: for otherwise the woman can have no children without prejudice to her authority. And universally, if the society of the male and female be such an union, as the one have subjected himselfe to the other, the children belong to him or her that commands.

VI. But in the state of nature, if a man, and woman contract so, as neither is subject to the command of the other, the children are the Mothers for the reasons above given in the third Article, unlesse by pacts it be otherwise provided. For the Mother may by pact dispose of her Right as she lists, as heretofore hath been done by the Amazons, who of those children which have been begotten by their neighbours, have by pact allowed them the males, and retained the females to themselves; but in a civill government, if there be a contract of marriage between a man and woman, the children are the Fathers; because in all Cities, viz. constituted of Fathers, not Mothers governing their families, the domesticall command belongs to the man, and such a contract, if it be made according to the civill Laws, is called MATRIMONY; but if they agree only to lye together, the children are the Fathers, or the Mothers variously, according to the differing civill Lawes of divers Cities.

VII. Now because by the third Article the Mother is originally Lord of her Children, and from her the Father, or some body else by derived Right, it is manifest that the Children are no lesse subject to those by whom they are nourisht, and brought up, than Servants to their Lords, and Subjects to him who beares the Supreme Rule; and that a Parent cannot be injurious to his Sonne as long as he is under his power. A Son also is freed from subjection on the same manner as a subject and servant are. For emancipation is the same thing with manumission, and abdication with banishment.

VIII. The enfranchised son, or released servant, doe now stand in lesse fear of their Lord and Father, being deprived of his naturall and lordly power over them, and (if regard be had to true and inward Honour) doe Honour him lesse, than before. For Honour (as hath been said in the section above) is nothing else but the estimation of anothers power; and therefore he that hath least power, hath alwayes least Honour. But it is not to be imagin'd that the enfranchiser ever intended so to match the enfranchised with himself, as that he should not so much as acknowledge a benefit, but should so carry himself in all things, as if he were become wholly his equall; It must therefore be ever understood, That he who is freed from subjection, whether he be a servant, sonne, or some colony, doth promise all those externall signes, at least whereby Superiours used to be Honour'd by their inferiours. From whence it followes, That the precept of honouring our Parents, belongs to the law of nature, not onely under the title of Gratitude, but also of Agreement.

IX. What then, will some one demand, is the difference between a sonne, or between a subject, and a servant? Neither doe I know that any Writer hath fully declared what liberty, and what slavery is. Commonly to doe all things according to our own phancies, and that without punishment, is esteem'd to be liberty; not to be able to doe this, is judg'd bondage; which in a Civill Government, and with the peace of mankind cannot possibly be done, because there is no City without a Command, and a restraining Right. LIBERTY, that we may define it, is nothing else but an absence of the lets, and hinderances of motion, as water shut up in a vessell is therefore not at liberty, because the vessell hinders it from running out, which the vessell being broken, is made free. And every man hath more or lesse liberty, as he hath more or lesse space in which he employes himself: as he hath more liberty, who is in a large, than he that is kept in a close prison. And a man may be free toward one part, and yet not toward another; as the traveller is bounded on this, and that side with hedges, or stone walls, lest he spoyle the vines, or corne, neighbouring on the high way. And these kinde of lets are externall, and absolute; in which sense all Servants, and Subjects are free, who are not fetter'd and imprisoned. There are others which are arbitrary, which doe not absolutely hinder motion, but by accident; to wit, by our own choyce, as he that is in a ship is not so hindered, but he may cast himselfe into the Sea, if he will: and here also the more wayes a man may move himselfe, the more liberty he hath, and herein consists civill liberty; for no man, whether subject, sonne, or servant, is so hindred by the punishments appointed by the City, the Father, or the Lord, how cruell soever, but that he may doe all things, and make use of all meanes necessary to the preservation of his life and health. For my part therefore I cannot finde what reason a meer servant hath to make complaints, if they relate onely to want of liberty, unlesse he count it a misery to be restrained from hurting himselfe, and to receive that life, (which by warre, or misfortune, or through his own idlenesse was forfeited) together with all manner of sustenance, and all things necessary to the conservation of health, on this condition only, that he will be rul'd: for he that is kept in by punishments layd before him, so as he dares not let loose the reines to his will in all things; is not opprest by servitude, but is governed and sustained. But this priviledge free subjects and sonnes of a family, have above servants, (in every government, and family, where servants are) that they may both undergoe the more honourable offices of the City or family, and also enjoy a larger possession of things superfluous. And herein layes the difference between a free subject, and a servant, that he is FREE indeed, who serves his City onely; but a SERVANT is he who also serves his fellow subject: all other liberty is an exemption from the Lawes of the City, and proper only to those that bear Rule.

X. A Father, with his sonnes and servants growne into a civill Person by vertue of his paternall jurisdiction, is called a FAMILY. This family, if through multiplying of children, and acquisition of servants, it becomes numerous, insomuch as without casting the uncertain dye of warre, it cannot be subdued, will be termed an Hereditary Kingdome; which though it differ from an institutive Monarchy, being acquired by force in the original, manner of its constitution; yet being constituted, it hath al the same properties, and the Right of authority is every where the same, insomuch as it is not needfull to speak any thing of them apart.

XI. It hath been spoken, by what Right supreme authorities are constituted. Wee must now briefly tell you by what right they may be continued. Now the Right by which they are continued, is that which is called the right of SUCCESSION. Now because in a Democratie, the supreme authority is with the People, as long as there be any subjects in being, so long it rests with the same Person; for the People hath no Successour. In like manner in an Aristocraty, one of the Nobles dying, some other by the rest is substituted in his place; and therefore except they all dye together, which I suppose will never happen, there is no succession. The Querie therefore of the Right of Succession takes place onely in an absolute Monarchy. For they who exercise the supreme power for a time onely, are themselves no Monarchs, but Ministers of state.

XII. But first, if a Monarch shall by Testament appoint one to succeed him, the Person appointed shall succeed; for if he be appointed by the People, he shall have all the Right over the City which the People had, as hath been shewed in the 7. Chap. Art. 11. But the People might choose him; by the same Right therefore may he choose another; But in an hereditary Kingdome there are the same Rights as in an institutive; Wherefore, every Monarch may by his will make a successour.

XIII. But what a man may transferre on another by Testament, that by the same Right may he yet living, give, or sell away; To whomsoever therefore he shall make over the supreme power, whether by gift, or sale, it is rightly made.

XIV. But if living, he have not declared his will concerning his successour by Testament, nor otherwise, it is supposed, First, that he would not have his Government reduced to an Anarchy, or the state of warre, (that is) to the destruction of his subjects; as well because he could not doe that without breach of the Lawes of nature, whereby he was obliged to the performance of all things necessarily conducing to the preservation of Peace, as also because if that had been his will, it had not been hard for him to have declared that openly. Next, because the Right passeth according to the will of the Father, we must judge of the successour according to the signes of his will. It is understood therefore, that he would have his subjects to be under a Monarchicall Government rather than any other, because he himselfe in ruling, hath before approved of that state by his example, and hath not afterward either by any word or deed condemned it.

XV. Furthermore, because by naturall necessity all men wish them better from whom they receive glory, and honour, than others; but every man after death receives honour and glory from his children, sooner than from the power of any other men: hence we gather, that a father intends better for his children, than any other persons. It is to be understood therefore, that the will of the father, dying without Testament, was, that some of his children should succeed him; yet this is to be understood with this proviso, that there be no more apparent tokens to the contrary: of which kind, after many successions, custome may be one, for he that makes no mention of his succession, is supposed to consent to the customes of his Realme.

XVI. Among children the Males carry the preheminence, in the beginning perhaps, because for the most part (although not alwayes) they are fitter for the administration of greater matters, but specially of wars; but afterwards, when it was grown a custome, because that custome was not contradicted; and therefore the will of the Father, unlesse some other custome or signe doe clearly repugne it, is to be interpreted in favour of them.

XVII. Now because the Sonnes are equall, and the power cannot be divided, the eldest shall succeed; for if there be any difference by reason of age, the eldest is supposed more worthy, for nature being judge, the most in years (because usually it is so) is the wisest. But other judge there cannot be had. But if the Brothers must be equally valued, the succession shall be by lot. But primogeniture is a naturall lot, and by this the eldest is already prefer'd; nor is there any that hath power to judge, whether by this, or any other kind of lots the matter is to be decided. Now the same reason which contends thus for the first–born sonne, doth no lesse for the first born daughter.

XVIII. But if he have no children, then the command shall pass to his Brothers Sisters, for the same reason, that the children should have succeeded if he had had them: for those that are nearest to us in nature, are supposed to be nearest in benevolence; and to his brothers, sooner than his sisters, and to the elder sooner than the yonger; for the reason is the same for these which it was for the children.

XIX. Furthermore, by the same reason that men succeed to the power, doe they also succeed to the Right of succession: for if the first–born dye before the Father, it will be judged, that he transferred his Right of succession unto his children, unless the Father have otherwise decreed it, and therefore the Nephewes will have a fairer pretence to the succession, than the Uncles. I say all these things will be thus, if the custome of the place (which the Father by not contradicting, will be judged to have consented to) doe not hinder them.

CHAPTER X. A COMPARISON BETWEEN THREE KINDS OF GOVERNMENT, ACCORDING TO THEIR SEVERALL INCONVENIENCES

I. What Democraty, Aristocraty, and Monarchy are, hath already been spoken, but which of them tends most to the preservation of the subjects Peace, and procuring their advantages, we must see by comparing them together. But first let us set forth the advantages, and disadvantages of a City in generall, lest some perhaps should think it better, that every man be left to live at his own will, than to constitute any civill society at all. Every man indeed out of the state of civill government hath a most entire, but unfruitfull liberty; because that he who by reason of his own liberty acts all at his own will, must also by reason of the same liberty in others, suffer all at anothers will; but in a constituted City, every subject retains to himselfe as much freedom as suffices him to live well, and quietly, there is so much taken away from others, as may make them not to be feared. Out of this state, every man hath such a Right to all, as yet he can enjoy nothing; in it, each one securely enjoyes his limited Right; Out of it, any man may rightly spoyle, or kill one another; in it, none but one. Out of it we are protected by our own forces; in it, by the power of all. Out of it no man is sure of the fruit of his labours; in it, all men are. Lastly, out of it, there is a Dominion of Passions, war, fear, poverty, slovinlinesse, solitude, barbarisme, ignorance, cruelty. In it, the Dominion of reason, peace, security, riches, decency, society, elegancy, sciences, and benevolence.

II. Aristotle, in his seventh book and fourteenth Chapter of his Politiques saith, that there are two sorts of governments, whereof the one relates to the benefit of the Ruler, the other to that of the Subjects; as if where Subjects are severely dealt with, there were one, and where more mildly, there were another form of government; which opinion may by no means be subscribed to, for all the profits and disprofits arising from government are the same, and common both to the Ruler, and the Subject; The Dammages which befall some particular subjects through misfortune, folly, negligence, sloth, or his own luxury, may very well be severed from those which concern the Ruler, but those relate not to the government it selfe, being such as may happen in any form of government whatsoever. If these same happen from the first institution of the City, they will then be truly called the inconveniencies of government, but they will be common to the Ruler with his subjects, as their benefits are common; but the first and greatest benefit, Peace, and defence, is common to both, for both he that commands, and he who is commanded, to the end that he may defend his life, makes use at once of all the forces of his fellow-subjects; and in the greatest inconvenience that can befall a City, namely the slaughter of subjects, arising from Anarchy, both the Commander, and the Parties commanded, are equally concerned. Next, if the Ruler levie such a summe of vast monies from his subjects, as they are not able to maintain themselves, and their families, nor conserve their bodily strength, and vigour, the disadvantage is as much his, as theirs, who with never so great a stock, or measure of riches, is not able to keep his authority or his riches without the bodies of his subjects; but if he raise no more than is sufficient for the due administration of his power, that is a benefit equall to himselfe and his subjects, tending to a common Peace, and defence. Nor is it imaginable which way publick treasures can be a grievance to private subjects, if they be not so exhausted, as to be wholly deprived from all possibility to acquire, even by their industry, necessaries to sustain the strength of their bodies, and mindes; for even thus the grievance would concern the Ruler; nor would it arise from the ill institution, or ordination of the government, (because in all manner of governments subjects may be opprest) but from the ill administration of a well established government.

III. Now that Monarchy of the foresaid forms, of Democraty, Aristocraty, and Monarchy, hath the preheminence, will best appear by comparing the conveniences and inconveniences arising in each one of them. Those arguments therefore that the whole universe is governed by one God; that the Ancients preferr'd the Monarchicall state before all others, ascribing the Rule of the Gods to one Jupiter; that in the beginning of affairs, and of Nations, the decrees of Princes were held for Laws; that paternall government instituted by God himselfe in the Creation, was Monarchicall; that other governments were compacted by the artifice of men [1] out of the ashes of Monarchy, after it had been ruined with seditions; and that the people of God were under the jurisdiction of Kings, although I say these doe hold forth Monarchy as the more eminent to us, yet because they doe it by examples and testimonies, and not by solid reason, we will passe them over.

IV. Some there are who are discontented with the government under one, for no other reason, but because it is under one; as if it were an unreasonable thing that one man among so many, should so farre excell in power, as to be able at his own pleasure to dispose of all the rest; these men sure, if they could, would withdraw themselves from under the Dominion of one God. But this exception against one is suggested by envie, while they see one man in possession of what all desire: for the same cause they would judge it to be as unreasonable, if a few commanded, unlesse they themselves either were, or hoped to be of the number; for if it be an unreasonable thing that all men have not an equall Right, surely an Aristocraty must be unreasonable also. But because we have shewed that the state of equality is the state of warre, and that therefore inequality was introduc'd by a generall consent; this inequality whereby he, whom we have voluntarily given more to, enjoyes more, is no longer to be accompted an unreasonable thing. The inconveniences therefore which attend the Dominion of one man, attend his Person, not his Unity. Let us therefore see whether brings with it the greater grievances to the subject, the command of one man, or of many.

V. But first, we must remove their opinion who deny that to be any City at all, which is compacted of never so great a number of servants under a common Lord. In the 9. Artic. of the 5. Chapter, a City is defined to be one Person made out of many men, whose will by their own contracts is to be esteemed as the wills of them all, insomuch as he may use the strength and faculties of each single Person for the publick Peace and safety; and by the same article of the same Chapter, One Person is that, when the wills of many are contained in the will of one. But the will of each servant is contained in the will of his Lord, as hath been declared in the 5. Article of the 8. Chapter, so as he may employ all their forces and faculties according to his own will, and pleasure; it followes therefore that that must needs be a city, which is constituted by a Lord, and many servants; neither can any reason be brought to contradict this which doth not equally combat against a City constituted by a Father, and his Sonnes; for to a Lord who hath no children, servants are in the nature of sonnes; for they are both his honour, and safeguard; neither are servants more subject to their Lords, than children to their Parents, as hath been manifested above in the 5. Article of the 8. Chapter.

VI. Among other grievances of supreme authority one is, that the Ruler, beside those monies necessary for publick charges, as the maintaining of publick Ministers, building, and defending of Castles, waging warres, honourable sustaining his own houshold, may also, if he will, exact others through his lust, whereby to enrich his sonnes, kindred, favourites, and flatterers too. I confesse this is a grievance, but of the number of those which accompany all kindes of government, but are more tolerable in a Monarchy than in a Democraty; for though the Monarch would enrich them, they cannot be many, because belonging but to one. But in a Democraty, look how many Demagoges, (that is) how many powerfull Oratours there are with the people (which ever are many, and daily new ones growing) so many Children, Kinsmen, friends, Flatterers, are to be rewarded; for every of them desire not onely to make their families as potent, as illustrious in wealth, as may be, but also to oblige others to them by benefits for the better strengthning of themselves. A Monarch may in great part satisfie his Officers and Friends, because they are not many, without any cost to his Subjects, I mean, without robbing them of any of those Treasures given in for the maintenance of War, and Peace; In a Democraty, where many are to be satisfied, and alwayes new ones, this cannot be done without the Subjects oppression. Though a Monarch may promote unworthy Persons, yet oft times he will not doe it; but in a Democraty all the popular men are therefore suppos'd to doe it, because it is necessary; for else, the power of them who did it would so encrease, as it would not onely become dreadfull to those others, but even to the whole City also.

VII. Another grievance is, that same perpetuall fear of death which every man must necessarily be in, while he considers with himself that the Ruler hath power not onely to appoint what punishments he lists on any Transgressions, but that he may also in his wrath, and sensuality, slaughter his innocent Subjects, and those who never offended against the Lawes. And truly this is a very great grievance in any forme of Government wheresoever it happens: (for it is therefore a grievance because it is; not, because it may be done) but it is the fault of the Ruler, not of the Government; For all the acts of Nero are not essentiall to Monarchie; yet Subjects are lesse often undeservedly condemn'd under one Ruler, than under the People: For Kings are onely severe against those who either trouble them with impertinent Counsells, or oppose them with reproachfull words, or controule their Wills; but they are the cause that that excesse of power which one Subject might have above another becomes harmlesse. Wherefore some Nero or Caligula reigning, no men can undeservedly suffer, but such as are known to him, namely Courtiers, and such as are remarkable for some eminent Charge; and not all neither, but they onely who are possessed of what he desires to enjoy; for they that are offensive, and contumelious, are deservedly punisht. Whosoever therefore in a Monarchy will lead a retired life, let him be what he will that Reignes, he is out of danger: for the ambitious onely suffer, the rest are protected from the injuries of the more potent. But in a popular Dominion there may be as many Nero's, as there are Oratours who sooth the People; for each one of them can doe as much as the People, and they mutually give way to each others appetite (as it were by this secret pact, Spare me to day, and Ile spare thee to morrow) while they exempt those from punishment, who to satisfie their lust, and private hatred, have undeservedly slain their fellow—subjects. Furthermore, there is a certain limit in private power, which if it exceed, it may prove pernicious to the Realme, and by reason whereof it is necessary sometimes for Monarchs to have a care that the common—weale do thence receive no prejudice. When therefore this power consisted in the multitude of Riches, they lessened it by diminishing their heaps; but if it were in popular applause, the powerfull party without any other crime laid to his charge, was taken from among them. The same was usually practised in Democraties; for the Athenians inflicted a punishment of ten yeares banishment on those that were powerfull, meerly because of their powers, without the guilt of any other crime; and those who by liberall gifts did seek the favour of the common people, were put to death at Rome, as men ambitious of a Kingdome. In this Democracy and Monarchy were eaven; yet differ'd they much in fame, because fame derives from the People, and what is done by many, is commended by many: and therefore what the Monarch does, is said to be done out of envie to their vertues, which if it were done by the People, would be accounted Politie.

VIII. There are some who therefore imagine Monarchy to bee more grievous than Democraty, because there is lesse liberty in that, than in this. If by liberty they mean an exemption from that subjection which is due to the Lawes (i.e.) the commands of the People, neither in Democraty, nor in any other state of government whatsoever, is there any such kind of liberty. If they suppose liberty to consist in this, that there be few lawes, few prohibitions, and those too such, that except they were forbidden, there could be no Peace; then I deny that there is more liberty in Democraty than Monarchy; for the one as truly consisteth with such a liberty, as the other. For although the word liberty, may in large, and ample letters be written over the gates of any City whatsoever, yet is it not meant the Subjects, but the Cities liberty, neither can that word with better Right be inscribed on a City which is governed by the people, than that which is ruled by a Monarch. But when private men or subjects demand liberty, under the name of liberty, they ask not for liberty, but dominion, which yet for want of understanding, they little consider; for if every man would grant the same liberty to another, which he desires for himselfe, as is commanded by the law of nature, that same naturall state would return again, in which all men may by Right doe all things, which if they knew, they would abhor, as being worse than all kind of civill subjection whatsoever. But if any man desire to have his single freedome, the rest being bound, what does he else demand but to have the Dominion? For who so is freed from all bonds, is Lord over all those that still continue bound. Subjects therefore have no greater liberty in a Popular, than in a Monarchicall State. That which deceives them, is the equall participation of command, and publique places; for where the authority is in the People, single subjects doe so far forth share in it as they are parts of the People ruling; and they equally partake in publique Offices so far forth as they have equall voices in choosing Magistrates, and publique Ministers. And this is that which Aristotle aim'd at, himself also, through the custome of that time, mis—calling Dominion liberty, in his sixth Book, and second Chapter of Politiques. In a popular State there is liberty by supposition; which is a speech of the vulgar, as if no man were free out of this State. From whence, by the way, we may collect, That those Subjects, who in a Monarchy deplore their lost liberty, doe onely stomack this, that they are not receiv'd to the steerage of the Common—weal.

IX. But perhaps for this very reason some will say, That a Popular State is much to be preferr'd before a Monarchicall; because that, where all men have a hand in publique businesses, there all have an opportunity to shew their wisedome, knowledge, and eloquence, in deliberating matters of the greatest difficulty and moment; which by reason of that desire of praise which is bred in humane nature, is to them who excell in such like faculties, and seeme to themselves to exceed others, the most delightfull of all things. But in a Monarchy, this same way to obtain praise, and honour, is shut up to the greatest part of Subjects; and what is a grievance, if this be none? Ile tell you: To see his opinion whom we scorne, preferr'd before ours; to have our wisedome undervalued before our own faces; by an uncertain tryall of a little vaine glory, to undergoe most certaine enmities (for this cannot be avoided, whether we have the better, or the worse); to hate, and to be hated, by reason of the disagreement of opinions; to lay open our secret Counsells, and advises to all, to no purpose, and without any benefit; to neglect the affaires of our own Family: These, I say, are grievances. But to be absent from a triall of wits, although those trialls are pleasant to the Eloquent, is not therefore a grievance to them, unlesse we will say, that it is a grievance to valiant men to be restrained from fighting, because they delight in it.

68

X. Besides, there are many reasons why deliberations are lesse successefull in great Assemblies, than in lesser Councells; whereof one is, that to advise rightly of all things conducing to the preservation of a Common—weal, we must not onely understand matters at home, but Forraign Affaires too: at Home, by what goods the Country is nourished, and defended, and whence they are fetched; what places are fit to make Garrisons of; by what means Souldiers are best to be raised, and maintained; what manner of affections the Subjects bear toward their Prince, or Governours of their Country, and many the like: Abroad, what the power of each neighbouring Country is, and wherein it consists; what advantage, or disadvantage we may receive from them; what their dispositions are both to us—ward, and how affected to each other among themselves, and what Counsell daily passeth among them. Now, because very few in a great Assembly of men understand these things, being for the most part unskilfull (that I say not incapable) of them, what can that same number of advisers with their impertinent Opinions contribute to good Counsells, other than meer letts and impediments?

XI. Another reason why a great Assembly is not so fit for consultation is, because every one who delivers his opinion holds it necessary to make a long continued Speech, and to gain the more esteem from his Auditours, he polishes, and adornes it with the best, and smoothest language. Now the nature of Eloquence is to make Good and Evill, Profitable and Unprofitable, Honest and Dishonest, appear to be more or lesse than indeed they are, and to make that seem just, which is unjust, according as it shall best suit with his end that speaketh. For this is to perswade; and though they reason, yet take they not their rise from true Principles, but from vulgar received opinions, which, for the most part, are erroneous; neither endeavour they so much to fit their speech to the nature of the things they speak of, as to the Passions of their mindes to whom they speak; whence it happens that opinions are delivered not by right reason, but by a certain violence of mind. Nor is this fault in the Man, but in the nature it selfe of Eloquence, whose end (as all the Masters of Rhetorick teach us) is not truth (except by chance) but victory, and whose property is not to inform, but to allure.

XII. The third reason why men advise lesse successfully in a great convent is, because that thence arise Factions in a commonweal, and out of Factions, Seditions, and Civill War; for when equall Oratours doe combat with contrary Opinions, and Speeches, the conquered hates the Conquerour, and all those that were of his side, as holding his Counsell, and wisedome in scorne: and studyes all meanes to make the advise of his adversaries prejudiciall to the State, for thus he hopes to see the glory taken from him, and restored unto himself. Farthermore, where the Votes are not so unequall, but that the conquered have hopes by the accession of some few of their own opinion at another sitting to make the stronger Party, the chief heads do call the rest together; they advise apart how they may abrogate the former judgment given; they appoint to be the first and earliest at the next convent; they determine what, and in what order each man shall speak, that the same businesse may again be brought to agitation, that so what was confirmed before by the number of their then present adversaries, the same may now in some measure become of no effect to them, being negligently absent. And this same kind of industry and diligence which they use to make a people, is commonly called a faction. But when a faction is inferiour in votes, and superiour, or not much inferiour in power, than what they cannot obtain by craft, and language, they attempt by force of armes, and so it comes to a civill warre. But some will say, these things doe not necessarily, nor often happen; he may as well say, that the chief Parties are not necessarily desirous of vain glory, and that the greatest of them seldom disagree in great matters.

XIII. It followes hence, that when the legislative power resides in such convents as these, the Laws must needs be inconstant, and change, not according to the alteration of the state of affaires, nor according to the changeablenesse of mens mindes, but as the major part, now of this, then of that faction, do convene; insomuch as the Laws do flote here, and there, as it were upon the waters.

XIV. In the fourth place, the counsels of great assemblies have this inconvenience, that whereas it is oft of great consequence, that they should be kept secret, they are for the most part discovered to the enemy before they can be brought to any effect, and their power, and will, is as soon known abroad, as to the People it selfe commanding at home.

XV. These inconveniences which are found in the deliberations of great assemblies do so farre forth evince Monarchy to be better than Democraty, as in Democraty affairs of great consequence are oftner trusted to be discussed by such like Committees, than in a Monarchy. Neither can it easily bee done otherwayes; for there is no reason why every man should not naturally rather minde his own private, than the publique businesse, but that here he sees a means to declare his eloquence, whereby he may gain the reputation of being ingenuous, and wise, and returning home to his friends, to his Parents, to his wife, and children, rejoyce, and triumph in the applause of his dexterous behaviour: As of old all the delight Marcus Coriolanus had in his warlike actions, was, to see his praises so well pleasing to his Mother. But if the People in a Democraty would bestow the power of deliberating in matters of Warre, and Peace, either on one, or some very few, being content with the nomination of Magistrates, and publique Ministers, that is to say, with the authority without the ministration, then it must be confest, that in this particular, Democraty and Monarchy would be equall.

XVI. Neither do the conveniencies or inconveniences which are found to be more in one kind of government than another, arise from hence, namely, because the government it self, or the administration of its affairs, are better committed to one, than many; or on the other side, to many, than to some few. For Government is the power, the administration of it is the act. Now the Power in all kind of government is equall; the acts only differ, that is to say the actions and motions of a common−weale, as they flow from the deliberations of many, or few, of skilfull, or impertinent men. Whence we understand, that the conveniences, or inconveniences of any government, depend not on him in whom the authority resides, but on his Officers; and therefore nothing hinders, but that the common−weale may be well governed, although the Monarch be a woman, or youth, or infant, provided that they be fit for affaires, who are endued with the publique Offices, and charges; And that which is said, Woe to the land whose King is a childe, doth not signifie the condition of a Monarchy to be inferiour to a Popular state, but contrariwise, that by accident it is the grievance of a Kingdome, that the King being a childe, it often happens, that many by ambition, and power, intruding themselves into publique counsels, the government comes to be administred in a Democraticall manner, and that thence arise those infelicities which for the most part accompany the Dominion of the People.

XVII. But it is a manifest sign, that the most absolute Monarchy is the best state of government, that not onely Kings, but even those Cities which are subject to the people, or to Nobles, give the whole command of warre to one only, and that so absolute, as nothing can be more (wherein by the way this must be noted also, that no King can give a Generall greater authority over his army, than he himselfe by Right may exercise over all his subjects). Monarchy therefore is the best of all governments in the Camps. But what else, are many Common−wealths, than so many Camps strengthened with armes, and men against each other, whose state (because not restrained by any common power, howsoever an uncertain peace, like a short truce, may passe between them) is to be accounted for the state of nature, which is the state of War.

XVIII. Lastly, since it was necessary for the preservation of our selves to be subject to some Man, or Councell, we cannot on better condition be subject to any, than one whose interest depends upon our safety, and welfare; and this then comes to passe when we are the inheritance of the Ruler; for every man of his own accord endeavours the preservation of his inheritance. But the Lands, and Monies of the Subjects are not onely the Princes Treasure, but their bodies, and active minds; which will be easily granted by those who consider at how great rates the Dominion of lesser Countries is valued, and how much easier it is for men to procure mony, than money men; nor doe we readily meet with any example that shewes us when any subject, without any default of his own, hath by his Prince been despoiled of his life, or goods, through the sole licenciousnesse of his Authority.

XIX. Hitherto we have compared a Monarchicall, with a Popular State; we have said nothing of Aristocracy; we may conclude of this, by what hath been said of those, that, that which is hereditary, and content with the election of Magistrates; which transmits its deliberations to some few, and those most able; which simply imitates the government of Monarchs most, and the People least of all, is for the Subjects both better, and more lasting than the rest.

1. Compacted by the artifice of men, It seems the Ancients who made that same fable of Prometheus pointed at this. They say, that Prometheus having stolne fire from the Sunne, formed a man out of clay, and that for this deed he was tortured by Jupiter with a perpetuall gnawing in his liver. Which is, that by humane invention (which is signified by Prometheus) Laws and Justice were by imitation taken from Monarchy, by vertue whereof (as by fire removed from its naturall orbe) the multitude (as the durt and dregs of men) was as it were quickned and formed into a civill Person, which is termed Aristocraty, or Democraty; but the Awthours and Abettors being found, who might securely and quietly have lived under the naturall jurisdiction of Kings, doe thus smart for it, that being exposed still to alteration, they are tormented with perpetuall cares, suspitions, and dissentions.

CHAPTER XI. PLACES AND EXAMPLES OF SCRIPTURE OF THE RIGHTS OF GOVERNMENT AGREEABLE TO WHAT HATH BEEN SAID BEFORE

I. We have in the 6. Chapter, and the 2. Article, so derived the Originall of institutive, or politicall Government from the consent of the Multitude, that it appears they must either all consent, or be esteem'd as Enemies. Such was the beginning of Gods Government over the Jewes instituted by Moses, If ye will obey my voice indeed, Ye shall be unto me a Kingdome of Priests, And Moses came, and called the Elders of the People, And all the people answered, and said: All that the Lord hath spoken we will do, Exod. 19. ver. 5, 6, 7, 8. Such also was the beginning of Moyses his power under God, or of his Vicegerency. And all the people saw the thunderings and lightenings, and the noyse of the Trumpet, And they said unto Moyses, speak thou unto us, and we will hear. Exod. 20:18,19. The like beginning also had Sauls Kingdome. When yee saw that Nahash King of the children of Ammon came out against you, yee said unto me, nay, but a King shall raign over us, when the Lord your God was your King; Now therefore behold the King whom yee have chosen, and whom yee have desired. 1 Sam. 12:12. But the major part only consenting, and not all (for there were certain Sons of Belial, who said, How shall this man save us? And they dispised him, 1 Sam. 10:27.) Those who did not consent were put to death as Enemies; And the people said unto Samuel, Who is he that said, shall Saul reign over us? Bring the men that we may put them to death. 1 Sam. 11.

II. In the same 6. Chapter, the 6. and 7. Articles, I have shewed, that all judgment and Wars depend upon the will and pleasure of him who beares the Supreme Authority; that is to say, in a Monarchy, on a Monarch, or King; and this is confirmed by the Peoples owne judgement. Wee also will be like all the Nations, and our King shall JUDGE us, and goe out before us, and fight our BATTELS. 1 Sam. 8:20. And what pertaines to judgements, and all other matters, whereof there is any controversie, whether they be Good, or Evill, is confirmed by the testimony of King Solomon. Give therefore thy Servant an understanding heart to JUDGE thy People, that I may discerne between GOOD and EVILL. 1. Kings 3:9. And that of Absolom, There is no man deputed of the King to heare thee. 2. Sam. 15:3.

III. That Kings may not be punished by their subjects, as hath been shewed above in the sixth Chapter, and the twelfth Article, King David also confirmes, who, though Saul sought to slay him, did notwithstanding refrain his hand from killing him, and forbad Abishai, saying, Destroy him, not; for who can stretch forth his hand against the Lords Anointed, and be innocent? 1 Sam: 4:9. And when he had cut off the skirt of his garment, The Lord forbid (saith he) that I should doe this thing unto my Master the Lords Anointed, to stretchforth mine hand against him. 1 Sam. 24:7. And commanded the Amalekite, who for his sake had slain Saul, to be put to death. 2 Sam. 1:15.

IV. That which is said in the 17. Chapter of Judges, at the 6. verse. In those dayes there was no King in Israel, but every man did that which was right in his own eyes (as though where there were not a Monarchy, there were an Anarchy or confusion of all things) may be brought as a testimony to prove the excellency of Monarchy above all other forms of government, unlesse that by the word King may perhaps be understood, not one man onely, but also a Court, provided that in it there reside a supreme power; which if it be taken in this sense, yet hence it may follow, that without a supreme and absolute power (which we have endeavoured to prove in the sixth Chapter) there will be a liberty for every man to doe what hee hath a minde, or whatsoever shall seem right to himselfe; which cannot stand with the preservation of mankinde, and therefore in all Government whatsoever, there is ever a supreme power understood to be somewhere existent.

V. We have in the 8. Chapter, the 7. and 8. Article, said, that Servants must yeeld a simple obedience to their Lords, and in the 9. Chapter, Article 7. that Sonnes owe the same obedience to their Parents. Saint Paul sayes the same thing concerning Servants, Servants obey in all things your Masters according to the flesh, not with eye service, as men−pleasers, but in singlenesse of heart, fearing God. Colos. 3:22. Concerning Sonnes, Children obey your Parents in all things, for this is well pleasing unto the Lord. Colos. 3:20. Now as wee by simple obedience understand ALL THINGS which are not contrary to the Lawes of God; so in those cited places of Saint Paul, after the word ALL THINGS, we must suppose, excepting those which are contrary to the Lawes of God.

VI. But that I may not thus by peecemeale prove the right of Princes, I will now instance those testimonies which altogether establish the whole power, (namely that there is an absolute and simple obedience due to them from their subjects). And first out of the new Testament. The Scribes and Pharisees sit in Moyses seat; all therefore, whatsoever they bid you observe, that observe, and doe. Mat. 23:2. Whatsoever they bid you, (sayes he) observe, that is to say, obey simply: Why? Because they sit in Moyses seat; namely, the civill Magistrates, not Aaron, the Priests. Let every soule be subject to the higher powers, for there is no Power but of God, the powers that be are ordained of God; whosoever therefore resisteth the Power, resisteth the ordinance of God, and they that resist shall receive to themselves damnation. Rom. 13:1. Now because the powers that were in Saint Pauls time were ordained of God, and all Kings did at that time require an absolute entire obedience from their subjects, it followes that such a power was ordained of God. Submit your selves unto every ordinance of man for the Lords sake, whether it bee to the King as supreme, or unto Governours, as unto them that are sent by him, for the punishment of wicked doers, and for the praise of them that doe well, for so is the will of God. 1 Pet. 2:13. Again Saint Paul to Titus, Put them in mind to bee subject to Principalities and Powers, to obey Magistrates, Chap. 3. vers. 1. What Principalities? Was it not to the Principalities of those times, which required an absolute obedience? Furthermore, that we may come to the example of Christ himselfe, to whom the Kingdome of the Jewes belonged by hereditary Right, derived from David himselfe; He when he lived in the manner of a subject, both paid tribute unto Caesar, and pronounced it to be due to him. Give unto Caesar (saith he) the things which are Caesars, and unto God, the things which are Gods. Mat. 22:21. When it pleased him to shew himselfe a King, he required entire obedience. Goe (said he) into the village over against you, and straightway yee shall finde an Asse tyed, and a Colt with her, loose them, and bring them unto me; and if any man say ought unto you, yee shall say the Lord hath need of them. Mat. 21:2,3. This he did therefore by the right of being Lord, or a King of the Jewes. But to take away a subjects goods on this pretence onely, because the Lord hath need of them, is an absolute power. The most evident places in the old Testament are these, Goe thou near, and heare ALL that the Lord our God shall say, and speak thou unto us all that the Lord our God shall speak unto thee, and we will hear it, and doe it. Deut. 5:27. But under the word all, is contained absolute obedience. Again to Joshua. And they answered Joshua saying, ALL that thou commandest us, we will doe, and whithersoever thou sendest us, we will goe; according as we hearkened unto Moyses in ALL things, so will we hearken unto thee, onely the Lord thy God be with thee, as he was with Moyses; whosoever hee be that doth rebell against thy Commandement, and will not hearken unto thy words in ALL that thou commandest him, he shall be put to death. Joshua 1:16–18. And the Parable of the Bramble. Then said all the trees unto the Bramble, Come thou, and reign over us; And the Bramble said unto the trees, If in truth yee anoint me King over you, then come and put your trust in my shadow; and if not, let fire come out of the Bramble, and devoure the Cedars of Lebanon. Judges 9. vers. 14,

15. The sense of which words is, that we must acquiese to their sayings, whom we have truly constituted to be Kings over us, unlesse we would chuse rather to be consumed by the fire of a civill warre. But the Regall authority is more particularly described by God himselfe, in the 1. Sam. 8. vers. 9. Shew them the Right of the King that shall reign over them, This shall be the Right of the King that shall reign over you; he will take your Sons, and appoint them for himself, for his Chariots, and to be his horsemen, and some shall runne before his Chariots, And he will take your daughters to be confectionaries, And he will take your vineyards, and give them to his Servants, Is not this power absolute? And yet it is by God himself styled the KINGS RIGHT; neither was any man among the Jewes, no not the High Priest himselfe, exempted from this obedience. For when the King (namely Solomon) said to Abiathar the Priest, Get thee to Anathoth unto thine own fields, for thou art worthy of death, but I will not at this time put thee to death, because thou barest the Ark of the Lord God before David my father, and because thou hast been afflicted in all wherein my Father was afflicted. So Solomon thrust out Abiathar from being Priest unto the Lord. 1 Kings. 2:26. It cannot by any argument be proved, that this act of his displeased the Lord; neither read we, that either Solomon was reproved, or that his Person at that time was any whit lesse acceptable to God.

CHAPTER XII. OF THE INTERNAL CAUSES, TENDING TO THE DISSOLUTION OF ANY GOVERNMENT

I. Hitherto hath been spoken by what causes, and Pacts, Common–weals are constituted, and what the Rights of Princes are over their subjects; Now we will briefly say somewhat concerning the causes which dissolve them, or the reasons of seditions. Now as in the motion of naturall bodies, three things are to be considered, namely, internall disposition, that they be susceptible of the motion to be produced; the externall Agent, whereby a certain and determined motion may in act be produced; and the action it selfe: So also in a

Common–weale where the subjects begin to raise tumults, three things present themselves to our regard; First the Doctrines and the Passions contrary to Peace, wherewith the mindes of men are fitted and disposed; next their quality and condition who sollicite, assemble, and direct them already thus disposed, to take up armes, and quit their allegiance; Lastly, the manner how this is done, or the faction it selfe. But one, and the first which disposeth them to sedition, is this, That the knowledge of good and evill belongs to each single man. In the state of nature indeed, where every man lives by equall Right, and have not by any mutuall Pacts submitted to the command of others, we have granted this to be true, nay in the first Chapter, Article 9. we have demonstrated it. But in the civil state it is false. For it was shown in chap. 6. art. 9. that the civill Lawes were the Rules of good and evill, just and unjust, honest and dishonest; that therefore what the Legislator commands, must be held for good, and what he forbids for evill; and the Legislator is ever that Person who hath the supreme power in the Commonweale, that is to say, the Monarch in a Monarchy. We have confirmed the same truth in the eleventh Chapter, Article 2. out of the words of Solomon; for if private men may pursue that as good, and shun that as evill which appears to them to be so, to what end serve those words of his?

Give therefore unto thy servant an understanding heart to judge thy People, that I may discern between good and evill. Since therefore it belongs to Kings to discerne betweene good and evill, wicked are those, though usuall sayings, that he onely is a King who does righteously, and that Kings must not be obeyed, unlesse they command us just things, and many other such like. Before there was any government, just and unjust had no being, their nature onely being relative to some command, and every action in its own nature is indifferent; that it becomes just, or unjust, proceeds from the right of the Magistrate: Legitimate Kings therefore make the things they command, just, by commanding them, and those which they forbid, unjust, by forbidding them; but private men while they assume to themselves the knowledge of good and evill, desire to be even as Kings, which cannot be with the safety of the Common weale. The most ancient of all Gods commands is, Gen.

2:15. Thou shalt not eat of the tree of knowledge of good and evill; and the most ancient of all diabolicall tentations, Chap. 3. vers. 5. Yee shall be as Gods, knowing good and evill; and Gods first expostulation with man, vers. 11. Who told thee that thou wert naked? Hast thou eaten of the tree, whereof I commanded thee that thou shouldest not eat? As if he had said, how comest thou to judge that nakedness, wherein it seemed good to me to create thee, to be shamefull, except thou have arrogated to thy selfe the knowledge of good and evill?

II. Whatsoever any man doth against his conscience is a sinne, for he who doth so, contemns the Law. But we must distinguish: That is my sinne indeed, which committing, I doe beleeve to be my sinne; but what I beleeve to be another mans sin, I may sometimes doe that without any sin of mine. For if I be commanded to doe that which is a sin in him who commands me, if I doe it, and he that commands me be by Right, Lord over me, I sinne not; for if I wage warre at the Commandement of my Prince, conceiving the warre to be unjustly undertaken, I doe not therefore doe unjustly, but rather if I refuse to doe it, arrogating to my selfe the knowledge of what is just and unjust, which pertains onely to my Prince. They who observe not this distinction, will fall into a necessity of sinning, as oft as any thing is commanded them, which either is, or seems to be unlawfull to them: for if they obey, they sin against their conscience, and if they obey not, against Right. If they sin against their conscience, they declare that they fear not the paines of the world to come; if they sinne against Right, they doe as much as in them lyes, abolish humane society, and the civill life of the present world. Their opinion therefore who teach, that subjects sinne when they obey their Princes commands, which to them seem unjust, is both erroneous, and to be reckoned among those which are contrary to civill obedience; and it depends upon that originall errour which we have observed above in the foregoing Article; for by our taking upon us to judge of good and evill, we are the occasion, that as well our obedience, as disobedience, becomes sin unto us.

III. The third seditious doctrine springs from the same root, That Tyrannicide is lawfull; Nay, at this day it is by many Divines, and of old it was by all the Philosophers, Plato, Aristotle, Cicero, Seneca, Plutarch, and the rest of the maintainers of the Greek, and Roman Anarchies, held not only lawful, but even worthy of the greatest praise. And under the title of Tyrants, they mean not onely Monarchs, but all those who bear the chief rule in any Government whatsoever; for not Pisistratus onely at Athens, but those thirty also who

succeeded him, and ruled together, were all called Tyrants. But he, whom men require to be put to death as being a Tyrant, commands either by Right, or without Right; if without Right, he is an enemy, and by Right to be put to death; but then this must not be called the killing a Tyrant, but an enemy: if by Right, then the divine interrogation takes place, Who hath told thee that he was a Tyrant, hast thou eaten of the tree whereof I commanded thee that thou shouldest not eat? For why doest thou call him a Tyrant, whom God hath made a King, except that thou being a private Person, usurpest to thy self the knowledge of good and evill? But how pernicious this opinion is to all governments, but especially to that which is Monarchicall, we may hence discerne, namely, that by it every King, whether good or ill, stands exposed to be condemned by the judgement, and slain by the hand of every murtherous villain.

IV. The fourth adversary opinion to Civill Society, is theirs, who hold, That they who bear Rule are Subject also to the Civill Lawes. Which hath been sufficiently proved before not to be true in the 6. Chap. Artic. 14. from this Argument, That a City can neither be bound to it self, nor to any subject; not to it selfe, because no man can be obliged except it be to another; not to any Subject, because the single wills of the Subjects are contained in the will of the City, insomuch, that if the City will be free from all such obligation, the Subjects will so too; and by consequence she is so. But that which holds true in a City, that must be supposed to be true in a man, or an assembly of men, who have the Supreme Authority, for they make a City, which hath no being but by their Supreme Power. Now that this Opinion cannot consist with the very being of Government, is evident from hence, that by it the knowledge of what is Good and Evill, that is to say, the definition of what is, and what is not against the Lawes, would return to each single Person: Obedience therefore will cease as oft as any thing seemes to be commanded contrary to the Civill Lawes, and together with it, all coercive jurisdiction, which cannot possibly be without the destruction of the very essence of Government. Yet this Errour hath great props, Aristotle, and others; who, by reason of humane infirmity, suppose the Supreme Power to be committed with most security to the Lawes onely; but they seem to have lookt very shallowly into the nature of Government, who thought that the constraining Power, the interpretation of Lawes, and the making of Lawes, (all which are powers necessarily belonging to Government) should be left wholly to the Lawes themselves. Now although particular Subjects may sometimes contend in judgement, and goe to Law with the Supreme Magistrate, yet this is onely then, when the question is not what the Magistrate may, but what by a certain Rule he hath declared he would doe. As, when by any Law the Judges sit upon the life of a Subject, the question is not whether the Magistrate could by his absolute Right deprive him of his life; but whether by that Law his will was that he should be deprived of it; but his will was, he should, if he brake the Law; else, his will was he should not: This therefore, that a Subject may have an action of Law against his Supreme Magistrate, is not strength of Argument sufficient to prove that he is tyed to his own Lawes. On the contrary, it is evident, that he is not tied to his owne Lawes, because no man is bound to himself. Lawes therefore are set for Titius, and Caius, not for the Ruler: however, by the ambition of Lawyers, it is so ordered, that the Lawes, to unskilfull men seeme not to depend on the Authority of the Magistrate, but their Prudence.

V. In the fifth place, That the Supreme Authority may be divided, is a most fatall Opinion to all Common—weales. But diverse men divide it diverse wayes. For some divide it so as to grant a Supremacy to the Civill Power in matters pertaining to Peace, and the benefits of this life, but in things concerning the salvation of the Soul they transfer it on others. Now, because justice is of all things most necessary to Salvation, it happens, that Subjects measuring justice, not as they ought, by the Civill Lawes, but by the precepts and doctrines of them who, in regard of the Magistrate, are either private mens or strangers, through a superstitious fear dare not perform the obedience due to their Princes, through fear falling into that which they most feared: Now what can be more pernicious to any state, than that men should, by the apprehension of everlasting torments, be deterred from obeying their Princes, that is to say, the Lawes, or from being just? There are also some who divide the Supreme Authority so as to allow the power of War, and Peace, unto one, (whom they call a Monarch) but the right of raising Monies they give to some others, and not to him: But because monies are the sinewes of War, and Peace, they who thus divide the Authority, doe either really not divide it at all, but place it wholly in them, in whose power the money is, but give the name of it to another, or if they doe really divide it, they dissolve the Government: for neither upon necessity can War be waged, nor can the publique Peace be preserved without Money.

VI. It is a common doctrine, That faith and holinesse are not acquired by study, and naturall reason, but are always supernaturally infused, and inspired into men: which, if it were true, I understand not why we should be commanded to give an account of our faith; or why any man, who is truly a Christian, should not be a Prophet; or lastly, why every man should not judge what's fit for him to doe, what to avoid, rather out of his own inspiration, than by the precepts of his Superiours, or right Reason. A return therefore must be made to the private knowledge of Good and Evil; which cannot be granted without the ruine of all Governments. This Opinion hath spread it self so largely through the whole Christian world, that the number of Apostates from natural reason is almost become infinite. And it sprang from sick—brained men, who having gotten good store of Holy Words by frequent reading of the Scriptures, made such a connexion of them usually in their preaching, that their Sermons, signifying just nothing, yet to unlearned men seemed most divine; for he whose non—sense appears to be a Divine speech, must necessarily seeme to be inspired from above.

VII. The seventh Doctrine opposite to Government, is this, That each subject hath an absolute Dominion over the goods he is in possession of. That is to say, such a propriety as excludes not only the right of all the rest of his fellow—subjects to the same goods, but also of the Magistrate himself. Which is not true; for they who have a Lord over them, have themselves no Lordship, as hath been proved, Chap. 8. Artic. 5. Now the Magistrate is Lord of all his Subjects, by the constitution of Government. Before the yoke of Civill Society was undertaken, no man had any Proper Right; all things were common to all men. Tell me therefore, how gottest thou this propriety but from the Magistrate? How got the Magistrates it, but that every man transferred his Right on him? And thou therefore hast also given up thy Right to him; thy Dominion therefore, and Propriety, is just so much as he will, and shall last so long as he pleases; even as in a Family, each Son hath such proper goods, and so long lasting, as seeme good to the Father. But the greatest part of men who professe Civill Prudence, reason otherwise; we are equall (say they) by nature; there is no reason why any man should by better Right take my goods from me, than I his from him; we know that mony sometimes is needfull for the defence and maintenance of the publique; but let them, who require it, shew us the present necessity, and they shall willingly receive it. They who talk thus, know not, that what they would have, is already done from the beginning in the very constitution of Government, and therefore speaking as in a dissolute multitude, and yet not fashioned Government, they destroy the frame.

VIII. In the last place, it's a great hindrance to Civill Government, especially Monarchicall, that men distinguish not enough between a People and a Multitude. The People is somewhat that is one, having one will, and to whom one action may be attributed; none of these can properly be said of a Multitude. The People rules in all Governments, for even in Monarchies the People Commands; for the People wills by the will of one man; but the Multitude are Citizens, that is to say, Subjects. In a Democraty, and Aristocraty, the Citizens are the Multitude, but the Court is the People. And in a Monarchy, the Subjects are the Multitude, and (however it seeme a Paradox) the King is the People. The common sort of men, and others who little consider these truthes, do alwayes speak of a great number of men, as of the People, that is to say, the City; they say that the City hath rebelled against the King (which is impossible) and that the People will, and nill, what murmuring and discontented Subjects would have, or would not have, under pretence of the People, stirring up the Citizens against the City, that is to say, the Multitude against the People. And these are almost all the Opinions wherewith Subjects being tainted doe easily Tumult. And forasmuch as in all manner of Government Majesty is to be preserv'd by him, or them who have the Supreme Authority, the crimen laesae Majestatis naturally cleaves to these Opinions.

IX. There is nothing more afflicts the mind of man than Poverty, or the want of those things which are necessary for the preservation of life, and honour; and though there be no man but knowes that riches are gotten with industry, and kept by frugality, yet all the poor commonly lay the blame on the Evill Government, excusing their own sloth, and luxury, as if their private goods forsooth were wasted by publique exactions; But men must consider, that they who have no patrimony, must not onely labour that they may live, but fight too, that they may labour. Every one of the Jewes, who in Esdras his time built the Walls of Jerusalem, did the work with one hand, and held the Sword in the other. In all Government we must conceive that the hand which holds the Sword is the King, or Supreme Councell, which is no lesse to be sustained, and nourisht, by the Subjects care and industry, than that wherewith each man procures himself a private fortune; and that Customes, and Tributes, are nothing else but their reward who watch in Armes for us, that the labours and endeavours of single men may not be molested by the incursion of enemies; and that their complaint, who impute their poverty to publick Persons, is not more just, than if they should say that they are become in want by paying of their debts: But the most part of men consider nothing of these things, for they suffer the same thing with them who have a disease they call an Incubus, which springing from Gluttony, it makes men believe they are invaded, opprest, and stifled with a great weight: Now it is a thing manifest of it selfe, that they who seeme to themselves to be burthened with the whole load of the Common−weal, are prone to be Seditious; and that they are affected with change, who are distasted at the present state of things.

X. Another noxious disease of the mind is theirs, who having little employment, want Honour and Dignity. All men naturally strive for Honour, and Preferment, but chiefly they who are least troubled with caring for necessary things. For these men are invited by their vacancy sometimes to disputation among themselves concerning the Common−weal, sometimes to an easie reading of Histories, Politiques, Orations, Poems, and other pleasant Books; and it happens, that hence they think themselves sufficiently furnisht both with wit, and learning, to administer matters of the greatest consequence. Now because all men are not what they appear to themselves, and if they were, yet all (by reason of the multitude) could not be received to publique Offices, its necessary that many must be passed by. These therefore conceiving themselves affronted, can desire nothing more, partly out of envy to those who were preferred before them, partly out of hope to overwhelm them, than ill successe to the publique Consultations; and therefore its no marvell if with greedy appetites they seek for occasions of innovations.

XI. The hope of overcomming is also to be numbred among other seditious inclinations. For let there be as many men as you wil, infected with opinions repugnant to Peace, and civill Government; let there be as many as there can, never so much wounded and torne with affronts, and calumnies, by them who are in Authority; yet if there be no hope of having the better of them, or it appear not sufficient, there will no sedition follow; every man will dissemble his thoughts, and rather content himself with the present burthen, than hazard an heavier weight. There are four things necessarily requisite to this hope: Numbers, Instruments, mutuall trust, and Commanders. To resist publique Magistrates without a great number, is not Sedition, but Desperation. By Instruments of war I mean all manner of armes, munition, and other necessary provision, without which Number can doe nothing, nor Arms neither without mutuall trust; Nor all these without union under some Commander, whom of their own accord, they are content to obey; not as being engaged by their submission to his command (for we have already in this very Chapter, supposed these kind of men not to understand, being obliged beyond that which seems right and good in their own eyes) but for some opinion they have of his vertue, or military skill, or resemblance of humours. If these four be near at hand to men grieved with the present state, and measuring the justice of their actions by their own judgements, there will be nothing wanting to sedition and confusion of the Realme, but one to stirre up and quicken them.

XII. Salust his Character of Catiline, (than whom there never was a greater Artist in raising seditions) is this, That he had great eloquence, and little wisdome. He separates wisdome from eloquence, attributing this as necessary to a man born for commotions, adjudging that as an instructresse of Peace, and quietnesse. Now, eloquence is twofold. The one is an elegant, and cleare expression of the conceptions of the mind, and riseth partly from the contemplation of the things themselves, partly from an understanding of words taken in their own proper, and definite signification; the other is a commotion of the Passions of the minde (such as are hope, fear, anger, pitty) and derives from a metaphoricall use of words fitted to the Passions: That forms a speech from true Principles, this from opinions already received, what nature soever they are of. The art of that is Logick, of this Rhetorick; the end of that is truth, of this victory. Each hath its use, that in deliberations, this in exhortations; for that is never disjoyned from wisdome, but this almost ever. But that this kind of powerfull eloquence, separated from the true knowledge of things, that is to say, from wisdome, is the true character of them who sollicite, and stirre up the people to innovations, may easily be gathered out of the work it selfe which they have to doe; for they could not poyson the people with those absurd opinions contrary to Peace and civill society, unlesse they held them themselves, which sure is an ignorance greater than can well befall any wise man. For he that knows not whence the Lawes derive their power, which are the Rules of just and unjust, honest and dishonest, good and evill; what makes and preserves Peace among men, what destroyes it; what is his, and what anothers; Lastly, what he would have done to himselfe (that he may doe the like to others) is surely to be accounted but meanly wise. But that they can turn their Auditors out of fools into madmen; that they can make things to them who are ill−affected seem worse, to them who are well−affected seem evil; that they can enlarge their hopes, lessen their dangers beyond reason: this they have from that sort of eloquence, not which explains things as they are, but from that other, which by moving their mindes, makes all things to appear to bee such as they in their mindes prepared before, had already conceived them.

XIII. Many men who are themselves very well affected to civill society, doe through want of knowledge, cooperate to the disposing of subjects mindes to sedition, whilst they teach young men a doctrine conformable to the said opinions in their Schooles, and all the people in their Pulpits. Now they who desire to bring this disposition into Act, place their whole endeavour in this, First, that they may joyn the ill affected together into faction and conspiracy; next, that themselves may have the greatest stroke in the faction: They gather them into faction, while they make themselves the relators, and interpretors of the counsels and actions of single men, and nominate the Persons and Places, to assemble and deliberate of such things whereby the present government may be reformed, according as it shall seem best to their interests. Now to the end that they themselves may have the chief rule in the faction, the faction must be kept in a faction, that is to say, they must have their secret meetings apart with a few, where they may order what shall afterward be propounded in a general meeting, and by whom, and on what subject, and in what order each of them shall speak, and how they may draw the powerfullest, and most popular men of the faction to their side: And thus when they have gotten a faction big enough, in which they may rule by their eloquence, they move it to take upon it the managing of affaires; and thus they sometimes oppresse the Commonwealth, namely where there is no other faction to oppose them, but for the most part they rend it, and introduce a civill warre. For folly and eloquence concurre in the subversion of government in the same manner (as the fable hath it) as heretofore the daughters of Pelias King of Thessaly, conspired with Medea against their father; They going to restore the decrepit old man to his youth again, by the counsell of Medea, they cut him into peeces, and set him in the fire to boyle, in vain expecting when he would live again; So the common people through their folly (like the daughters of Pelias) desiring to renew the ancient government, being drawne away by the eloquence of ambitious men, as it were by the witchcraft of Medea, divided into faction, they consume it rather by those flames, than they reforme it.

CHAPTER XIII. CONCERNING THE DUTIES OF THEM WHO BEAR RULE

I. By what hath hitherto been said, the duties of Citizens and in any kind of government whatsoever, and the Power of the supreme Ruler over them are apparent; but we have as yet said nothing of the duties of Rulers, and how they ought to behave themselves towards their Subjects; We must then distinguish between the Right, and the exercise of supreme authority, for they can be divided; as for example, when he who hath the Right, either cannot, or will not be present in judging trespasses, or deliberating of affaires: For Kings sometimes by reason of their age cannot order their affaires, sometimes also though they can doe it themselves, yet they judge it fitter, being satisfied in the choyce of their Officers and Counsellors, to exercise their power by them. Now where the Right and exercise are severed, there the government of the Commonweale, is like the ordinary government of the world, in which God, the mover of all things,

produceth naturall effects by the means of secondary causes; but where he, to whom the Right of ruling doth belong, is himselfe present in all judicatures, consultations, and publique actions, there the administration is such, as if God beyond the ordinary course of nature, should immediately apply himself unto all matters. We will therefore in this Chapter summarily and briefly speak somewhat concerning their duties, who exercise authority, whether by their own or others Right. Nor is it my purpose to descend into those things, which being divers from others, some Princes may doe, for this is to be left to the Politicall Practices of each Common weale.

II. Now all the duties of Rulers are contained in this one sentence, The safety of the people is the supreme Law; for although they who among men obtain the chiefest Dominion, cannot be subject to Lawes properly so called, that is to say, to the will of men, because to be chief, and subject, are contradictories; yet is it their duty in all things, as much as possibly they can, to yeeld obedience unto right reason, which is the naturall, morall, and divine Law. But because dominions were constituted for Peaces sake, and Peace was sought after for safeties sake, he, who being placed in authority, shall use his power otherwise than to the safety of the people, will act against the reasons of Peace, that is to say, against the Lawes of nature; Now as the safety of the People dictates a Law by which Princes know their duty, so doth it also teach them an art how to procure themselves a benefit; for the power of the Citizens, is the power of the City, that is to say, his that bears the chief Rule in any state.

III. By the people in this place we understand, not one civill Person, namely the City it selfe which governs, but the multitude of subjects which are governed; for the City was not instituted for its own, but for the subjects sake; and yet a particular care is not required of this or that man; for the Ruler (as such) provides no otherwise for the safety of his people, than by his Lawes, which are universall; and therefore he hath fully discharged himselfe, if he have throughly endeavoured by wholesome constitutions, to establish the welfare of the most part, and made it as lasting as may be; and that no man suffer ill, but by his own default, Or by some chance which could not be prevented; but it sometimes conduces to the safety of the most part, that wicked men doe suffer.

IV. But by safety must be understood, not the sole preservation of life in what condition soever, but in order to its happines. For to this end did men freely assemble themselves, and institute a government, that they might, as much as their humane condition would afford, live delightfully. They therefore who had undertaken the administration of power in such a kinde of government, would sinne against the Law of nature (because against their trust who had committed that power unto them) if they should not study, as much as by good Laws could be effected, to furnish their subjects abundantly, not only with the good things belonging to life, but also with those which advance to delectation. They who have acquired Dominion by arms, doe all desire that their subjects may be strong in body and mind, that they may serve them the better; wherefore if they should not endeavour to provide them, not only with such things whereby they may live, but also with such whereby they may grow strong and lusty, they would act against their own scope and end.

V. And first of all, Princes doe beleeve that it mainly concerns eternall salvation, what opinions are held of the Deity, and what manner of worship he is to be adored with; which being supposed, it may be demanded, whether chief Rulers, and whosoever they be, whether one or more, who exercise supreme authority, sin not against the Law of nature, if they cause not such a doctrine, and worship, to be taught and practised (or permit a contrary to be taught and practised) as they beleeve necessarily conduceth to the eternall salvation of their subjects? It is manifest that they act against their conscience, and that they will, as much as in them lies, the eternall perdition of their subjects; for if they willed it not, I see no reason why they should suffer, (when being supreme they cannot be compelled) such things to be taught and done, for which they beleeve them to be in a damnable state. But we will leave this difficulty in suspence.

VI. The benefits of subjects respecting this life only, may be distributed into foure kindes. 1. That they be defended against forraign enemies. 2. That Peace be preserved at home. 3. That they be enrich't as much as may consist with publique security. 4. That they enjoy a harmelesse liberty; For supreme Commanders can conferre no more to their civill happinesse, than that being preserved from forraign and civill warres, they may quietly enjoy that wealth which they have purchased by their own industry.

VII. There are two things necessary for the Peoples defence; To be warned, and to be forearmed; for the state of Common-wealths considered in themselves, is natural, that is to say, hostile; neither if they cease from fighting, is it therefore to be called Peace, but rather a breathing time, in which one enemy observing the motion and countenance of the other, values his security not according to the Pacts, but the forces and counsels of his adversary; And this by naturall Right, as hath been shewed in the second Chapter, 10. Artic. from this, that contracts are invalid in the state of nature, as oft as any just fear doth intervene; It is therefore necessary to the defence of the City, First, that there be some who may as near as may be, search into, and discover the counsels and motions of all those who may prejudice it. For discoverers to Ministers of State, are like the beames of the Sunne to the humane soule, and we may more truly say in vision politicall, than naturall, that the sensible, and intelligible Species of outward things, not well considered by others, are by the ayre transported to the soule, (that is to say to them who have the Supreme Authority) and therefore are they no lesse necessary to the preservation of the State, than the rayes of the light are to the conservation of man; or if they be compared to Spiders webs, which extended on all sides by the finest threds, doe warn them, keeping in their small holds, of all outward motions; They who bear Rule can no more know what is necessary to be commanded for the defence of their Subjects without Spies, than those Spiders can when they shall goe forth, and whether they shall repair, without the motion of those threds.

VIII. Farthermore, its necessarily requisite to the peoples defence, that they be fore-armed. Now to be fore-armed is to be furnisht with Souldiers, Armes, Ships, Forts and Monies, before the danger be instant; for the listing of Souldiers, and taking up of Armes after a blow is given, is too late at least, if not impossible. In like manner, not to raise Forts, and appoint Garrisons in convenient places, before the Frontiers are invaded, is to be like those Country Swains (as Demosthenes said) who ignorant of the art of Fencing, with their Bucklers guarded those parts of the body where they first felt the smart of the strokes. But they who think it then seasonable enough to raise Monies for the maintenance of Souldiers, and other Charges of War, when the danger begins to shew it self, they consider not surely how difficult a matter it is to wring suddainly out of close—fisted men so vast a proportion of Monies; for almost all men, what they once reckon in the number of their goods, doe judge themselves to have such a right and propriety in it, as they conceive themselves to be injured whensoever they are forced to imploy but the least part of it for the publique good. Now a sufficient stock of monies to defend the Country with Armes, will not soon be raised out of the treasure of Imposts, and Customes; we must therefore, for fear of War, in time of Peace hoord up good summs, if we intend the safety of the Common—weal. Since therefore it necessarily belongs to Rulers for the Subjects safety to discover the Enemies Counsell, to keep Garrisons, and to have Money in continuall readinesse, and that Princes are by the Law of Nature bound to use their whole endeavour in procuring the welfare of their Subjects, it followes, that its not onely lawfull for them to send out Spies, to maintain Souldiers, to build Forts, and to require Monies for these purposes, but also, not to doe thus, is unlawfull. To which also may be added, whatsoever shall seeme to conduce to the lesning of the power of forraigners whom they suspect, whether by sleight, or force. For Rulers are bound according to their power to prevent the evills they suspect, lest peradventure they may happen through their negligence.

IX. But many things are required to the conservation of inward Peace, because many things concur (as hath been shewed in the foregoing Chapter) to its perturbation. We have there shewed, that some things there are which dispose the minds of men to sedition, others which move and quicken them so disposed. Among those which dispose them, we have reckoned in the first place certaine perverse doctrines. Its therefore the duty of those who have the chief Authority; to root those out of the mindes of men, not by commanding, but by teaching; not by the terrour of penalties, but by the perspicuity of reasons; the Lawes whereby this evill may be withstood are not to be made against the Persons erring, but against the Errours themselves. Those errours which in the foregoing Chapter we affirmed were inconsistent with the quiet of the Common—weal, have

crept into the mindes of ignorant men, partly from the Pulpit, partly from the daily discourses of men, who by reason of little employment, otherwise, doe finde leasure enough to study; and they got into these mens mindes by the teachers of their youth in publique schooles. Wherefore also, on the other side, if any man would introduce sound Doctrine, he must begin from the Academies: There, the true, and truly demonstrated foundations of civill Doctrine are to be laid, wherewith young men being once endued, they may afterward both in private and publique instruct the vulgar. And this they will doe so much the more cheerfully, and powerfully, by how much themselves shall be more certainly convinced of the truth of those things they profess, and teach; for seeing at this day men receive propositions, though false, and no more intelligible, than if a man should joyne together a company of termes drawn by chance out of an urne, by reason of the frequent use of hearing them; how much more would they for the same reason entertain true doctrines suitable to their own understandings, and the nature of things? I therefore conceive it to be the duty of Supreme Officers to cause the true elements of civill Doctrine to be written, and to command them to be taught in all the Colledges of their severall Dominions.

X. In the next place we shewed that grief of mind arising from want did dispose the Subjects to Sedition, which want, although deriv'd from their own luxury, and sloth, yet they impute it to those who govern the Realm, as though they were drained and opprest by publique Pensions. Notwithstanding it may sometimes happen that this complaint may be just, namely, when the burthens of the Realm are unequally imposed on the Subjects; For that which to all together is but a light weight, if many withdraw themselves, it wil be very heavy, nay, even intollerable to the rest: Neither are men wont so much to grieve at the burthen it self, as at the inequality. With much earnestnes therefore men strive to be freed from taxes, in this conflict the lesse happy, as being overcome, do envy the more fortunate. To remove therefore all just complaint, its the interest of the publique quiet, and by consequence it concernes the duty of the Magistrate, to see that the publique burthens be equally born. Furthermore, since what is brought by the subjects to publick use, is nothing else but the price of their bought Peace, its reason good, that they who equally share in the peace, should also pay an equall part either by contributing their Monies, or their labours to the Common−weal. Now it is the Law of Nature (by the 15. Article of the 3. Chapter) that every man in distributing right to others, doe carry himself equall to all; wherefore Rulers are by the naturall Law obliged to lay the burthens of the Common−weal equally on their Subjects.

XI. Now in this place we understand an equality, not of Money, but of Burthen, that is to say, an equality of reason between the Burthens, and the Benefits. For although all equally enjoy Peace, yet the benefits springing from thence, are not equall to all; for some get greater possessions, others lesse; and againe, some consume lesse, others more. It may therefore be demanded whether Subjects ought to contribute to the publique, according to the rate of what they gain, or of what they spend, that is to say, whether the persons must be taxt, so as to pay contribution according to their wealth, or the goods themselves, that every man contribute according to what he spends. But if we consider, where Monies are raised according to wealth, there they who have made equall gain, have not equall possessions, because that one preserves what he hath got by frugality, another wastes it by luxury, and therefore equally rejoycing in the benefit of Peace, they doe not equally sustaine the Burthens of the Common−weal: and on the other side, where the goods themselves are taxt, there every man, while he spends his private goods, in the very act of consuming them he undiscernably payes part due to the Common−weal, according to, not what he hath, but what by the benefit of the Realm he hath had. It is no more to be doubted, but that the former way of commanding monies is against equity, and therefore against the duty of Rulers, the latter is agreeable to reason, and the exercise of their authority.

XII. In the third place, we said that that trouble of minde which riseth from ambition was offensive to publique Peace. For there are some who seeming to themselves to be wiser than others, and more sufficient for the managing of affaires than they who at present doe govern, when they can no otherwise declare how profitable their vertue would prove to the Common−weale, they shew it, by harming it; but because ambition and greedinesse of honours cannot be rooted out of the mindes of men, its not the duty of Rulers to endeavour it; but by constant application of rewards, and punishments, they may so order it, that men may know that the way to honour is, not by contempt of the present government, nor by factions, and the popular ayre, but by the contraries. They are good men who observe the Decrees, the Lawes and Rights of their Fathers; if with a constant order we saw these adorned with honours, but the factious punisht, and had in contempt by those who bear command, there would be more ambition to obey, than withstand. Notwithstanding it so happens sometimes, that as we must stroke a horse by reason of his too much fiercenesse, so a stiffe−neckt subject must be flatter'd for fear of his power; but as that happens when the rider, so this, when the Commander is in danger of falling. But we speak here of those, whose authority and power is intire. Their duty (I say) it is to cherish obedient subjects, and to depresse the factious all they can; nor can the publique power be otherwise preserved, nor the subjects quiet without it.

XIII. But if it be the duty of Princes to restrain the factious, much more does it concern them to dissolve and dissipate the factions themselves. Now I call a faction, a multitude of subjects gathered together, either by mutuall contracts among themselves, or by the power of some one, without his or their authority who bear the supreme Rule: A faction therefore is as it were a City in a City; for as by an Union of men in the state of nature a City receives its being, so by a new union of subjects, there ariseth a faction. According to this definition, a multitude of subjects who have bound themselves simply to obey any forreign Prince, or Subject, or have made any Pacts, or Leagues of mutuall defence between themselves against all men, not excepting those who have the supreme power in the City, is a faction. Also favour with the vulgar if it be so great, that by it an Army may be rais'd, except publique caution be given, either by hostages, or some other pledges, contains faction in it; The same may be said of private wealth, if it exceed, because all things obey mony. Forasmuch therefore as it is true, that the state of Cities among themselves is naturall, and hostile, those Princes who permit factions, doe as much as if they received an enemy within their walls, which is Contrary to the subjects safety, and therefore also against the Law of nature.

XIV. There are two things necessary to the enriching of Subjects, Labour and thrift; there is also a third which helps, to wit the naturall increase of the earth and water; and there is a fourth too, namely the Militia, which sometimes augments, but more frequently lessens the subjects stock. The two first are only necessary. For a City constituted in an Island of the Sea, no greater than will serve for dwelling, may grow rich without sowing, or fishing, by merchandize, and handicrafts only; but there is no doubt if they have a territory, but they may be richer with the same number, or equally rich, being a greater number. But the fourth, namely the Militia, was of old reckoned in the number of the gaining Arts, under the notion of Booting or taking Prey; and it was by mankind, (disperst by families) before the constitution of civill societies, accounted just and honourable; for preying, is nothing else but a warre waged with small forces; And great Common—weales, namely that of Rome, and Athens, by the spoyles of warre, forraigne tribute, and the territories they have purchased by their armes, have sometimes so improved the Common—wealth, that they have not onely not required any publique monies from the poorer sort of subjects, but have also divided to each of them both monies and lands. But this kind of increase of riches, is not to be brought into rule and fashion: For the Militia in order to profit, is like a Dye wherewith many lose their estates, but few improve them. Since therefore there are three things only, the fruits of the earth and water, Labour and Thrift, which are expedient for the enriching of subjects, the duty of Commanders in chief, shall be conversant onely about those three. For the first, those lawes will be usefull which countenance the arts that improve the increase of the earth, and water, such as are husbandry, and fishing. For the second, all Lawes against idlenesse, and such as quicken industry, are profitable; the art of Navigation (by help whereof the commodities of the whole world, bought almost by labour only, are brought into one City) and the Mechanicks, (under which I comprehend all the arts of the most excellent workmen) and the Mathematicall sciences, the fountains of navigatory and mechanick employments, are held in due esteem and honour. For the third, those lawes are usefull, whereby all inordinate expence, as well in meats, as in clothes, and universally in all things which are consumed with usage, is forbidden. Now because such lawes are beneficiall to the ends above specified, it belongs also to the Office of supreme Magistrates, to establish them.

XV. The liberty of subjects consists not in being exempt from the Lawes of the City, or that they who have the supreme power cannot make what Laws they have a mind to; but because all the motions and actions of subjects, are never circumscribed by Lawes, nor can be, by reason of their variety, it is necessary that there be infinite cases, which are neither commanded, nor prohibited, but every man may either doe, or not doe them, as he lists himselfe. In these, each man is said to enjoy his liberty, and in this sense liberty is to be understood in this place, namely, for that part of naturall Right, which is granted and left to Subjects by the civill Lawes. As water inclosed on all hands with banks, stands still and corrupts; having no bounds, it spreds too largely, and the more passages it findes, the more freely it takes its current; so subjects, if they might doe nothing without the commands of the Law would grow dull, and unwildly, if all, they would be disperst, and the more is left undetermined by the Lawes, the more liberty they enjoy. Both extremes are faulty, for Lawes were not invented to take away, but to direct mens actions, even as nature ordained the banks, not to stay, but to guide the course of the streame. The measure of this liberty is to be taken from the subjects, and the Cities good. Wherefore in the first place it is against the charge of those who command, and have the authority of making lawes, that there should be more lawes than necessarily serve for good of the Magistrate, and his Subjects; for since men are wont commonly to debate what to do, or not to do, by naturall reason, rather than any knowledge of the Lawes, where there are more Lawes than can easily be remembred, and whereby such things are forbidden, as reason of it selfe prohibites not of necessity, they must through ignorance, without the least evill intention, fall within the compasse of Lawes, as gins laid to entrap their harmelesse liberty, which supreme Commanders are bound to preserve for their subjects by the Lawes of nature.

XVI. It is a great part of that liberty, which is harmlesse to civill government, and necessary for each subject to live happily, that there be no penalties dreaded, but what they may both foresee, and look for; and this is done, where there are either no punishments at all defined by the Lawes, or greater not required than are defined. Where there are none defined, there he that hath first broken the Law, expects an indefinite or arbitrary punishment, and his feare is supposed boundlesse, because it relates to an unbounded evill; now the Law of nature commands them who are not subject to any civill Lawes, (by what we have said in the third Chapter, Artic. 11.) and therefore supreme Commanders, that in taking revenge and punishing, they must not so much regard the past evill, as the future good, and they sin, if they entertain any other measure in arbitrary punishment than the publique benefit. But where the punishment is defined, either by a Law prescribed, as when it is set down in plain words, that he that shall doe thus, or thus, shall suffer so and so; or by practice, as when the penalty, (not by any Law prescribed, but arbitrary from the beginning) is afterward determined by the punishment of the first delinquent (for naturall equity commands that equall transgressors be equally punished); there to impose a greater penalty than is defined by the Law, is against the Law of nature. For the end of punishment is not to compell the will of man, but to fashion it, make it such as he would have it who hath set the penalty. And deliberation is nothing else but a weighing, as it were in scales, the conveniencies, and inconveniencies of the fact we are attempting; where, that which is more weighty, doth necessarily according to its inclination prevaile with us. If therefore the Legislator doth set a lesse penalty on a crime, than will make our feare more considerable with us, than our lust; that excesse of lust above the feare of punishment, whereby sinne is committed, is to be attributed to the Legislator (that is to say) to the supreme; and therefore if he inflict a greater punishment, than himselfe hath determined in his Lawes, he punisheth that in another, in which he sinned himselfe.

XVII. It pertaines therefore to the harmlesse and necessary liberty of subjects, that every man may without feare, enjoy the rights which are allowed him by the Lawes; for it is in vain to have our own distinguisht by the Lawes from anothers, if by wrong judgement; robbery, theft, they may bee again confounded. But it falls out so, that these doe happen where Judges are corrupted; for the fear whereby men are deterred from doing evill, ariseth not from hence, namely, because penalties are set, but because they are executed; for we esteeme the future by what is past, seldome expecting what seldome happens. If therefore Judges corrupted either by Gifts, Favour, or even by pitty it self, do often forbear the execution of the Penalties due by the Law, and by that meanes put wicked men in hope to passe unpunisht: honest Subjects encompast with murtherers, theeves and knaves, will not have the liberty to converse freely with each other, nor scarce to stirre abroad without hazard; nay, the City it self is dissolved, and every mans right of protecting himself at his own will returnes to him. The Law of Nature therefore gives this precept to Supreme Commanders, that they not onely doe righteousnesse themselves, but that they also by penalties cause the Judges, by them appointed, to doe the same; that is to say, that they hearken to the complaints of their Subjects; and as oft as need requires, make choice of some extraordinary Judges, who may hear the matter debated concerning the ordinary ones.

CHAPTER XIV. OF LAWES AND TRESPASSES

I. They who lesse seriously consider the force of words, doe sometimes confound Law with Counsell, sometimes with Covenant, sometimes with Right. They confound Law with Counsell, who think, that it is the duty of Monarchs not onely to give ear to their Counsellours, but also to obey them, as though it were in vaine to take Counsell, unlesse it were also followed. We must fetch the distinction between Counsell, and Law, from the difference between Counsell, and Command. Now COUNSELL is a precept in which the reason of my obeying it, is taken from the thing it self which is advised; but COMMAND is a precept in which the cause of my obedience depends on the will of the Commander. For it is not properly said, Thus I will, and thus I Command, except the will stand for a Reason. Now when obedience is yielded to the Lawes, not for the thing it self, but by reason of the advisers will, the Law is not a Counsell, but a Command, and is defined thus, LAW is the command of that Person (whether Man, or Court) whose precept containes in it the reason of obedience; as the Precepts of God in regard of Men, of Magistrates in respect of their Subjects, and universally of all the powerfull in respect of them who cannot resist, may be termed their Lawes. Law and Counsell therefore differ many ways; Law belongs to him who hath power over them whom he adviseth, Counsell to them who have no power. To follow what is prescribed by Law, is duty, what by Counsell, is free—will. Counsell is directed to his end that receives it; Law, to his that gives it. Counsell is given to none but the willing; Law even to the unwilling. To conclude, the right of the Counsellour is made void by the will of him to whom he gives Counsell, the right of the Law—giver is not abrogated at the pleasure of him who hath a Law imposed.

II. They confound Law, and Covenant, who conceive the Lawes to be nothing else but certain omologemata or forms of living, determined by the common consent of men: Amongst whom is Aristotle, who defines Law on this manner, Nomos esti logos orismenos kath omologian koinen poleos, minuon pos dei prattein ekasta, that is to say, Law is a speech, limited according to the common consent of the City, declaring every thing that we ought to doe. Which definition is not simply of Law, but of the Civill Law; for it is manifest that the Divine Lawes sprang not from the consent of men, nor yet the Lawes of Nature; for if they had their originall from the consent of men, they might also by the same consent be abrogated; but they are unchangeable. But indeed that's no right definition of a Civill Law; for in that place a City is taken either for one civill person, having one will, or for a multitude of men who have each of them the liberty of their private wills. If for one person, those words, common consent, are ill placed here, for one person hath no common consent; neither ought he to have said, (declaring what was needfull to be done) but commanding; for what the City declares, it commands its Subjects. He therefore by a City understood a multitude of men declaring by common consent (imagine it a writing confirm'd by Votes) some certain formes of living; but these are nothing else but some mutuall contracts which oblige not any man (and therefore are no Lawes) before that a Supreme Power being constituted which can compell, have sufficient remedy against the rest, who otherwise are not likely to keep them. Lawes therefore, according to this definition of Aristotle, are nothing else, but naked, and weak contracts, which then at length, when there is one who by right doth exercise the Supreme Power, shall either become Lawes, or no Lawes, at his will and pleasure: Wherefore he confounds Contracts with Lawes, which he ought not to have done; for Contract is a promise, Law a command. In Contracts we say, I will do this; In Lawes, Doe this. Contracts oblige us, [1] Lawes tie us fast, being obliged. A Contract obligeth of it self, The Law holds the party obliged by vertue of the universall Contract of yeelding obedience; Therefore in Contract its first determined what is to be done, before we are obliged to doe it; But in Law we are first obliged to performe, and what is to be done, is determined afterwards. Aristotle therefore ought to have defined a civill law thus, A civill law is a speech limited by the will of the City, commanding every thing behoofefull to be done, which is the same with that we have given above in the 6. Chap. art. 9. to wit, that the civill lawes are the command of him (whether man, or Court of men) who is endued with supreme Power in the city, concerning the future actions of his Subjects.

III. They confound Lawes with Right, who continue still to doe what is permitted by divine Right, notwithstanding it be forbidden by the civill Law: That which is prohibited by the divine Law, cannot bee permitted by the civill, neither can that which is commanded by the divine Law, be prohibited by the civill. Notwithstanding that which is permitted by the divine Right, that is to say, that which may be done by divine Right, doth no whit hinder why the same may not be forbidden by the civill Lawes; for inferiour Lawes may restrain the liberty allowed by the superiour, although they cannot enlarge them. Now naturall liberty is a Right not constituted, but allowed by the Lawes. For the Lawes being removed, our liberty is absolute; This is first restrained by the naturall, and divine Lawes, the residue is bounded by the civill Law, and what remains may again be restrained by the constitutions of particular Towns, and Societies. There is great difference therefore between Law, and Right; For Law is a fetter, Right is freedome, and they differ like contraries.

IV. All Law may be divided, first according to the diversity of its Authors into Divine and humane. The Divine, according to the two wayes whereby God hath made known his will unto men, is twofold, naturall (or morall) and positive; naturall is that which God hath declared to all men by his eternall word borne with them, to wit, their naturall Reason; and this is that Law which in this whole book I have endeavoured to unfold. Positive is that, which God hath revealed to us by the word of Prophesie, wherein he hath spoken unto men as a man: Such are the Lawes which he gave to the Jewes concerning their government, and divine worship, and they may be termed the Divine civill Lawes, because they were peculiar to the civill government of the Jewes, his peculiar people. Again, the naturall Law may be divided into that of Men, which alone hath obtained the title of the Law of nature, and that of Cities, which may be called that of Nations, but vulgarly it is termed the Right of Nations. The precepts of both are alike, but because Cities once instituted doe put on the personall proprieties of men, that Law, which speaking of the duty of single men, we call naturall, being applyed to whole Cities, and Nations, is called the Right of Nations. And the same Elements of naturall law, and Right, which have hitherto been spoken of, being transferred to whole Cities and Nations, may be taken for the Elements of the lawes, and Right of Nations.

V. All humane law is civill. For the state of men considered out of civill society, is hostile, in which, because one is not subject to another, there are no other Lawes, beside the dictates of naturall reason, which is the divine Law. But in civill government the City onely, that is to say, that man, or Court, to whom the supreme power of the City is committed, is the Legislator, and the Lawes of the City are civill. The civill Lawes may be divided according to the diversity of their subject matter, into sacred, or secular; sacred are those which pertain to Religion, that is to say, to the ceremonies, and worship of God (to wit what Persons, things, places, are to be consecrated, and in what fashion, what opinions concerning the Deity are to be taught publiquely, and with what words, and in what order supplications are to be made, and the like) and are not determined by any divine positive Law. For the civill sacred Lawes are the humane Lawes (which are also called Ecclesiasticall) concerning things sacred; but the secular under a generall notion, are usually called the civill Lawes.

89

VI. Again, the civill Law (according to the two offices of the Legislator, whereof one is to judge; the other to constrain men to acquiesce to his judgements) hath two parts; the one distributive, the other vindicative, or penall. By the distributive it is, that every man hath his proper Right, that is to say, it sets forth Rules for all things, whereby we may know what is properly ours, what another mans; so as others may not hinder us from the free use and enjoyment of our own; and we may not interrupt others in the quiet possession of theirs; and what is lawfull for every man to doe or omit, and what is not lawfull. Vindicative is that whereby it is defined what punishment shall be inflicted on them who break the Law.

VII. Now distributive, and vindicative, are not two severall Species of the Lawes, but two parts of the same Law. For if the Law should say no more, but (for example) whatsoever you take with your net in the Sea, be it yours, its in vain; For although another should take that away from you which you have caught, it hinders not, but that it still remains yours; for in the state of nature where all things are common to all, yours, and others, are all one, insomuch as what the Law defines to be yours, was yours even before the Law, and after the Law ceases not to bee yours, although in another mans possession. Wherefore the Law doth nothing, unlesse it bee understood to bee so yours, as all other men be forbidden to interrupt your free use, and secure enjoyment of it at all times, according to your own will, and pleasure. For this is that which is required to a propriety of goods, not that a man may be able to use them, but to use them alone, which is done by prohibiting others to be an hinderance to him. But in vain doe they also prohibit any men, who doe not withall strike a fear of punishment into them; in vain therefore is the Law, unlesse it contain both parts, that which forbids injuries to be done, and that which punisheth the doers of them. The first of them which is called distributive, is Prohibitory, and speaks to all; the second which is styled vindicative, or paenary, is mandatory, and onely speaks to publique Ministers.

VIII. From hence also we may understand, that every civill Law hath a penalty annexed to it, either explicitly, or implicitly; For where the penalty is not defined, neither by any writing, nor by example of any one who hath suffered the punishment of the transgressed Law there the penalty is understood to be arbitrary, namely, to depend on the will of the Legislator, that is to say, of the supreme Commander. For in vain is that Law which may be broken without punishment.

IX. Now because it comes from the civill Lawes, both that every man have his proper Right, and distinguisht from anothers, and also that he is forbidden to invade anothers Rights, it followes, that these Precepts (Thou shalt not refuse to give the honour defin'd by the Lawes unto thy Parents: Thou shalt not kill the man whom the Lawes forbid thee to kill: Thou shalt avoid all copulation forbidden by the Laws: Thou shalt not take away anothers goods against the Lords will: Thou shalt not frustrate the Laws and Judgements by false testimony) are Civill Lawes. The naturall Lawes command the same things but implicitly. For the law of nature (as hath been said in the 3. Chap. Art. 2.) commands us to keep contracts, and therefore also to performe obedience when we have covenanted obedience, and to abstaine from anothers goods when it is determin'd by the civill Law what belongs to another. But all Subjects (by the 13. Art. of the 6. Chap.) do covenant to obey his commands who hath the supreme power, that is to say the civill Lawes, in the very constitution of government, even before it is possible to break them. For the Law of nature did oblige in the state of nature, where first (because nature hath given all things to all men) nothing did properly belong to another, and therefore it was not possible to invade anothers right; next, where all things were common, and therefore all carnall copulations lawfull; Thirdly, where was the state of Warre, and therefore lawfull to kill; Fourthly, where all things were determined by every mans own judgement, and therefore paternall respects also: Lastly, where there were no publique judgements, and therefore no use of bearing witnesse, either true, or false.

X. Seeing therefore our obligation to observe those Laws is more ancient than the promulgation of the Laws themselves, as being contained in the very constitution of the City, by the vertue of the naturall Law which forbids breach of Covenant, the Law of nature commands us to keep all the civill Laws; for where we are tyed to obedience, before we know what will be commanded us, there we are universally tyed to obey in all things. Whence it followes, that no civil Law whatsoever, which tends not to a reproach of the Deity (in respect of whom, Cities themselves have no right of their own, and cannot be said to make Lawes) can possibly be against the Law of nature; for though the Law of nature forbid theft, adultery, yet if the civill Law command us to invade any thing, that invasion is not theft, adultery, For when the Lacedemonians of old permitted their youths by a certaine Law, to take away other mens goods, they commanded that these goods should not bee accounted other mens, but their own who took them; and therefore such surreptions were no thefts. In like manner, copulations of heathen Sexes, according to their Lawes, were lawfull marriages.

XI. Its necessary to the essence of a Law, that the Subjects be acquainted with two things, First, what man or Court hath the supreme power, that is to say, the Right of making Lawes. Secondly, what the Law it self sayes; for he that neither knew either to whom or what he is tyed to, cannot obey, and by consequence is in such a condition, as if he were not tyed at all. I say not that it is necessary to the essence of a Law, that either one, or the other be perpetually known, but onely that it be once knowne; and if the Subject afterward forget either the Right he hath who made the Law, or the Law it self, that makes him no lesse tyed to obey, since he might have remembred it, had he had a will to obey.

XII. The knowledge of the Legislator depends on the Subject himselfe; for the right of making Lawes could not be conferr'd on any man without his owne consent, and covenant, either exprest, or suppos'd; exprest, when from the beginning the Citizens doe themselves constitute a forme of governing the City, or when by promise they submit themselves to the Dominion of any one; or suppos'd at least, as when they make use of the benefit of the Realme, and Lawes, for their protection and conservation against others. For to whose Dominion we require our fellow Subjects to yeeld obedience for our good, his Dominion we acknowledge to be legitimate by that very request. And therefore ignorance of the power of making Lawes, can never be a sufficient excuse; for every man knowes what he hath done himselfe.

XIII. The knowledge of the lawes depends on the Legislator, who must publish them, for otherwise they are not Lawes; for Law is the command of the Law—maker, and his command is the Declaration of his Will; it is not therefore a Law, except the will of the Law—maker be declar'd, which is done by promulgation. Now in promulgation two things must be manifest, whereof one is, that he or they who publish a Law, either have a right themselves to make Lawes, or that they doe it by authority deriv'd from him or them who have it; the other is the sense of the Law it selfe. Now, that the first, namely publisht Lawes proceed from him who hath the supreme command, cannot be manifest (speaking exactly and philosophically) to any, but them who have received them from the mouth of the Commander; the rest beleeve, but the reasons of their beliefe are so many, that it is scarce possible they should not believe. And truly in a Democratical City where every one may be present at the making of Laws if he will, he that shall be absent, must beleeve those that were present; but in monarchies and Aristocraties, because its granted but to few to be present, and openly to heare the commands of the monarch or the Nobles, it was necessary to bestow a power on those few of publishing them to the rest. And thus we beleeve those to be the Edicts and Decrees of Princes, which are propounded to us for such, either by the writings, or voices of them, whose office it is to publish them. But yet when we have these causes of beliefe, that we have seen the Prince, or supreme Councell constantly use such Counsellors, Secretaries, Publishers, and Seales, and the like arguments for the declaring of his will; that he never took any authority from them; that they have bin punisht who not giving credit to such like promulgations have transgrest the Law; not onely he who thus believing shall not obey the Edicts and Decrees set forth by them is every where accus'd, but he that not believing, shall not yield obedience, is punisht. For the constant permission of these things is a manifest signe enough, and evident declaration of the Commanders will; provided there be nothing contain'd in the Law, Edict or Decree, derogatory from his supreme power. For it is not to be imagin'd that he would have ought taken from his power by any of his Officers as long as he retaines a will to governe. Now the sense of the law, when there is any doubt made of it, is to be taken from them to whom the supreme authority hath committed the knowledge of causes, or Judgements; for to judge is nothing else than by interpretation to apply the lawes to particular cases. Now we may know who they are that have this Office granted them, in the same manner, as we know who they be that have authority given them to publish Laws.

XIV. Againe the civill law according to its two fold manner of publishing, is of two sorts, written unwritten; By written, I understand that which wants a voice, or some other signe of the will of the Legislator that it may become a Law. For all kind of Laws are of the same age with mankinde, both in nature, and time, and therefore of more antiquity than the invention of letters, and the Art of writing. Wherefore not a writing, but a voice is necessary for a written law; this alone is requisite to the being, that to the Remembrance of a Law; for we reade, that before letters were found out for the help of memory, that Lawes contracted into Meetre, were wont to be sung. The unwritten is that which wants no other publishing than the voice of nature, or naturall reason; such are the lawes of nature. For the naturall Law although it be distinguisht from the civill, for as much as it commands the Will, yet so farre forth as it relates to our actions it is civill; for example, this same, Thou shalt not covet, which onely appertaines to the minde, is a naturall Law, onely; but this, Thou shalt not invade, is both naturall and civill. For seeing it is impossible to prescribe such universall Rules, whereby all future contentions which perhaps are infinite, may be determined, its to be understood that in all cases not mentioned by the written lawes, the law of naturall equity is to be followed, which commands us to distribute equally to equals; and this by the vertue of the civill law, which also punisheth those who knowingly and willingly doe actually transgresse the lawes of nature.

XV. These things being understood, it appeares first, That the Lawes of Nature, although they were describ'd in the Books of some Philosophers, are not for that reason to be termed Written lawes: and that the Writings of the Interpreters of the Lawes, were no Lawes, for want of the Supreme Authority; nor yet those orations of the Wise, (that is to say) Judges, but so farre forth as by the consent of the Supreme power they part into custome; and that then they are to be received among the Written lawes, not for the Customes sake (which by its own force doth not constitute a Law) but for the Will of the Supreme Commander, which appeares in this, that he hath suffer'd his Sentence, whether equall, or unequall, to passe into custome.

XVI. Sinne, in its largest signification, comprehends every deed, word and thought, against right reason. For every man by reasoning seeks out the meanes to the end which he propounds to himselfe. If therefore he reason right (that is to say, beginning from most evident principles, he makes a discourse out of consequences continually necessary,) he will proceede in a most direct way; otherwise hee'l goe astray, that is to say, he will either doe, say, or endeavour, somewhat against his proper end: which when he hath done, he will indeed in reasoning be said to have erred, but in action and will to have sinned; for sin followes errour, just as the Will doth the understanding: And this is the most generall acception of the word, under which is contain'd every imprudent action, whether against the Law, as to overthrow another mans house, or not against the Law, as to build his owne upon the Sand.

XVII. But when we speak of the Lawes, the word Sinne is taken in a more strict sense, and signifies not every thing done against right reason, but that onely which is blameable, and therefore is call'd malum culpae, the evill of fault; but yet if any thing be culpable it is not presently to be term'd a sinne, or fault, but onely if it be blameable with reason. We must therefore enquire what is to be blameable with reason, what against reason. Such is the nature of man, that every one calls that good which he desires, and evill which he eschewes; and therefore through the diversity of our affections, it happens that one counts that good, which another counts evill; and the same man what now he esteem'd for good, he immediately looks on as evill; and the same thing which he calls good in himselfe, he tearmes evill in another. For we all measure good and evill by the pleasure or paine we either feele at present, or expect hereafter. Now seeing the prosperous actions of enemies (because they increase their honours, goods, and power) and of equalls, (by reason of that strife of honours which is among them) both seeme and are irkesome, and therefore evill to all; and men use to repute those evill, that is to say, to lay some fault to their charge from whom they receive evill; its impossible to be determined by the consent of single men whom the same things doe not please and displease, what actions are, and what not to be blam'd. They may agree indeed in some certaine generall things, as that theft, adultery, and the like are sinnes, as if they should say that all men account those things evill to which they have given names which are usually taken in an evill sense; but we demand not whether theft be a Sinne, but what is to be term'd theft, and so concerning other in like manner. For as much therefore as in so great a diversity of censurers, what is by reason blameable, is not to bee measur'd by the reason of one man more than another, because of the equality of humane nature, and there are no other reasons in being, but onely those of particular men, and that of the City, it followes, that the City is to determine what with reason is culpable: So as a fault, that is to say, a SINNE, is that, which a man do's, omits, sayes, or wills, against the reason of the City, that is, contrary to the Lawes.

XVIII. But a man may doe somewhat against the Lawes through humane infirmity, although he desire to fulfill them, and yet his action as being against the Lawes, is rightly blam'd, and call'd a Sinne. But there are some, who neglect the Lawes, and as oft as any hope of gain and impunity doth appear to them, no conscience of contracts and betrothed faith can withhold them from their violation. Not only the deeds, but even the mindes of these men are against the Lawes. They who sinne onely through infirmity, are good men even when they sinne; but these even when they doe not sin, are wicked. For though both the action, and the mind be repugnant to the Lawes, yet those repugnancies are distinguisht by different appellations, for the irregularity of the action is called adikema, unjust deed; that of the mind adikia, and kakia, injustice, and malice; that is, the infirmity of a disturbed soule, this the pravity of a sober mind.

XIX. But seeing there is no sin which is not against some Law, and that there is no Law which is not the command of him who hath the supreme power, and that no man hath a supreme power which is not bestowed on him by our own consent; in what manner will he be said to sinne, who either denies that there is a God, or that he governs the world, or casts any other reproach upon him? For he will say, that he never submitted his will to Gods will, not conceiving him so much as to have any being. And granting that his opinion were erroneous, and therefore also a sin, yet were it to be numbred among those of imprudence or ignorance, which by right cannot be punished. This speech seems so farre forth to be admitted, that though this kind of sin be the greatest and most hurtful, yet is it to be refer'd to sins of imprudence; [2] but that it should be excused by imprudence or ignorance, is absurd. For the Atheist is punisht either immediately by God himselfe, or by Kings constituted under God; not as a Subject is punished by a King, because he keeps not the Lawes, but as one enemy by another, because he would not accept of the Lawes; that is to say, by the Right of warre, as the Giants warring against God: For whosoever are not subject either to some common Lord, or one to another, are enemies among themselves.

XX. Seeing that from the vertue of the Covenant whereby each Subject is tyed to the other to perform absolute and universall obedience (such as is defined above Chap. 6. art. 13.) to the City, that is to say, to the Soveraign power, whether that be one man or Councel, there is an obligation derived to observe each one of the civill Lawes, so that that Covenant contains in it self all the Laws at once; it is manifest that the subject who shall renounce the generall Covenant of obedience, doth at once renounce all the Lawes. Which trespasse is so much worse than any other one sinne, by how much to sinne alwayes, is worse than to sinne once. And this is that sin which is called TREASON; and it is a word or deed whereby the Citizen, or Subject, declares that he will no longer obey that man or Court to whom the supreme power of the City is entrusted. And the Subject declares this same will of his by deed, when he either doth, or endeavours to do violence to the Soveraigns Person, or to them who execute his commands; of which sort are Traytors, Regicides, and such as take up armes against the City, or during a warre, flye to the enemies side. And they shew the same will in word, who flatly deny that themselves or other subjects are tyed to any such kind of obedience, either in the whole, as he who should say that wee must not obey him (keeping the obedience which we owe to God intire) simply, absolutely, and universally; or in part, as he who should say, that he had no Right to wage warre at his own will, to make Peace, list souldiers, levie monies, electing Magistrates, and publique Ministers, enacting Lawes, deciding controversies, setting penalties, or doing ought else, without which the State cannot stand. And these and the like words and deeds are Treason by the naturall, not the civill Law. But it may so happen, that some action which before the civill Law was made, was not Treason, yet will become such, if it be done afterwards. As if it be declared by the Law, that it shall be accounted for a sign of renouncing publique obedience (that is to say for Treason) if any man shall coyn monies, or forge the Privie Seale, he that after that Declaration shall doe this, will be no lesse guilty of Treason than the other. Yet he sinnes lesse, because he breakes not all the Laws at once, but one Law only; for the Law by calling that Treason which by nature is not so, doth indeed by Right set a more odious name, and perhaps a more grievous punishment on the guilty persons, but it makes not the sinne it selfe more grievous.

XXI. But that sinne which by the Law of nature is Treason, is a Transgression of the naturall, not the civill Law. For since our obligation to civill obedience, by vertue whereof the civill Lawes are valid, is before all civill Law, and the sin of Treason is naturally nothing else but the breach of that obligation; it followes that by the sin of Treason, that Law is broken which preceded the civill Law, to wit, the naturall, which forbids us to violate Covenants, and betrothed faith. But if some Soveraign Prince should set forth a Law on this manner, Thou shalt not rebell, he would effect just nothing: For except Subjects were before obliged to obedience, that is to say, not to rebell, all Law is of no force; now the obligation which obligeth to what we were before obliged to, is superfluous.

XXII. Hence it followes, that Rebels, Traytors, and all others convicted of Treason, are punisht not by civill, but naturall Right; that is to say, not as civill Subjects, but as Enemies to the Government, not by the Right of Soveraignty, and Dominion, but by the Right of Warre.

XXIII. There are some who think that those acts which are done against the Law, when the punishment is determined by the Law it selfe, are expiated, if the punished willingly undergoe the punishment; and that they are not guilty before God of breaking the naturall Law (although by breaking the civill Lawes, we break the naturall too, which command us to keep the civill) who have suffered the punishment which the Law required; as if by the Law, the fact were not prohibited, but a punishment were set instead of a price, whereby a licence might be bought of doing what the Law forbids. By the same reason they might inferre too, that no transgression of the Law were a sin, but that every man might enjoy the liberty which he hath bought by his own perill. But we must know that the words of the Law may be understood in a twofold sense, the one as containing two parts (as hath been declared above in the seventh Art.) namely that of absolutely prohibiting, as, Thou shalt not doe this; and revenging, as, he that doth this, shall be punisht; The other, as containing a condition, for example, Thou shalt not doe this thing, unlesse thou wilt suffer punishment; and thus, the Law forbids not simply, but conditionally. If it be understood in the first sense, he that doth it, sins, because he doth what the Law forbids to be done; if in the second, he sins not, because he cannot be said to doe what is forbidden him, that performes the condition; For in the first sense, all men are forbidden to doe it; in the second, they only who keep themselves from the punishment. In the first sense, the vindicative part of the Law obligeth not the guilty, but the Magistrate to require punishment; in the second, he himselfe that owes the punishment is obliged to exact it, to the payment whereof, if it be capitall, or otherwise grievous, he cannot be obliged. But in what sense the Law is to be taken, depends on the will of him who hath the Soveraignty. When there is therefore any doubt of the meaning of the Law, since we are sure they sinne not who doe it not, it will be sin if we doe it, howsoever the Law may afterward be explained; for so to doe that which a man doubts whether it be a sin or not, when he hath freedome to forbear it, is a contempt of the Lawes, and therefore by the 28. Art. of the third Chapter, a sin against the Law of nature. Vain therefore is that same distinction of obedience into Active and Passive, as if that could be expiated by penalties constituted by humane decrees, which is a sinne against the Law of nature, which is the Law of God; or as though they sinned not, who sinne at their own perill.

1. Contracts oblige us. To be obliged, and to be tyed being obliged, seems to some men to be one, and the same thing, and that therefore here seems to be some distinction in words, but none indeed. More cleerly therefore, I say thus, That a man is obliged by his contracts, that is, that he ought to performe for his promise sake; but that the Law tyes him being obliged, that is to say, it compells him to make good his promise, for fear of the punishment appointed by the Law.

2. Yet is it to be referred to sins of imprudence. Many find fault that I have referr'd Atheisme to imprudence, and not to injustice; yea by some it is taken so, as if I had not declared my selfe an enemy bitter enough against Atheists: They object farther, that since I had elsewhere said that it might be knowne there is a God, by naturall reason, I ought to have acknowledged that they sin at least against the Law of nature, and therefore are not only guilty of imprudence, but injustice too. But I am so much an enemy to Atheists, that I have both diligently sought for, and vehemently desired to find some Law whereby I might condemne them of injustice; but when I found none, I enquired next what name God himselfe did give to men so detested by him. Now God speaks thus of the Atheist: The fool hath said in his heart, there is no God.

Wherefore I placed their sinne in that rank which God himselfe referres to; next, I shew them to be enemies of God. But I conceive the name of an enemy to be sometimes somewhat sharper, than that of an unjust man. Lastly, I affirme that they may under that notion be justly punisht both by God, and supreme Magistrates, and therefore by no meanes excuse or extenuate this sinne. Now that I have said that it might be known by naturall reason that there is a God, is so to be understood, not as if I had meant that all men might know this, except they think that because Archimedes by naturall reason found out what proportion the circle hath to the square, it followes thence, that every one of the vulgar could have found out as much. I say therefore, that although it may be knowne to some by the light of reason that there is a God, yet men that are continually engaged in pleasures, or seeking of riches and honour, also men that are not wont to reason aright, or cannot do it, or care not to doe it, lastly, fools, in which number are Atheists, cannot know this.

Religion

96

CHAPTER XV. OF THE KINGDOME OF GOD, BY NATURE

I. Wee have already in the foregoing Chapters, proved both by reason, and testimonies of holy Writ, that the estate of nature, that is to say, of absolute liberty, such as is theirs, who neither govern, nor are governed, is an Anarchy, or hostile state; that the precepts whereby to avoyd this state, are the Lawes of nature; that there can be no civill government without a Soveraigne; and that they who have gotten this Soveraigne command must be obey'd simply, that is to say, in all things which repugne not the Commandments of God: There is this one thing only wanting to the complete understanding of all civill duty, that is, to know which are the Laws and Commandments of God. For else we cannot tell whether that which the civill power commands us, be against the Lawes of God, or not; whence it must necessarily happen, that either by too much obedience to the civill authority, we become stubborne against the divine Majesty; or for feare of sinning against God, we runne into disobedience against the civill power: To avoid both these rocks, its necessary to know the Divine Lawes. Now because the knowledge of the Lawes, depends on the knowledge of the Kingdome, we must in what followes, speak somewhat concerning the Kingdome of God.

II. The Lord is King, the earth may be glad there of; saith the Psalmist, Psal. 97 v. 1. And againe the same Psalmist, Psal. 99. v. 1. The Lord is King, be the People never so unpatient; he sitteth betweene the Cherubins, be the Earth never so unquiet; to wit, whether men will, or not, God is THE King over all the Earth, nor is he mov'd from his Throne, if there be any who deny either his existence, or his providence. Now although God governe all men so by his power, that none can doe any thing which he would not have done, yet this, to speake properly, and accurately, is not to reigne; for he is sayed to reigne, who rules not by acting, but speaking, that is to say, by precepts and threatnings. And therefore we account not inanimate, nor irrationall bodies, for Subjects in the Kingdome of God, although they be subordinate to the Divine power; because they understand not the commands, and threats of God; nor yet the Atheists, because they beleeve not that there is a God; nor yet those who beleeving there is a God, doe not yet beleeve that he rules these Inferiour things; for even these, although they be govern'd by the power of God, yet doe they not acknowledge any of his Commands, nor stand in awe of his threats. Those onely therefore are suppos'd to belong to Gods Kingdome, who acknowledge him to be the Governour of all things, and that he hath given his Commands to men, and appointed punishments for the transgressours; The rest, we must not call Subjects, but Enemies of God.

III. But none are said to governe by commands, but they who openly declare them to those who are govern'd by them; for the Commands of the Rulers are the Lawes of the Rul'd. But lawes they are not, if not perspicuously publisht, in so much as all excuse of Ignorance may be taken away. Men indeed publish their Lawes by word or voice, neither can they make their will universally knowne any other way; But Gods lawes are declar'd after a threefold manner: first, by the tacit dictates of Right reason; next, by immediate revelation, which is suppos'd to be done either by a supernaturall voice, or by a vision or dreame, or divine inspiration; Thirdly, by the voice of one man whom God recommends to the rest, as worthy of beliefe, by the working of true miracles. Now he whose voice God thus makes use of to signifie his will unto others, is called a PROPHET. These three manners may be term'd the threefold word of God, to wit the Rationall word, the sensible word, and the word of Prophecy: To which answer, the three manners whereby we are said to heare God; Right reasoning, sense, and faith. Gods sensible word hath come but to few; neither hath God spoken to men by Revelation except particularly to some, and to diverse diversely; neither have any Lawes of his Kingdome beene publisht on this manner unto any people.

IV. And according to the difference which is between the Rationall word and the word of Prophecy, we attribute a twofold Kingdome unto God: Naturall, in which he reignes by the dictates of right reason, and which is universall over all who acknowledge the Divine power, by reason of that rationall nature which is common to all; and Propheticall, in which he rules also by the word of Prophecy, which is peculiar, because he hath not given positive Lawes to all men, but to his peculiar people, and some certaine men elected by him.

V. God in his naturall Kingdome hath a Right to rule, and to punish those who break his Lawes, from his sole irresistable power. For all Right over others is either from nature, or from Contract. How the Right of governing springs from Contract, we have already shewed in the 6. Chapter. And the same Right is derived from nature, in this very thing, that it is not by nature taken away. For when by nature all men had a Right over all things, every man had a Right of ruling over all as ancient as nature it selfe; but the reason why this was abolisht among men, was no other but mutuall fear; as hath been declared above in the second Chapter, the 3. art; reason namely dictating that they must foregoe that Right for the preservation of mankinde, because the equality of men among themselves according to their strength and naturall powers was necessarily accompanied with warre, and with warre joynes the destruction of mankinde. Now if any man had so farre exceeded the rest in power, that all of them with joyned forces could not have resisted him, there had been no cause why he should part with that Right which nature had given him; The Right therefore of Dominion over all the rest, would have remained with him, by reason of that excesse of power whereby he could have preserved both himselfe and them. They therefore whose power cannot be resisted, and by consequence God Almighty, derives his Right of Soveraignty from the Power it selfe. And as oft as God punisheth, or slayes a sinner, although he therefore punish him because he sinned, yet may we not say that he could not justly have punisht or killed him although he had not sinned. Neither, if the will of God in punishing, may perhaps have regard to some sin antecedent, doth it therefore follow, that the Right of afflicting, and killing, depends not on divine Power, but on mens sins.

VI. That question made famous by the disputations of the Antients, why evill things befell the good, and good things the evill, is the same with this of ours, by what Right God dispenseth good and evill things unto men. And with its difficulty, it not only staggers the faith of the vulgar concerning the divine providence, but also of Philosophers, and which is more, even of holy men. Psal. 73. v. 1, 2, 3. Truly God is good to Israel, even to such as are of a clean heart; but as for me, my feet were almost gone, my steps had well nigh slipt. And why? I was grieved at the wicked, I doe also see the ungodly in such prosperity. And how bitterly did Job expostulate with God, that being just, he should yet be afflicted with so many calamities? God himselfe with open voyce resolved this difficulty in the case of Job, and hath confirmed his Right by arguments drawn not from Jobs sinne, but from his own power. For Job and his friends had argued so among themselves, that they would needs make him guilty, because he was punisht; and he would reprove their accusation by arguments fetcht from his own innocence: But God when he had heard both him and them, refutes his expostulation, not by condemning him of injustice, or any sin, but by declaring his own power, Job. 38. v. 4.

Where wast thou (sayes he) when I laid the foundation of the earth, And for his friends, God pronounces himself angry against them, Job. 42. v. 7. Because they had not spoken of him the thing that is right, like his servant Job. Agreeable to this is that speech of our Saviours in the mans case who was born blind, when, his Disciples asking him whether he or his Parents had sinned, that he was born blind, he answered, John 9. v. 3. Neither hath this man sinned, nor his Parents, but that the works of God should be manifest in him. For though it be said, Rom. 5:12. That death entred into the world by sinne, it followes not, but that God by his Right might have made men subject to diseases, and death, although they had never sinned, even as he hath made the other animalls mortall, and sickly, although they cannot sinne.

VII. Now if God have the Right of Soveraignty from his power, it is manifest, that the obligation of yeelding him obedience lyes on men by reason of their weaknesse; [1] for that obligation which rises from Contract, of which we have spoken in the second Chapter, can have no place here, where the Right of Ruling (no Covenant passing between) rises only from nature. But there are two Species of naturall obligation, one when liberty is taken away by corporall impediments, according to which we say that heaven and earth, and all Creatures, doe obey the common Lawes of their Creation: The other when it is taken away by hope, or fear, according to which the weaker despairing of his own power to resist, cannot but yeeld to the stronger. From this last kinde of obligation, that is to say from fear, or conscience of our own weaknesse (in respect of the divine power) it comes to passe, that we are obliged to obey God in his naturall Kingdome; reason dictating to all, acknowledging the divine power and providence, that there is no kicking against the pricks.

VIII. Because the word of God ruling by nature onely, is supposed to be nothing else but right reason, and the Laws of Kings can be known by their word only, its manifest that the Laws of God ruling by nature alone, are onely the naturall Lawes; namely those which we have set down in the second and third Chapters, and deduced from the dictates of reason, Humility, Equity, Justice, Mercy, and other Morall vertues befriending Peace, which pertain to the discharge of the duties of men one toward the other, and those which right reason shall dictate besides, concerning the honour and worship of the Divine Majesty. We need not repeat what those Naturall Laws, or Morall vertues are; but we must see what honours, and what divine worship, that is to say, what sacred Lawes, the same naturall reason doth dictate.

IX. Honour, to speak properly, is nothing else but an opinion of anothers Power joyned with goodnesse; and to honour a man, is the same with highly esteeming him, and so honour is not in the Party honoured, but in the honourer. Now three Passions do necessarily follow honour thus placed in opinion; Love, which referres to goodnesse; hope, and feare, which regard Power. And from these arise all outward actions, wherewith the powerfull are appeased, and become Propitious, and which are the effects, and therefore also the naturall signes of honour it selfe. But the word honour is transferred also to those outward effects of honour, in which sense, we are said to honour him, of whose power we testifie our selves, either in word, or deed, to have a very great respect; insomuch as honour is the same with worship. Now WORSHIP is an outward act, the sign of inward honour; and whom we endeavour by our homage to appease, if they be, angry or howsoever to make them favourable to us, we are said to worship.

X. All signes of the mind are either words or deeds, and therefore all worship consists either in words or deeds. Now both the one and the other are referred to three kindes; whereof the first is Praise, or publique declaration of goodnesse; The second, a publique declaration of Present Power, which is to magnify, megalunein; The third, is a publique declaration of happinesse, or of Power, secure also for the future, which is called, makariomos. I say, that all kindes of honour may be discerned, not in words only, but in deeds too. But we then praise, and celebrate in words, when we doe it by way of Proposition, or Dogmatically, that is to say by Attributes, or Titles, which may be termed praysing, and celebrating, categorically, and plainly, as when we declare him whom we honour to be liberall, strong, wise; And then, in deeds, when it is done by consequence, or by hypothesis, or supposition, as by Thanksgiving, which supposeth goodnesse; or by Obedience, which supposeth Power; or by Congratulation, which supposeth happinesse.

XI. Now whether we desire to praise a man in words, or deeds, we shall find some things which signify honour with all men, such as among attributes, are the generall words of vertues and powers, which cannot be taken in ill sense, As Good, Faire, Strong, Just, and the like; and among actions, Obedience, Thanksgiving, Prayers, and others of that kinde, by which an acknowledgement of vertue and power is ever understood: Others, which signify honour, but with some, and scorne with others, or else neither; such as in Attributes, are those words which according to the diversity of opinions, are diversly referred to vertues or vices, to honest or dishonest things; As that a man slew his enemy, that he fled, that he is a Philosopher, or an Orator, and the like, which with some are had in honour, with others in contempt. In deeds, such as depend on the custome of the place, or prescriptions of civill Lawes, as in saluting to be bareheaded, to put off the shoes, to bend the body, to petition for any thing standing, prostrate, kneeling, forms of ceremony, and the like. Now that worship which is alwayes, and by all men accounted honourable, may be called Naturall; the other, which followes places, and customes, Arbitrary.

XII. Furthermore, worship may be enjoyned, to wit by the command of him that is worshiped, and it may bee voluntary, namely such as seems good to the worshipper: If it be enjoyned, the actions expressing it, do not signify honour, as they signify actions, but as they are enjoyned: for they signify obedience immediately, obedience power; insomuch as worship enjoyned consists in obedience. Voluntary is honourable onely in the nature of the actions, which if they doe signify honour to the beholders, it is worship, if not, it is Reproach. Again worship may be either publique or private. But publique, respecting each single worshipper, may not be voluntary; respecting the City it may. For seeing that which is done voluntarily, depends on the will of the Doer, there would not one worship be given, but as many worships as worshippers, except the will of all men were united by the command, of one. But Private worship may be voluntary, if it be done secretly; for what is done openly is restrained, either by Lawes, or through modesty, which is contrary to the nature of a voluntary action.

XIII. Now that we may know what the scope and end of worshipping others is, we must consider the cause why men delight in worship: And we must grant what we have shewed elsewhere, that Joy consists in this, that a man contemplate vertue, strength, science, beauty, friends, or any Power whatsoever, as being, or as though it were his own; and it is nothing else but a Glory, or Triumph of the mind conceiving it selfe honoured, that is to say, lov'd and fear'd, that is to say, having the services and assistances of men in readinesse. Now because men beleeve him to be powerfull whom they see honoured (that is to say) esteemed powerfull by others, it falls out that honour is increased by worship; and by the opinion of power, true power is acquired. His end therefore who either commands, or suffers himself to be worshipt, is, that by this means he may acquire as many as he can, either through love, or fear, to be obedient unto him.

XIV. But that we may understand what manner of Worship of God naturall reason doth assigne us, let us begin from his Attributes: where, first it is manifest, that existence is to be allowed him; for there can be no will to honour him, who, we think, hath no being. Next, those Philosophers who said, that God was the World, or the worlds Soul, (that is to say, a part of it) spake unworthily of God, for they attribute nothing to him, but wholly deny his being. For by the word God we understand the Worlds cause; but in saying that the World is God, they say, that it hath no cause, that is as much, as there is no God. In like manner, they who maintain the world not to be created, but eternall; because there can be no cause of an eternall thing, In denying the world to have a Cause, they deny also that there is a God. They also have a wretched apprehension of God, who imputing idlenesse to him, doe take from him the Government of the world, and of mankind. For say they should acknowledge him omnipotent, yet if he minde not these inferiour things, that same thred—bare Sentence will take place with them, Quod supra nos, nihil ad nos; What is above us, doth not concern us. And seeing there is nothing for which they should either love, or fear him, truly he will be to them as though he were not at all. Moreover in Attributes which signifie Greatnesse, or Power, those which signifie some finite, or limited thing, are not signes at all of an honouring mind. For we honour not God worthily if we ascribe lesse Power, or greatnesse to him than possibly we can; but every finite thing is lesse than we can, for most easily we may alwayes assigne and attribute more to a finite thing; No shape therefore

must be assigned to God, for all shape is finite; nor must he be said to be conceived, or comprehended by imagination, or any other faculty of our soul; for whatsoever we conceive is finite: And although this word Infinite signifie a conception of the mind, yet it followes not, that we have any conception of an infinite thing: For when we say that a thing is infinite, we signifie nothing really, but the impotency in our owne mind, as if we should say we know not whether, or where it is limited: Neither speak they honourably enough of God, who say we have an Idea of him in our mind; for an Idea is our conception, but conception we have none, except of a finite thing: Nor they, who say that he hath Parts, or that he is some certaine intire thing; which are also attributes of finite things: Nor that he is in any place; for nothing can be said to be in a place, but what hath bounds and limits of its greatnesse on all sides: Nor that he is moved, or is at rest; for either of them suppose a being in some place: Nor that there are more Gods; because not more infinites. Farthermore concerning attributes of happinesse, those are unworthy of God which signify sorrow (unlesse they be taken not for any Passion, but by a Metonomy for the effect) such as Repentance, Anger, Pity: Or Want, as Appetite, Hope, Concupiscence, and that love which is also called lust, for they are signes of Poverty, since it cannot be understood, that a man should desire, hope, and wish for ought, but what he wants and stands in need of. Or any Passive faculty; for suffering belongs to a limited power, and which depends upon another.

When we therefore attribute a will to God, it is not to be conceived like unto ours, which is called a rationall desire; for if God desires, he wants, which for any man to say, is a contumelie; but we must suppose some resemblance which we cannot conceive. In like manner when wee attribute sight and other acts of the senses to him, or knowledge, or understanding, which in us are nothing else but a tumult of the minde raised from outward objects pressing the Organes, wee must not think that any such thing befalls the Deity; for it is a signe of power depending upon some other, which is not the most blessed thing. He therefore who would not ascribe any other titles to God, than what reason commands, must use such as are either Negative, as infinite, eternall, incomprehensible, or superlative, as most good, most great, most powerfull, or Indefinite, as good, just, strong, Creatour, King, and the like; in such sense, as not desiring to declare what he is (which were to circumscribe him within the narrow limits of our phantasie), but to confesse our own admiration, and obedience, which is the property of humility, and of a minde yeelding all the honour it possibly can doe. For Reason dictates one name alone, which doth signify the nature of God (i.e.) Existent, or simply, that he is; and one in order to, and in relation to us, namely God, under which is contained both King, and Lord, and Father.

XV. Concerning the Outward actions wherewith God is to be worshipped (as also concerning his Titles) its a most generall command of Reason, that they be signes of a mind yeelding honour; under which are contained in the first place, Prayers;

Qui fingit sacros auro, vel marmore vultus, Non facit ille Deos, qui rogat, ille facit.

For Prayers are the signes of hope, and hope is an acknowledgement of the divine Power, or goodnesse.

In the second place, Thanksgiving; which is a signe of the same affection, but that prayers goe before the benefit, and thanks follow it.

In the third, Guifts, that is to say oblations and sacrifices, for these are thanksgivings.

In the fourth, not to sweare by any other. For a mans Oath is an Imprecation of his wrath against him if he deceive, who both knowes whether he doe, or not, and can punish him if he doe, though he be never so powerfull; which only belongs to God: for if there were any man from whom his subjects malice could not lye hid, and whom no humane power could resist, plighted faith would suffice without swearing, which, broken, might be punisht by that Man; and for this very reason there would be no need of an Oath.

In the fifth place, To speak warily of God; for that is a sign of fear, and feare is an acknowledgement of Power. It followes from this precept: That we may not take the name of God in vain, or use it rashly; for either are inconsiderate. That wee must not swear where there is no need; for that is in vain; but need there is none, unlesse it be between Cities to avoyd or take away contention by force, which necessarily must arise, where there is no faith kept in promises, or in a City, for the better certainty of Judicature. Also, That we must not dispute of the Divine nature: For it is supposed that all things in the naturall Kingdom of God are enquired into by reason only, that is to say, out of the Principles of naturall Science; but we are so far off by these to attain to the knowledge of the nature of God, that we cannot so much as reach to the full understanding of all the qualities of our own bodies, or of any other Creatures. Wherefore there comes nothing from these disputes, but a rash imposition of names to the divine Majesty, according to the small measure of our conceptions. It followes also (which belongs to the Right of Gods Kingdome) that their speech is inconsiderate, and rash, who say, That this, or that, doth not stand with divine justice; for even men count it an affront that their children should dispute their Right, or measure their justice otherwise than by the rule of their Commands.

In the sixth, Whatsoever is offered up in Prayers, thanksgivings, and sacrifices, must in its kind be the best, and most betokening honour; namely, Prayers must not be rash, or light, or vulgar, but beautifull, and well composed. For though it were absurd in the Heathen to worship God in an image, yet was it not against reason to use Poetry, and Musick, in their Churches.

Also Oblations must be clean, and Presents sumptuous, and such as are significative either of submission, or gratitude, or commemorative of benefits received; for all these proceed from a desire of honouring.

In the seventh, That God must be worshipt not privately onely, but openly, and publiquely in the sight of all men; because that worship is so much more acceptable, by how much it begets honour, and esteem in others (as hath been declared before in the 13. art.). Unlesse others therefore see it, that which is most pleasing in our worship, vanisheth.

In the last place, That we use our best endeavour to keep the Lawes of Nature. For the undervaluing of our Masters command, exceeds all other affronts whatsoever; as on the other side, Obedience is more acceptable than all other sacrifices. And these are principally the naturall Lawes concerning the worship of God, those I mean which Reason dictates to every Man; but to whole Cities, every one whereof is one Person, the same naturall Reason farther commands an uniformity of publique worship. For the actions done by particular Persons, according to their private Reasons, are not the Cities actions, and therefore not the Cities worship; but what is done by the City, is understood to be done by the command of him, or them who have the Soveraignty, wherefore also together with the consent of all the subjects, that is to say, Uniformly.

XVI. The naturall Lawes set down in the foregoing Article concerning the divine worship, only command the giving of naturall signes of honour; but we must consider that there are two kindes of signes, the one naturall, the other done upon agreement, or by expresse, or tacite composition. Now because in every language, the use of words, and names, come by appointment, it may also by appointment be altered; for that which depends on, and derives its force from the will of men, can by the will of the same men agreeing be changed again, or abolisht. Such names therefore as are attributed to God by the appointment of men, can by the same appointment be taken away; now what can be done by the appointment of men, that the City may doe; The City therefore by Right (that is to say, they who have the power of the whole City) shall judge what names or appellations are more, what lesse honourable for God, that is to say, what doctrines are to be held and profest concerning the nature of God, and his operations. Now actions doe signify not by mens appointment, but naturally, even as the effects are signes of their causes; whereof some are always signes of Scorn to them before whom they are committed, as those, whereby the bodies uncleannesse is discovered, and whatsoever men are ashamed to doe before those whom they respect; Others are always signes of honour, as to draw near, and discourse decently and humbly, to give way, or to yeeld in any matter of private benefit: In these actions the City can alter nothing. But there are infinite others, which, as much as belongs to honour, or reproach, are indifferent; now these, by the institution of the City, may both be made signes of honour, and being made so, doe in very deed become so. From whence we may understand, that we must obey the City in whatsoever it shall command to be used for a sign of honouring God, that is to say, for Worship; provided it can be instituted for a sign of honour, because that is a sign of honour, which by the Cities command is us'd for such.

XVII. We have already declared which were the Laws of God, as wel sacred as secular, in his government by the way of Nature onely. Now because there is no man but may be deceived in reasoning, and that it so falls out, that men are of different opinions concerning the most actions, it may be demanded farther, whom God would have to be the Interpreter of right Reason, that is to say, of his Lawes. And as for the Secular Lawes, I mean those which concern justice, and the carriage of men towards men; by what hath been said before of the constitution of a City, we have demonstratively shewed it agreeable to reason, that all Judicature belongs to the City, and that Judicature is nothing else but an Interpretation of the Laws, and by consequence, that everywhere Cities, that is to say, those who have the Soveraign power, are the Interpreters of the Lawes. As for the Sacred Lawes, we must consider what hath been before demonstrated in the fifth Chap. the 13. art. that every Subject hath transferr'd as much right as he could on him, or them, who had the supreme authority, but he could have transferred his right of judging the manner how God is to be honoured, and therefore also he hath done it; That he could, it appeares hence, that the manner of honouring God before the constitution of a City was to be fetcht from every mans private Reason; but every man can subject his private Reason to the Reason of the whole City. Moreover, if each Man should follow his own reason in the worshipping of God, in so great a diversity of worshippers, one would be apt to judge anothers worship uncomely, or impious; neither would the one seem to the other to honour God: Even that therefore which were most consonant to reason, would not be a worship, because that the nature of worship consists in this, that it be the sign of inward honour; but there is no sign but whereby somewhat becomes known to others, and therefore is there no sign of honour but what seems so to others. Again, that's a true sign which by the consent of men becomes a sign; therefore also that is honourable, which by the consent of men, that is to say, by the command of the City, becomes a sign of honour. It is not therefore against the will of God, declared by the way of reason onely, to give him such signs of honour as the City shall command. Wherefore Subjects can transferre their Right of judging the manner of Gods worship on him or them who have the Soveraign power. Nay, they must doe it, for else all manner of absurd opinions, concerning the nature of God, and all ridiculous ceremonies which have been used by any Nations, will bee seen at once in the same City. Whence it will fall out, that every man will beleeve that all the rest doe offer God an affront; so that it cannot be truly said of any that he worships God; for no man worships God, that is to say, honours him outwardly, but he who doth those things, whereby hee appeares to others for to honour him. It may therefore bee concluded, that the Interpretation of all Lawes, as well Sacred, as Secular, (God ruling by the way of nature only) depends on the authority of the City, that is to say, that man, or councell, to whom the Soveraign power is committed; and that whatsoever God commands, he commands by his voyce. And on the other side, that whatsoever is commanded by them, both concerning the manner of honouring God, and concerning secular affaires, is commanded by God himselfe.

XVIII. Against this, some Man may demand, first, Whether it doth not follow, that the City must be obeyed if it command us directly to affront God, or forbid us to worship him? I say, it does not follow, neither must we obey. For to affront, or not to worship at all, cannot by any Man be understood for a manner of worshipping; neither also had any one, before the constitution of a City, of those who acknowledge God to rule, a Right to deny him the honour which was then due unto him; nor could he therefore transfer a Right on the City of commanding any such things. Next, if it be demanded whether the City must be obeyed if it command somewhat to be said, or done, which is not a disgrace to God directly, but from whence by reasoning disgracefull consequences may be derived: as for example, if it were commanded to worship God in an image, before those who account that honourable? Truly it is to be done. [2] For Worship is instituted in signe of Honour; but to Worship him thus, is a signe of honour, and increaseth Gods Honour among those who do so account of it. Or if it be commanded to call God by a name which we know not what it signifies, or how it can agree with this word, God? That also must be done; for what we do for Honours sake, (and we know no better), if it be taken for a signe of Honour, it is a signe of Honour; and therefore if we refuse to doe it, we refuse the enlarging of Gods Honour. The same judgement must be had of all the Attributes and Actions about the meerly rationall Worship of God which may be controverted, and disputed; for though these kind of commands may be sometimes contrary to right reason, and therefore sins in them who command them, yet are they not against right reason, nor sins in Subjects, whose right reason in points of Controversie is that, which submits its selfe to the reason of the City. Lastly, if that Man, or Councell, who hath the Supreme Power, command himselfe to be Worshipt with the same Attributes, and Actions, wherewith God is to be Worshipt, the question

104

is, whether we must obey? There are many things which may be commonly attributed both to God, and Men; for even Men may be Praised, and Magnified; and there are many actions whereby God, and Men, may be Worshipt. But the significations of the Attributes, and Actions, are onely to be regarded: Those Attributes therefore, whereby we signify our selves to be of an opinion, that there is any man endued with a Soveraignty independent from God, or that he is immortall, or of infinite power, and the like, though commanded by Princes, yet must they be abstained from. As also from those Actions signifying the same, as Prayer to the absent; to aske those things which God alone can give, as Rain, and Fair weather; to offer him what God can onely accept, as Oblations, Holocausts; or to give a Worship, than which a greater cannot be given, as Sacrifice. For these things seeme to tend to this end, that God may not be thought to rule, contrary to what was supposed from the beginning. But genuflection, prostration, or any other act of the body whatsoever, may be lawfully used even in civill Worship. for they may signifie an acknowledgment of the civill power onely. For Divine Worship is distinguisht from civill, not by the motion, placing, habit, or gesture of the Body, but by the declaration of our opinion of him whom we doe Worship; as if we cast down our selves before any man, with intention of declaring by that Signe that we esteeme him as God, it is Divine Worship; if we doe the same thing as a Signe of our acknowledgment of the civill Power, it is civill Worship. Neither is the Divine Worship distinguished from Civill by any action usually understood by the words latreia and douleia, whereof the former marking out the Duty of Servants, the latter their Destiny, they are words of the same action in degree.

XIX. From what hath been said may be gathered, that God reigning by the way of naturall reason onely, Subjects doe sinne, First, if they break the morall Laws, which are unfolded in the second and third Chapters. Secondly, if they break the Lawes, or commands of the City in those things which pertain to Justice. Thirdly, if they worship not God, kata ta nomika. Fourthly, if they confesse not before men, both in words, and deeds, that there is one God most good, most great, most blessed, the Supreme King of the World, and of all worldly Kings; that is to say, if they doe not worship God. This fourth sinne in the naturall Kingdome of God, by what hath been said in the foregoing Chapter, in the second Article, is the sinne of Treason against the Divine Majesty; for it is a denying of the Divine Power, or Atheisme. For sinnes proceed here, just as if we should suppose some man to be the Soveraign King, who being himselfe absent, should rule by his Vice—Roy; against whom sure they would transgresse who should not obey his Vice—Roy in all things, except he usurpt the Kingdome to himself, or would give it to some other; but they who should so absolutely obey him, as not to admit of this exception, might be said to be guilty of Treason.

1. By reason of their weaknesse. If this shall seem hard to any man, I desire him with a silent thought to consider, if there were two Omnipotents, whether were bound to obey; I beleeve he will confesse that neither is bound: if this be true, then it is also true what I have set down, that men are subject unto God because they are not omnipotent. And truly our Saviour admonishing Paul (who at that time was an enemy to the Church) that he should not kick against the pricks, seems to require obedience from him for this cause, because he had not Power enough to resist.

2. Truly it is to be done. We said in the 14. Article of this Chapter, That they who attributed limits to God, transgrest the naturall Law concerning Gods Worship. Now they who worship him in an Image, assigne him limits; wherefore they doe that which they ought not to doe, and this place seemes to contradict the former.

105

We must therefore know first, that they who are constrained by Authority, doe not set God any bounds, but they who command them; for they who worship unwillingly, doe worship in very deed, but they either stand or fall there, where they are commanded to stand or fall by a lawfull Soveraign. Secondly, I say it must be done, not at all times, and every where, but on supposition that there is no other rule of worshipping God beside the dictates of humane reason; for then the will of the City stands for Reason. But in the Kingdome of God by way of Covenant, whether old, or new, where idolatry is expressely forbid, though the City commands us to worship thus, yet must we not do it. Which, if he shall consider, who conceived some repugnancy between this, and the 14. Article, will surely cease to think so any longer.

CHAPTER XVI. OF THE KINGDOME OF GOD UNDER THE OLD COVENANT

I. Mankind, from conscience of its own weaknesse, and admiration of naturall events, hath this, that most men beleeve God to be the invisible Maker of all visible things, whom they also fear, conceiving that they have not a sufficient protection in themselves; but the imperfect use they had of their Reason, the violence of their Passions did so clowd them, that they could not rightly worship him. Now the fear of invisible things, when it is sever'd from right reason is superstition. It was therefore almost impossible for men without the speciall assistance of God to avoyd both Rocks of Atheisme and Superstition: for this proceeds from fear without right reason, that, from an opinion of right reason, without feare. Idolatry therefore did easily fasten upon the greatest part of men, and almost all nations did worship God in Images, and resemblances of finite things; and they worshipt spirits, or vain visions, perhaps out of fear calling them Devills. But it pleased the Divine Majesty (as we read it written in the sacred history) out of all mankind to call forth Abraham, by whose means he might bring men to the true worship of him, and to reveal himselfe supernaturally to him, and to make that most famous Covenant with him and his seed, which is called the old Covenant, or Testament. He therefore is the head of true Religion; he was the first that after the Deluge taught, that there was one God, the Creatour of the Universe; And from him the Kingdome of God by way of Covenants, takes its beginning. Joseph. Antiq. Jewes. lib. I. cap. 7.

II. In the beginning of the world God reigned indeed, not onely naturally, but also by way of Covenant, over Adam, and Eve; so as it seems he would have no obedience yeelded to him, beside that which naturall Reason should dictate, but by the way of Covenant, that is to say, by the consent of men themselves. Now because this Covenant was presently made void, nor ever after renewed, the originall of Gods Kingdom (which we treat of in this place) is not to be taken thence. Yet this is to be noted by the way, that by that precept of not eating of the tree of the knowledge of good and evill (whether the judicature of good and evill, or the eating of the fruit of some tree were forbidden) God did require a most simple obedience to his commands, without dispute whether that were good, or evill, which was commanded; for the fruit of the tree, if the Command be wanting, hath nothing in its own nature, whereby the eating of it could be morally evill, that is to say, a sinne.

III. Now the Covenant between God and Abraham, was made in this manner. Gen. 17. v. 7, 8. I will establish my Covenant between me and thee, and thy seed after thee in their generations, for an everlasting Covenant, to be a God unto thee, and to thy seed after thee. And I will give unto thee, and to thy seed after thee, the Land wherein thou art a stranger, all the Land of Canaan, for an everlasting possession, and I will be their God. Now it was necessary to institute some sign whereby Abraham and his seed should retain the memory of this Covenant; wherefore Circumcision was added to the Covenant, but yet as a sign onely. vers 10: This is my Covenant which yee shall keep between me and thee, and thy seed after thee, every man−child among you shall be circumcised, and ye shall circumcise the flesh of your foreskin, and it shall be a token of the Covenant between me and you. It is therefore Covenanted, that Abraham shall acknowledge God to be his God, and the God of his seed; that is to say, that he shall submit himselfe to be governed by him, and that God shall give unto Abraham the inheritance of that Land wherein he then dwelt, but as a Pilgrim, and that Abraham for a memoriall sign of this Covenant, should take care to see himselfe, and his male seed circumcised.

IV. But seeing that Abraham even before the Covenant acknowledged God to be the Creatour and King of the world, (for he never doubted either of the being, or the Providence of God) how comes it not to be superfluous, that God would purchase to himself with a price, and by contract, an obedience which was due to him by nature; namely by promising Abraham the Land of Canaan, upon condition that he would receive him for his God, when by the Right of nature he was already so? By those words therefore, To be a God unto thee and to thy seed after thee, wee understand not that Abraham satisfied this Covenant by a bare acknowledgement of the power, and Dominion which God had naturally over men, that is to say, by acknowledging God indefinitely, which belongs to naturall reason; but he must definitely acknowledge him, who said unto him, Gen. 12. v. 1. Get thee out of thy Country, Gen. 13. v. 14. Lift up thine eyes. who appear'd unto him, Gen. 18. v. 1. in the shape of three celestiall men, and Gen. 15. v. 1. In a vision; and vers.

13. In a dream, which is matter of faith. In what shape God appeared unto Abraham, by what kinde of sound he spake to him, is not exprest, yet it is plain that Abraham beleeved that voyce to be the voyce of God, and a true Revelation; and would have all his to worship him, who had so spoken unto him, for God the Creatour of the world; and that his faith was grounded on this, not that he beleeved God to have a being, or that he was true in his promises, that which all men beleeve, but that he doubted not him to be God, whose voice, and promises he had heard; and that the God of Abraham signified not simply God, but that God which appeared unto him, even as the worship which Abraham owed unto God in that notion, was not the worship of reason, but of Religion, and Faith, and that, which not reason, but God had supernaturally revealed.

V. But we read of no Lawes given by God to Abraham, or by Abraham to his family, either then, or after, secular, or sacred (excepting the Commandement of Circumcision, which is contained in the Covenant it selfe); whence it is manifest, that there were no other Lawes, or worship, which Abraham was obliged to, but the Lawes of nature, rationall worship, and circumcision.

VI. Now Abraham was the Interpreter of all Lawes, as well sacred as secular, among those that belonged to him, not meerly naturally, as using the Lawes of nature onely, but even by the form of the Covenant it selfe, in which obedience is promised by Abraham not for himselfe onely, but for his seed also; which had been in vain, except his children had been tyed to obey his Commands: And how can that be understood, which God sayes Gen. 18. vers. 18, 19. (All the Nations of the earth shall be blessed in him; for I know him, that he will command his children, and his houshold after him, and they shall keep the way of the Lord to doe justice, and judgement) unlesse his children and his houshold were supposed to be obliged to yeeld obedience unto his Commands.

VII. Hence it followes, that Abrahams subjects could not sinne in obeying him, provided that Abraham commanded them not, to deny Gods Existence, or Providence, or to doe somewhat expresly contrary to the honour of God. In all other things, the word of God was to be fetcht from his lips only, as being the Interpreter of all the Lawes, and words of God. For Abraham alone could teach them who was the God of Abraham, and in what manner he was to be worshipped. And they who after Abrahams death were subject to the Soveraignty of Isaac or Jacob, did by the same reason obey them in all things without sin, as long as they acknowledged, and profest the God of Abraham to be their God. For they had submitted themselves to God simply, before they did it to Abraham; and to Abraham before they did it to the God of Abraham;

againe, to the God of Abraham before they did it to Isaac. In Abrahams subjects therefore, To deny God was the only Treason against the Divine Majesty; but in their posterity it was also Treason to deny the God of Abraham, that is to say, to worship God otherwise than was instituted by Abraham, to wit, in Images made with hands, [1] as other Nations did, which for that reason were called Idolators. And hitherto subjects might easily enough discern what was to be observed, what avoyded in the Commands of their Princes.

VIII. To goe on now, following the guidance of the holy Scripture, The same Covenant was renewed, Gen.

26. vers. 3, 4. with Isaac, and Gen. 28. vers. 14. with Jacob, where God stiles himselfe not simply God, whom nature doth dictate him to be, but distinctly the God of Abraham and Isaac; afterward being about to renew the same Covenant, by Moyses, with the whole People of Israel, Exod. 3. v. 6. I am, saith he, the God of thy Father, the God of Abraham, the God of Isaac, and the God of Jacob. Afterward when that People, not only the freest, but also the greatest enemy to humane subjection, by reason of the fresh memory of their AEgyptian bondage, abode in the wildernesse near mount Sinai, that antient Covenant was propounded to them all to be renewed in this manner, Exod. 19. ver. 5. Therefore if yee will obey my voice indeed, and keep my Covenant, (to wit, that Covenant which was made with Abraham, Isaac, and Jacob) then shall yee be a peculiar Treasure unto me, above all People; for all the earth is mine, and yee shall be to me a Kingdome of Priests, and an holy Nation. And all the People answered together, and said, All that the Lord hath spoken, will we doe, vers. 8.

IX. In this Covenant, among other things, we must consider well the appellation of Kingdom not used before. For although God both by nature by Covenant made with Abraham, was their King, yet owed they him an obedience and worship only naturall, as being his subjects; religious such as Abraham instituted, as being the Subjects of Abraham, Isaac, Jacob, their naturall Princes; For they had received no word of God beside the naturall word of right reason, neither had any Covenant past between God and them, otherwise than as their wils were included in the will of Abraham, as their Prince. But now by the Covenant made at mount Sinai, the consent of each man being had, there becomes an institutive Kingdome of God over them. That Kingdom of God so renowned in Scriptures and writings of Divines, took its beginning from this time, and hither tends that which God said to Samuel, when the Israelites asked a King, 1. Sam. 8:7. They have not rejected thee, but they have rejected me, that I should not reign over them; and that which Samuel told the Israelites, 1. Sam. 12:12. Yee said unto me, nay, but a King shall reign over us, when the Lord your God was your King; and that which is said, Jer. 31. vers. 31. I will make a new Covenant, Although I was an Husband unto them; And the doctrine also of Judas Galilaeus, where mention is made in Joseph. Antiq. of the Jewes, 18. Book, 2. Chap. in these words: But Judas Galilaeus was the first authour of this fourth way of those who followed the study of wisdome. These agree in all the rest with the Pharisees, excepting that they burn with a most constant desire of liberty, beleeving God alone to be held for their Lord and Prince, and will sooner endure even the most exquisite kinds of torments, together with their kinsfolks, and dearest friends, than call any mortall man their Lord.

X. The Right of the Kingdome being thus constituted by way of Covenant, let us see in the next place, what lawes God propounded to them; now those are knowne to all, to wit, the Decalogue, and those other, as well judiciall as ceremoniall lawes, which we find from the 20. Chap. of Exodus to the end of Deuteronomie, and the death of Moyses. Now of those lawes deliver'd in generall by the hand of Moyses, some there are which oblige naturally, being made by God, as the God of nature, and had their force even before Abrahams time; others there are which oblige by vertue of the Covenant made with Abraham, being made by God as the God of Abraham, which had their force even before Moyses his time, by reason of the former Covenant; but there are others which oblige by vertue of that Covenant onely which was made last with the people themselves, being made by God, as being the Peculiar King of the Israelites. Of the first sort are all the Precepts of the Decalogue which pertaine unto manners, such as, Honour thy Parents, thou shalt not Kill, thou shalt not commit Adultery, thou shalt not Steale, thou shalt not beare false witnesse, thou shalt not Covet; For they are the Lawes of nature; Also the precept of not taking Gods name in vaine, for it is a part of naturall worship, as hath beene declar'd in the foregoing Chap. Art. 15. In like manner the second Commandement of not worshipping by way of any Image made by themselves; for this also is a part of naturall Religion, as hath beene shewed in the same Article. Of the second sort is the first Commandment of the Decalogue, of not having any other Gods; for in that consists the essence of the Covenant made with Abraham, by which God requires nothing else, but that he should be his God, and the God of his seede: Also the Precept of keeping holy the Sabbath; for the Sanctification of the seventh day is instituted in memoriall of the six dayes Creation, as appeares out of these words, Exod. 31. ver. 16, 17. It is a perpetuall Covenant, (meaning the Sabbath) and a signe betweene me, and the Children of Israel for ever, for in six dayes the Lord made Heaven, and Earth, and on the seventh day he rested, and was refreshed. Of the third kind are the Politique, judiciall and

Ceremoniall lawes, which onely belong'd to the Jewes. The lawes of the first and second sort written in Tables of stone, to wit the Decalogue, was kept in the Ark it selfe. The rest written in the volume of the whole Law, were laid up in the side of the Arke. Deut. 31. ver. 26. For these retaining the faith of Abraham might be chang'd, those could not.

XI. All Gods Lawes are Gods Word; but all Gods Word is not his Law. I am the Lord thy God which brought thee out of the Land of AEgypt, is the word of God, it is no Law: Neither is all that which for the better declaring of Gods Word is pronounc't, or written together with it, instantly to be taken for Gods Word: For, Thus saith the Lord, is not the voice of God, but of the Preacher or Prophet. All that, and onely that, is the word of God which a true Prophet hath declar'd God to have spoken. Now the writings of the Prophets comprehending as well those things which God, as which the Prophet himselfe speaks, are therefore called the word of God, because they containe the word of God. Now because all that, and that alone, is the Word of God which is recommended to us for such, by a true Prophet, it cannot be knowne what Gods Word is, before we know who is the true Prophet; nor can we beleeve Gods Word, before we beleeve the Prophet. Moyses was beleev'd by the People of Israel for two things, His Miracles, and his Faith; for how great, and most evident Miracles soever he had wrought, yet would they not have trusted him, at least he was not to have beene trusted, if he had call'd them out of AEgypt to any other worship than the worship of the God of Abraham, Isaac, and Jacob their Fathers. For it had beene contrary to the Covenant made by themselves with God. In like manner two things there are, to wit, supernaturall Prediction of things to come, which is a mighty miracle; and Faith in the God of Abraham their deliverer out of AEgypt, which God propos'd to all the Jews to be kept for marks of a true Prophet. He that wants either of these is no Prophet, nor is it to be receiv'd for Gods word which he obtrudes for such. If Faith be wanting, he is rejected in these words, Deut. 13. ver. 1, 2, 3, 4, 5. If there arise among you a Prophet, or a dreamer of dreams, and giveth thee a signe, or a wonder, and the signe or the wonder come to Passe, whereof he spake unto thee, saying, Let us goe after other Gods, That Prophet, or that dreamer of dreames shall be put to death. If Praediction of events be wanting, he is condemn'd by these, Deut. 18. ver. 21, 22. And if thou say in thine heart, how shall we know the word which the Lord hath not spoken? When a Prophet speaketh in the name of the Lord, if the thing follow not, nor come to Passe, that is the thing which the Lord hath not spoken, but the Prophet hath spoken it presumptuously. Now, that that is the word of God which is publisht for such by a true Prophet, and that he was held to be a true Prophet among the Jewes, whose faith was true, and to whose praedictions the events answer'd, is without controversie. But what it is to follow other Gods, and whether the events which are affirm'd to answer their praedictions, doe truly answer them, or not, may admit many controversies, specially in praedictions which obscurely, aenigmatically foretell the Event, such as the praedictions of almost all the Prophets are, as who saw not God apparently like unto Moyses, but in darke speeches, and in figures. Numb.

12. ver. 8. But of these we cannot judge otherwise than by the way of naturall reason; because that Judgment depends on the Prophets interpretation, and on its proportion with the Event.

XII. The Jewes did hold the booke of the whole Law which was called Deuteronomie, for the written word of God, and that onely, (forasmuch as can be collected out of sacred history) untill the Captivity; for this booke was deliver'd by Moyses himselfe to the Priests to be kept, and layd up in the side of the Ark of the Covenant, and to be copyed out by the Kings; and the same a long time after by the authority of King Josiah acknowledg'd againe for the Word of God. Kings 23. ver. 2. But it is not manifest when the rest of the books of the Old Testament were first receiv'd into Canon. But what concernes the Prophets, Isaiah and the rest, since they foretold no other things than what were to come to passe, either in or after the Captivity, their writings could not at that time be held for Prophetique, by reason of the Law cited above. Deut. 18. ver. 21,

22. Whereby the Israelites were commanded not to account any man for a true Prophet but him whose Prophecies were answer'd by the events; And hence peradventure it is that the Jews esteem'd the writings of those whom they slew when they Prophesied, for Prophetique afterward, that is to say, for the word of God.

XIII. It being known what Lawes there were under the old Covenant, and that Word of God receiv'd from the beginning; we must farthermore consider with whom the authority of judging, whether the writings of the

Prophets arising afterward, were to be receiv'd for the Word of God, that is to say, whether the Events did answer their praedictions or not, and with whom also the authority of interpreting the Lawes already receiv'd, and the written Word of God, did reside; which thing is to be trac't through all the times, and severall changes of the Commonwealth of Israel. But it is manifest that this power during the life of Moyses, was intirely in himselfe; for if he had not been the Interpreter of the Lawes and Word, that office must have belong'd either to every private Person, or to a congregation, or Synagogue of many, or to the High–Priest, or to other Prophets. First, that that office belong'd not to private men, or any Congregation made of them, appeares hence, that they were not admitted, nay they were prohibited, with most heavy threats, to heare God speake, otherwise than by the means of Moyses; for it is written, Let not the Priests and the people break through to come up unto the Lord, lest he break forth upon them. So Moyses went downe unto the people, and spake unto them. Exod. 19:24,25. It is farther manifestly, and expresly declar'd, upon occasion given by the Rebellion of Core, Dathan and Abiram, and the two hundred and fifty Princes of the Assembly, that neither private men, nor the Congregation should pretend that God had spoken by them, and by Consequence that they had the right of interpreting Gods Word; for they contending, that God spake no lesse by them than by Moyses, argue thus, Yee take too much upon you, seeing all the Congregation are holy, every one of them, and the Lord is among them; wherefore then lift yee up your selves above the Congregation of the Lord?

Numb. 16. ver. 3. But how God determin'd this controversie is easily understood by the 33. and 35. verses of the same Chapter, where Corah, Dathan, and Abiram went downe alive into the Pit, and there came out fire from the Lord, and consumed the two hundred and fifty men that offer'd Incense: Secondly, that Aaron the high Priest had not this authority, is manifest by the like controversie betweene him (together with his Sister Miriam) and Moyses; For the question was, whether God spake by Moyses only, or by them also, that is to say, whether Moyses alone, or whether they also were interpreters of the Word of God. For thus they said, Hath the Lord indeed spoken onely by Moyses? Hath he not also spoken by us? Numb. 12. ver. 2. But God reprov'd them, and made a distinction betweene Moyses and other Prophets, saying, If there be a Prophet among you, I the Lord will make my selfe knowne unto him in a vision, and will speake unto him in a dreame: My Servant Moyses is not so, For with him will I speake mouth to mouth, even apparently, and not in darke speeches, and the Similitude of the Lord shall he behold; wherefore then were yee not afraid to speake against my Servant Moyses? Ibid. ver. 6, 7, 8. Lastly, that the interpretation of the Word of God as long as Moses liv'd, belong'd not to any other Prophets whatsoever, is collected out of that place which we now cited concerning his eminency above all others, and out of naturall reason, for as much as it belongs to the same Prophet who brings the Commands of God to unfold them too; but there was then no other Word of God, beside that which was declar'd by Moyses. And out of this also, that there was no other Prophet extant at that time, who Prophesied to the people, excepting the 70 Elders who Prophesied by the Spirit of Moyses; and even that Joshuah, who was then Moyses his Servant, his successour afterward, beleev'd to be injuriously done, till he knew it was by Moyses his Consent; which thing is manifest by Text of Scripture, And the Lord came downe in a clowd, and tooke of the spirit that was upon Moyses, and gave it unto the 70 Elders. Numb.

11. ver. 25. Now after it was told that they Prophesied, Joshuah said unto Moyses, Forbid them my Lord. But Moyses answered, Why enviest thou for my sake? Seeing therefore Moyses alone was the Messenger of Gods Word, and that the authority of interpreting it pertain'd neither to private men, nor to the Synagogue, nor to the High Priest, nor to other Prophets; it remaines, that Moyses alone was the Interpreter of Gods Word, who also had the supreme power in civill matters; And that the conventions of Corah with the rest of his complices against Moses and Aaron; and of Aaron with his Sister against Moyses, were rais'd, not for the salvation of their soules, but by reason of their ambition, and desire of Dominion over the People.

XIV. In Joshuahs time the interpretation of the Lawes, and of the Word of God, belong'd to Eleazar the High Priest, who was also under God, their absolute King. Which is collected first of all out of the Covenant it selfe, in which the Common−wealth of Israel is called a Priestly Kingdome, or as it is recited in the 1 Pet. 2:9. A Royall Priesthood; which could in no wise be sayd, unlesse by the institution and Covenant of the People, the regall power were understood to belong to the High Priest. Neither doth this repugne what hath beene said before, where Moyses, and not Aaron, had the Kingdome under God; since it is necessary that when one man institutes the forme of a future Common−wealth, that one should governe the Kingdome which he institutes, during his life, (whether it be Monarchie, Aristocraty, or Democraty) and have all that power for the present, which he is bestowing on others for the future. Now, that Eleazar the Priest, had not onely the Priesthood, but also the Soveraignty, is expressely set downe in Joshuahs call to the administration; for thus it is written. Take thee Joshuah the Son of Nun, a man in whom is the Spirit, and lay thine hand upon him, and set him before Eleazer the Priest, and before all the Congregation, and give him a charge in their sight, and thou shalt put some of thine honour uPon him, that all the Congregation of the Children of Israel may be obedient, and he shall stand before Eleazar the Priest, who shall aske Counsell for him after the judgment of Urim, before the Lord: at his word shall they goe out, and at his word shall they come in, and all the Children of Israel with him, even all the Congregation. Num. 27. ver. 18, 19, 20, 21. where to aske Counsell of God for whatsoever is to be done, (that is) to interpret Gods word, and in the name of God to Command in all matters, belongs to Eleazar; and to goe out, and, to come in at his word, that is to say, to obey, belongs both to Joshuah, and to all the People. Its to be observ'd also, that that speech, Part of thy glory; clearly denotes that Joshuah had not a power equall with that which Moyses had. In the meane time it is manifest, that even in Joshuahs time, the Supreme power and authority of interpreting the word of God, were both in one Person.

XV. After Joshuahs death follow the times of the Judges untill King Saul, in which it is manifest that the right of the Kingdome instituted by God, remained with the High Priest. For the Kingdome was by Covenant Priestly, that is to say, Gods government by Priests; and such ought it to have been untill that form with Gods consent were changed by the people themselves: which was not done, before that requiring a King God consented unto them, and said unto Samuel, Hearken unto the voyce of the people in all that they say unto thee; for they have not rejected thee, but they have rejected me that I should not reign over them. 1. Sam. 8:7. The supreme civill power was therefore Rightly due by Gods own institution to the High−Priest; but actually that power was in the Prophets, to whom (being raysed by God in an extraordinary manner) the Israelites (a people greedy of the Prophets) submitted themselves to be protected, and judged, by reason of the great esteem they had of Prophecies. The Reason of this thing, was, because that though penalties were set, and Judges appointed in the institution of Gods priestly Kingdome, yet, the Right of inflicting punishment, depended wholly on private judgement; and it belonged to a dissolute multitude, and each single Person, to punish or not to punish according as their private zeale should stirre them up. And therefore Moyses by his own command punisht no man with death; but when any man was to be put to death, one or many stirred up the multitude against him or them, by divine authority, and saying, Thus saith the Lord. Now this was conformable to the nature of Gods peculiar Kingdome. For there God reignes indeed where his Lawes are obeyed, not for fear of men, but for fear of himselfe. And truly, if men were such as they should be, this were an excellent state of civill government; but as men are, there is a coercive power (in which I comprehend both right and might) necessary to rule them. And therefore also God from the beginning prescribed Lawes by Moyses for the future Kings. Deut. 17. vers. 14. and Moyses foretold this in bis last words to the people, saying, I know that after my death ye will utterly corrupt your selves, and turn aside from the way that I have commanded you, Deut. 31:29. When therefore according to this prediction there arose another generation who knew not the Lord, nor yet the works which he had done for Israel, the children of Israel did evill in the sight of the Lord, and served Balaam, Jud. 2:10,11. to wit, they cast off Gods government, that is to say, that of the Priest, by whom God ruled, and afterward, when they were overcome by their enemies, and opprest with bondage, they looked for Gods will, not at the hands of the Priest any more, but of the Prophets. These therefore actually judged Israel, but their obedience was rightly due to the High Priest; Although therefore the Priestly Kingdome after the death of Moyses, Joshuah, was without power, yet was it not without Right. Now that the interpretation of Gods word did belong to the same High Priest, is manifest by this, That God, after the Tabernacle, the Ark of the Covenant was consecrated, spake no more in mount

113

Sinai, but in the Tabernacle of the Covenant, from the propitiatory which was between the Cherubims, whether it was not lawfull for any to aproach except the High Priest. If therefore regard be had to the Right of the Kingdome, the supreme civill Power, and the authority of interpreting Gods word, were joyned in the High Priest; If we consider the fact, they were united in the Prophets who judged Israel. For as Judges, they had the civill authority, as Prophets, they interpreted Gods word, and thus every way hitherto these two powers continued inseparable.

XVI. Kings being once constituted, its no doubt but the civill authority belonged to them, for the Kingdome of God by the way of Priesthood, (God consenting to the request of the Israelites) was ended; which Hierom also marks speaking of the books of Samuel: Samuel (sayes he) Eli being dead, and Saul slain, declares the old Law abolisht; Furthermore the Oaths of the new Priesthood, and new Soveraignty in Zadok, and David, do testifie, that the Right whereby the Kings did rule, was founded in the very concession of the People. The Priest could rightfully do only what God had commanded, but the King had by right whatsoever power over every man that each man by right had over himself; for the Israelites granted him a Right to judge of all things, and to wage warre for all men; in which two are contained all Right whatsoever can be conceived from man to man. Our King (say they) shall judge us, and goe out before us, and fight our battails, 1. Sam. 8:20. Judicature therefore belonged to the Kings; but to judge is nothing else than by interpreting to apply the facts to the Lawes; to them therefore belonged the interpretation of Lawes too. And because there was no other written word of God acknowledged beside the Law of Moyses, untill the Captivity, the authority of interpreting Gods word, did also belong to the Kings; Nay, forasmuch as the word of God must be taken for a Law, if there had been another written word beside the Mosaicall Law, seeing the interpretation of Lawes belonged to the Kings, the interpretation of it must also have belonged to them. When the book of Deuteronomie (in which the whole Mosaicall Law was contained) being a long time lost, was found again, the Priests indeed asked Counsell of God concerning that book; but not by their own authority, but by the Commandement of Josiah, and not immediately neither, but by the meanes of Holda the Prophetesse. Whence it appears that the authority of admitting books for the word of God, belonged not to the Priest; neither yet followes it that that authority belonged to the Prophetesse, because others did judge of the Prophets whether they were to be held for true, or not. For to what end did God give signes, and tokens to all the People, whereby the true Prophets might be discerned from the false, namely, the event of predictions, and conformity with the Religion establisht by Moyses, if they might not use those marks? The authority therefore of admitting books for the word of God belonged to the King, thus that book of the Law was approved, and received again by the authority of King Josiah, as appears by the fourth book of the Kings, Chap. 22, 23. where it is reported that he gathered together all the severall degrees of his Kingdome, the Elders, Priests, Prophets, and all the people, and he read in their eares all the words of the Covenant, that is to say, he caused that Covenant to be acknowledged for the Mosaicall Covenant, that is to say, for the word of God, and to be again received, and confirmed by the Israelites. The civill power therefore, and the power of discerning Gods word from the word of men, and of interpreting Gods word even in the dayes of the Kings was wholly belonging to themselves. Prophets were sent not with authority, but in the form, and by the Right of Proclaimers, and Preachers, of whom the hearers did judge; and if perhaps these were punisht who did not listen to them plainly, teaching easie things, it doth not thence follow, that the Kings were obliged to follow all things which they in Gods name did declare, were to be followed. For though Josiah the good King of Judah were slain because he obeyed not the word of the Lord from the mouth of Necho King of AEgypt, that is to say, because he rejected good Counsell though it seemed to come from an enemy, yet no man I hope will say that Josiah was by any bond either of divine, or humane Lawes obliged to beleeve Pharoah Necho King of

AEgypt, because he said that God had spoken to him. But what some man may object against Kings, that for want of learning, they are seldome able enough to interpret those books of antiquity in the which Gods word is contained, and that for this cause it is not reasonable that this office should depend on their authority, he may object as much against the Priests, and all mortall men, for they may erre; and although Priests were better instructed in nature, and arts than other men, yet Kings are able enough to appoint such interpreters under them; and so, though Kings did not themselves interpret the word of God, yet the office of interpreting them might depend on their authority; and they who therefore refuse to yeeld up this authority to Kings, because they cannot practise the office it selfe, doe as much as if they should say that the authority of teaching Geometry must not depend upon Kings, except they themselves were Geometricians. We read that Kings have prayed for the People, that they have blest the people, that they have consecrated the Temple, that they have commanded the Priests, that they have removed Priests from their office, that they have constituted others. Sacrifices indeed they have not offered, for that was hereditary to Aaron, and his sonnes; but it is manifest, as in Moyses his life time, so throughout all ages from King Saul to the captivity of Babylon, that the Priesthood was not a Maistry, but a Ministry.

XVII. After their returne from Babylonian bondage, the Covenant being renewed, and sign'd, the Priestly Kingdome was restor'd to the same manner it was in from the death of Joshuah to the beginning of the Kings; excepting that it is not expresly set downe that the return'd Jewes did give up the Right of Soveraignty either to Esdras (by whose directions they ordred their State) or to any other, beside God himselfe. That reformation seemes rather to be nothing else than the bare promises, and vowes of every man to observe those things which were written in the booke of the Law. Notwithstanding, (perhaps not by the Peoples intention) by virtue of the Covenant which they then renewed, (for the Covenant was the same with that which was made at Mount Sinai) that same state was a Priestly Kingdome, that is to say, the supreme civill authority, and the sacred were united in the Priests. Now, howsoever through the ambition of those who strove for the Priesthood, and by the interposition of forraigne Princes, it was so troubled till our Saviour Jesus Christs time, that it cannot be understood out of the histories of those times, where that authority resided; yet it's plaine, that in those times, the power of interpreting Gods Word was not severed from the supreme civill power.

XVIII. Out of all this, we may easily know how the Jewes in all times from Abraham unto Christ were to behave themselves in the Commands of their Princes. For as in Kingdomes meerly humane men must obey a subordinate Magistrate in all things, excepting when his Commands containe in them some Treason; so in the Kingdome of God, the Jewes were bound to obey their Princes, Abraham, Isaac, Jacob, Moyses, the Priest, the King, every one during their time in all things, except when their commands did containe some treason against the Divine Majesty. Now treason against the Divine Majesty was, first, the deniall of his divine providence, for this was to deny God to be a King by nature; next, Idolatry, or the worship not of other (for there is but one God) but of strange Gods, that is to say, a worship though of one God, yet under other Titles, Attributes, and Rites, than what were establisht by Abraham, and Moyses. For this was to deny the God of Abraham to be their King by Covenant made with Abraham, and themselves. In all other things they were to obey; and if a King or Priest having the Soveraign authority, had commanded somewhat else to be done which was against the Lawes, that had been his sinne, and not his subjects, whose duty it is, not to dispute, but to obey the Commands of his superiours.

1. In Images made with hands. In the 15. Chap. 14. Article, There wee have shewed such a kinde of worship to be irrationall; but if it be done by the command of a City to whom the written word of God is not known, nor received, we have then shewed this worship in the 15. Chap. art. 18. to be rationall. But where God reigns by way of Covenant, in which it is expresly warned not to worship thus, as in the Covenant made with Abraham, there, whether it be with, or without the Command of the City, it is ill done.

CHAPTER XVII. OF THE KINGDOME OF GOD BY THE NEW COVENANT

I. There are many cleare prophesies extant in the old Testament concerning our Saviour Jesus Christ, who was to restore the Kingdome of God by a new Covenant, partly foretelling his regall Dignity, partly his Humility and Passion. Among others concerning his Dignity, these; God blessing Abraham, makes him a promise of his sonne Isaac, and addes, And Kings of People shall be of him, Gen. 17. vers. 16. Jacob blessing his sonne Judah, The Scepter (quoth he) shall not depart from Judah, Gen. 49. vers. 10. God to Moyses, A Prophet (saith he) will I raise them up from among their brethren like unto thee, and will put my words in his mouth, and he shall speak unto them all that I shall command him, and it shall come to Passe, that whosoever will not hearken unto my words, which he shall speak in my name, I will require it of him, Deut. 18. vers. 18.

Isaias, The Lord himselfe shall give thee a signe, Behold a Virgin shall conceive, and bear a Sonne, and shall call his name Emanuel, Isai. 7. v. 14. The same Prophet, Unto us a child is born, unto us a Sonne is given, and the government shall be upon his shoulders; and his name shall be called Wonderfull, Counsellour, the mighty God, the Everlasting Father, the Prince of Peace, Isai. 9. vers. 6. And again, There shall come forth a Rod out of the stemme of Jesse, and a branch shall grow out of his roots; the spirit of the Lord shall rest upon him, he shall not judge after the sight of his eyes, neither reprove after the hearing of his eares, but with righteousnesse shall he judge the Poor, and he shall smite the earth with the rod of his mouth, and with the breath of his lips shall he slay the wicked, Isai. 11. vers. 1, 2, 3, 4, 5. Furthermore in the 51, 52, 53, 54, 56, 60, 61, 62. Ch. of the same Isaiah, there is almost nothing else contained but a description of the coming, and the works of Christ. Jeremias, Behold the days come, saith the Lord, that I will make a new Covenant with the house of Israel, and with the house of Judah, Jerem. 31:31. And Baruch, This is our God. Afterward did he shew himselfe upon earth, and conversed with men; Baruch 3. vers. 35, 37. Ezekiel, I will set up one Shepheard over them, and he shall feed them, even my Servant David, And I will make with them a Covenant of Peace, Ezek. 34. vers. 23–25. Daniel, I saw in the night visions, and behold one like the Sonne of man came with the clouds of heaven, and came to the antient of dayes, and they brought him near before him, and there was given him Dominion, and Glory, and a Kingdome, that all People, Nations, and Languages should serve him, his Dominion is an everlasting Dominion, Dan. 7. vers. 13, 14. Haggai, Yet once it is a little while, and I will shake the Heaven, and the Earth, and the Sea, and the drye Land, and I will shake all Nations, and the desire of all Nations shall come, Haggai 2. v. 8. Zachariah, Under the type of Joshuah the High Priest: I will bring forth my servant the Branch, Zach. 3. v. 8. And again, Behold the man whose name is the Branch, Zach. 6. v. 12. And again, Rejoyce greatly O Daughter of Sion, Shout O Daughter of Jerusalem, behold thy King cometh to thee, he is just, having salvation, Zach. 9. v. 9. The Jewes moved by these, and other Prophesies, expected Christ their King to be sent from God, who should redeem them, and furthermore bear rule over all Nations. Yea this Prophesie had spread over the whole Roman Empire (which Vespasian too, though falsly, interpreted in favour of his own enterprises) That out of Judea should come he that should have dominion.

II. Now the Prophesies of Christs Humility and Passion, amongst others are these. Isa. 53. v. 4 He hath born our griefes, and carried our sorrowes; yet we did esteem him stricken, smitten of God, afflicted, and by and by, He was oppressed, he was afflicted, yet he opened not his mouth; He is brought as a Lamb to the slaughter, and as a sheep before her Shearer is dumb, so opened he not his mouth, vers. 7. And again, He was cut out of the Land of the living, for the transgression of my People was he stricken, vers. 8. Therefore will I divide him a portion with the great, and he shall divide the spoyle with the strong, because he hath poured out his soule unto death, and he was numbred with the transgressours, and he bare the sinne of many, and made intercession for the transgressours, vers. 12. And that of Zachary, He is lowly, riding upon an Asse, and upon a Colt the foale of an Asse. Zach. 9. vers. 9.

III. In the reign of Tiberius Caesar, JESUS our Saviour a Galilaean began to preach, the sonne (as was supposed) of Joseph, declaring to the people of the Jewes, that the Kingdome of God expected by them, was now come; and that himselfe was a King, that is to say, THE CHRIST: Explaining the Law; choosing twelve Apostles, and seventy Disciples, after the number of the Princes of the Tribes, and seventy Elders (according to the pattern of Moyses) to the Ministry; teaching the way of salvation by himselfe and them; purging the Temple; doing great signes, and fulfilling all those things which the Prophets had foretold of Christ to come. That this man, hated of the Pharisees, (whose false doctrine and hypocriticall sanctity he had reproved) and by their means, of the People accused of unlawfull seeking for the Kingdome, and crucified, was the true CHRIST, and King promised by God, and sent from his father to renew the new Covenant between them and God, both the Evangelists doe shew (describing his Genealogie, nativity, life, doctrine, death, and resurrection) and by comparing the things which he did, with those which were foretold of him, all Christians doe consent to.

IV. Now from this, That CHRIST was sent from God his Father to make a Covenant between him and the people, it is manifest, that though Christ were equall to his Father according to his nature, yet was he inferior according to the Right of the Kingdom; for this office to speak properly, was not that of a King, but of a Vice–roy, such as Moyses his Government was. For the Kingdom was not his, but his Fathers; which CHRIST himselfe signified when he was baptized as a subject, and openly profest, when he taught his Disciples to pray, Our Father, Thy Kingdome come, And when he said, I will not drink of the blood of the grape, untill that day when I shall drink it new with you in the Kingdome of my Father, Mat. 26. vers. 29. And Saint Paul. As in Adam all die, so in Christ shall all be made alive; but every man in his own order; Christ the first fruits, afterward they that are Christs, who beleeved in his coming; Then cometh the end when he shall have delivered up the Kingdom to God even his Father, 1. Cor. 15. vers. 22, 23, 24. The same notwithstanding is also called the Kingdome of Christ: for both the Mother of the sonnes of Zebedie petitioned Christ, saying, Grant that these my two sonnes may sit, the one on thy right hand, the other on thy left, in thy Kingdome, Mat. 20. vers. 21. And the Theef on the Cross, Lord remember me when thou comest into thy Kingdom, Luke 23. vers. 42. And Saint Paul, For this know yee, that no whormonger, shall enter into the Kingdome of God, and of Christ, Ephes. 5. ver. 5. And elsewhere, I charge thee before God, and the Lord Jesus Christ, who shall judge the quick and dead at his appearing, and his Kingdome, 2 Tim. 4. ver. 1. And the Lord shall deliver me from every evill worke, and will Preserve me unto his heavenly Kingdome, ver. 18. Nor is it to be marvelled at, that the same Kingdome is attributed to them both, since both the Father, and the Son, are the same God; and the new Covenant concerning Gods Kingdome, is not propounded in the Name of the FATHER, but in the name of the FATHER, of the SON, and of the HOLY–GHOST, as of one God.

V. But the Kingdome of God, for restitution whereof CHRIST was sent from God his Father, takes not its beginning before his second comming, to wit, from the day of Judgement, when he shall come in Majesty accompanied with his Angels: For it is promis'd the Apostles, that in the Kingdome of God, they shall judge the twelve tribes of Israel. Ye which have followed me in the regeneration, when the Sonne of man shall sit in the Throne of his glory, ye also shall sit upon twelve Thrones judging the twelve tribes of Israel, Mat. 19. ver.

28. which is not to be done till the day of judgement; CHRIST therefore is not yet in the throne of his Majesty, nor is that time when CHRIST was conversant here in the world call'd a Kingdome, but a regeneration, that is to say a renovation, or restitution of the Kingdome of God, and a calling of them who were hereafter to be receiv'd into his Kingdome; And where it is said, When the Son of man shall come in his glory, and all the holy Angels with him, then shall he sit upon the throne of his glory, and before him shall be gathered all Nations, and he shall separate them one from another, as a Shepheard divideth his Sheep from the Goates, Mat. 25. ver. 31. we may manifestly gather, that there will be no Locall separation of Gods Subjects from his Enemies, but that they shall live mixt together untill CHRISTS second comming. Which is also confirm'd by the comparison of the Kingdome of heaven, with wheat mingled with Darnell; and with a net containing all sorts of fish. But a multitude of men, Enemies and Subjects, living promiscuously together, cannot properly be term'd a Kingdome. Besides, the Apostles, when they askt our Saviour, Whether he would at that time when he ascended into heaven, restore the Kingdome unto Israel? Did openly testifie, that they then, when CHRIST ascended, thought the Kingdome of God not to be yet come. Farthermore, the words of CHRIST, My Kingdome is not of this world; And, I will not drinke, till the Kingdome of God come: And, God hath not sent his Son into the World, to judge the World, but that the World through him might be sav'd. And, If any man heare not my words, and keepe them, I judge him not; for I came not to judge the World, but to save the World. And, Man, who made me a judge or divider betweene you? And the very Appellation of the Kingdome of Heaven testifies as much. The same thing is gathered out of the words of the Prophet Jeremiah, speaking of the Kingdome of God by the new Covenant, They shall teach no more every man his Neighbour, saying, Know the Lord, for they shall all know me from the least of them, to the greatest of them, saith the Lord, Jer. 31. v. 34. which cannot be understood of a Kingdome in this World. The Kingdome of God therefore, for the restoring whereof CHRIST came into the world, of which the Prophets did Prophesie, and of which praying wee say, Thy Kingdome come, (if it must have Subjects locally separated from Enemies, if judicature, if Majesty, according as hath beene foretold,) shall begin from that time, wherein God shall separate the Sheep from the Goats; wherein the Apostles shall judge the twelve Tribes of Israel; wherein

CHRIST shall come in Majesty, and glory; wherein Lastly, all men shall so know God, that they shall not need to be taught, that is to say, at CHRIST his second comming, or the day of Judgement. But if the Kingdome of God were now already restor'd, no reason could be rendered why CHRIST having compleated the work for which he was sent, should come againe, or why we should pray, Thy Kingdome come.

VI. Now, although the Kingdome of God by CHRIST to be establisht with a new Covenant, were Heavenly, we must not therefore thinke, that they, who beleeving in CHRIST would make that Covenant, were not so to be govern'd here on the Earth too, as that they should persevere in their faith, and obedience promis'd by that Covenant. For in vaine had the Kingdome of heaven beene promis'd, if we were not to have been led into it. But none can be led, but those who are directed in the way. Moyses, when he had instituted the Priestly Kingdome, himselfe though he were no Priest, yet rul'd, and conducted the People all the time of their Peregrination untill their entrance into the promis'd Land. In the same manner is it our Saviours office (whom God in this thing would have like unto Moyses) as he was sent from his Father, so to governe the future Subjects of his heavenly Kingdome in this life, that they might attaine to, and enter into that, although the Kingdome were not properly his, but his Fathers. But the government whereby CHRIST rules the faithfull ones in this life, is not properly a Kingdome, or Dominion, but a Pastorall charge, or the Right of teaching, that is to say, God the father gave him not a power to judge of Meum and Tuum as he doth to the Kings of the Earth; nor a Coercive power; nor legislative; but of shewing to the world, and teaching them the way, and knowledge of Salvation, that is to say, of Preaching, and declaring what they were to doe, who would enter into the Kingdome of Heaven. That CHRIST had receiv'd no power from his father to judge in questions of Meum and Tuum, that is to say, in all questions of Right among those who beleev'd not; those words above cited doe sufficiently declare: Man, who made me a judge, or divider betweene you? And it is confirm'd by reason; for seeing CHRIST was sent to make a Covenant between God and men, and no man is oblig'd to performe obedience before the Contract be made, if he should have judg'd of questions of Right, no man had been tyed to obey his sentence. But that the discerning of Right was not committed to CHRIST in this world, neither among the faithfull, nor among infidels, is apparent in this, that that Right without all controversie belongs to Princes as long as it is not by, But it is not derogated God himselfe derogated from their authority; before the day of Judgement, as appears by the words of Saint Paul, speaking of the day of Judgement, Then commeth the end when He shall have delivered up the Kingdome to God even the Father, when He shall have put downe all rule, and all authority, and Power, 1 Cor. 15. ver. 24. Secondly, the words of our Saviour reproving James, and John, when they had said, Wilt thou that we call for Fyer from Heaven, that it may consume them (namely the Samaritans, who had denyed to receive him going up to Jerusalem) and replying, The Son of Man is not come to destroy soules, but to save them; And those words, Behold I send you as Sheep among Wolves; Shake off the dust of your Feet, and the like; And those words, God sent not his Son into the world, to judge the world, but that the world through him might be sav'd; and those, If any man heare my words, and keep them not, I judge him not, for I came not to judge the world, doe all shew, that he had no power given him, to condemne or punish any man. We reade indeed that the Father judgeth no Man, but hath committed all judgement to the Son, but since that both may, and must be understood of the day of future judgement, it doth not at all repugne what hath beene sayed before. Lastly, that he was not sent to make new Lawes, and that therefore by his Office, and mission, he was no Legislatour properly so called, nor Moyses neither, but a bringer and Publisher of his Fathers Lawes, (for God only, and neither Moyses, nor CHRIST, was a King by Covenant) is collected hence, that he sayed, I came not to destroy (to wit the Lawes before given from God by Moyses, which he presently interprets) but to fulfill; And, He that shall break one of the least of these Commandements, and shall teach men so, He shall be called least in the Kingdome of Heaven. CHRIST therefore had not a Royall, or Soveraigne power committed to him from his Father in this world, but consiliary, and doctrinall onely; which himselfe signifies, as well then when he call his Apostles, not Hunters, but Fishers of men; as when he compares the Kingdome of God to a graine of mustard seed, and to a little Leaven hid in meale.

VII. God promis'd unto Abraham first, a numerous seed, the possession of the Land of Canaan, and a blessing upon all Nations in his seed, on this Condition, that he, and his seed should serve him; next unto the seed of

Abraham according to the flesh, a Priestly Kingdome, a Government most free, in which they were to be Subject to no humane power, on this Condition, that they should serve the God of Abraham on that fashion which Moyses should teach. Lastly, both to them, and to all Nations, a heavenly, and eternall Kingdome, on Condition that they should serve the God of Abraham, on that manner which Christ should teach. For by the new, that is to say, the Christian Covenant, it's covenanted on mens part, to serve the God of Abraham, on that manner which JESUS should teach: On Gods part, to pardon their sinnes, and bring them into his caelestiall Kingdome. We have already spoken of the quality of the heavenly Kingdome above in the 5.

Article; but it is usually call'd, sometimes the Kingdome of Heaven, sometimes the Kingdome of Glory, sometimes the life Eternall. What's required on mens part, namely to serve God as CHRIST should teach, containes two things, Obedience to be performed to God, (for this is to serve God) and Faith in JESUS, to wit, That we beleeve JESUS TO BE THAT CHRIST who was promis'd by God: for that only is the cause why his Doctrine is to be followed, rather than any others. Now in holy Scriptures, Repentance is often put in stead of Obedience, because Christ teacheth every where, that with God the Will is taken for the deed; but Repentance is an infallible sign of an obedient mind. These things being understood, it will most evidently appear out of many places of sacred Scripture, that those are the Conditions of the Christian Covenant which we have nam'd, to wit, giving remission of sins, and eternall life on Gods part; and Repenting, and Beleeving in JESUS CHRIST, on Mens part. First, the words, The Kingdome of God is at hand. Repent yee and beleeve the Gospell, Mark 1:15. contain the whole Covenant: In like manner those, Thus it is written, and thus it behoved Christ to suffer, and to rise from the dead the third day; and that repentance, and remission of sinnes should be preached in his Name among all Nations, begining at Jerusalem, Luke 24. vers. 46, 47. And those, Repent and be converted, that your sins may be blotted out, when the times of refreshing shall come, Acts 3. vers. 19. And sometimes one part is expresly propounded, and the other understood, as here, He that beleeveth in the Sonne, hath everlasting life; He that beleeveth not the Sonne, shall not see life, but the wrath of God abideth on him, John 3. vers. 36, Where Faith is exprest, Repentance not mentioned. And in CHRISTS preaching, Repent, for the Kingdome of heaven is at hand, Mat. 4:17. Where Repentance is exprest, Faith is understood. But the parts of this new Contract are most manifestly, and formally set down there, where a certain Ruler bargaining as it were for the Kingdome of God, asketh our Saviour, Good Waster, what shall I doe to inherit eternall life, Luke 18. v. 18. But CHRIST first propounds one part of the price, namely observation of the Commandements, or obedience, which when he answered that he had kept, he adjoynes the other, saying, Yet lackest thou one thing; Sell all that thou hast, and distribute to the Poor, and thou shalt have Treasure in Heaven, and come, follow me, v. 22. This was matter of Faith. He therefore not giving sufficient credit to CHRIST, and his heavenly Treasures, went away sorrowfull. The same Covenant is contained in these words: Hee that beleeveth, and is baptized, shall be saved, he that beleeveth not, shall be damned, Mark 16. vers. 15, 16. Where Faith is exprest, Repentance is supposed in those that are baptized; and in these words, Except a man be born again of water, and the Holy Ghost, he cannot enter into the Kingdome of Heaven, John 3. vers. 5. Where to be born of water, is the same with regeneration, that is to say, Conversion to CHRIST. Now that Baptisme is required in the two places cited just before, and in divers others, we must understand, that what Circumcision was to the old Covenant, that Baptisme is to the new: Seeing therefore, that was not of the Essence, but served for a memoriall of the old Covenant, as a Ceremony or signe (and was omitted in the wildernesse) in like manner this also is used, not as pertaining to the Essence, but in memory, and for a signe of the New Covenant which wee make with God; and provided the will be not wanting, the Act through necessity may be omitted; but Repentance and Faith, which are of the Essence of the Covenant, are alwayes required.

VIII. In the Kingdome of God after this life there will be no Lawes; partly because there is no roome for Lawes, where there is none for sinne; partly because Laws were given us from God, not to direct us in Heaven, but unto Heaven. Let us now therefore enquire what Laws

CHRIST (establisht not himselfe, for he would not take upon him any Legislative authority, as hath been declared above in the sixth Article, but) propounded to us for his Fathers. Wee have a place in Scripture, where he contracts all the Lawes of God publisht till that time, into two Preceps, Thou shalt love the Lord thy God with all thine heart, with all thy soul, and with all thy minde: this is the greatest, and first Commandement. And the second is like unto it:

Thou shalt love thy Neighbour as thy selfe. On these two Commandements hangs all the Law, and the Prophets, Mat. 22. vers. 37, 38, 39, 40. The first of these was given before by Moyses in the same words, Deut. 6. vers. 5. And the second even before Moyses; for it is the naturall Law, having its begining with rationall nature it selfe. And both together is the summe of all Lawes: for all the Lawes of divine naturall worship, are contained in these words, Thou shalt love God; and all the Lawes of divine worship due by the old Covenant, in these words, Thou shalt love thy God, that is to say, God as being the peculiar King of Abraham, and his seed; and all the Lawes naturall, and civill, in these words, Thou shalt love thy Neighbour as thy selfe. For he that loves God and his neighbour, hath a minde to obey all Lawes, both divine, and humane. But God requires no more than a minde to obey. Wee have another place, where CHRIST interprets the Lawes, namely, the fifth, sixth, and seventh entire Chapters of Saint Matthewes Gospell. But all those Lawes are set down, either in the Decalogue, or in the morall Law, or are contained in the faith of Abraham; as that Law of not putting away a wife is contained in the faith of Abraham: for that same, Two shall be one flesh, was not delivered either by CHRIST first, or by Moyses, but by Abraham, who first publisht the Creation of the world. The Lawes therefore which CHRIST contracts in one place, and explaines in another, are no other than those to which all mortall men are obliged, who acknowledge the God of Abraham. Beside these, we read not of any Law given by CHRIST, beside the institution of the Sacraments of Baptisme, and the Eucharist.

IX. What may be said then of these kinde of Precepts: Repent, Be Baptized, Keep the Commandements, Beleeve the Gospell, Come unto me, Sell all that thou hast, give to the Poor, follow me, and the like? We must say that they are not Lawes, but a calling of us to the faith, such as is that of Isa. Come, buy wine, and milk without monie, and without Price, Isai. 55. vers. 1. Neither if they come not, doe they therefore sinne against any Law, but against prudence onely; neither shall their infidelity be punisht, but their former sinnes. Wherefore Saint John saith of the unbeleever, The wrath of God abideth on him; he saith not, The wrath of God shall come upon him; And, He that beleeveth not, is already judged; he saith not, shall be judged, but is already judged. Nay it cannot be well conceived, that remission of sinnes should be a benefit arising from faith, unlesse we understand also on the other side, that the punishment of sinnes is an hurt proceeding from infidelity.

X. From hence, that our Saviour hath prescribed no distributive Lawes, to the Subjects of Princes, and Citizens of Cities, that is to say, hath given no rules whereby a Subject may know, and discerne what is his owne, what another mans, not by what forms, words, or circumstances, a thing must be given, delivered, invaded, possest, that it may be known by Right to belong to the Receiver, Invader, or Possessour, we must necessarily understand that each single subject (not only with unbeleevers, among whom CHRIST himselfe denyed himselfe to be a judge and distributer, but even with Christians) must take those rules from his City, that is to say, from that Man, or Councell, which hath the supreme power. It followes therefore, that by those Lawes, Thou shalt not kill, Thou shalt not commit adultery, Thou shalt not steale, Honour thy Father and Mother, nothing else was commanded, but that Subjects, and Citizens, should absolutely obey their Princes in all questions concerning Meum Tuum, their own and others Right. For by

122

that Precept, Thou shalt not kill, all slaughter is not prohibited; for he that said, Thou shalt not kill, said also, Whosoever doth work upon the Sabbath, shall be put to death, Exod 35. vers. 2. No, nor yet all slaughter the cause not being heard; for he said, Slay every man his Brother, and every man his Companion, and every man his Neighbour, Exo. 32. v.

27. And there fell of the People about three thousand men, v. 28. Nor yet all slaughter of an innocent Person; for Jephte vowed, Whosoever cometh forth, I will offer him up for a burnt offering unto the Lord, Jud. 11. vers. 31. and his vow was accepted of God. What then is forbidden? Onely this: that no man kill another, who hath not a Right to kill him, that is to say, that no man kill, unlesse it belong to him to doe so. The Law of CHRIST therefore concerning killing, and consequently all manner of hurt done to any man, and what penalties are to be set, commands us to obey the City only. In like manner, by that Precept, Thou shalt not commit adultery, all manner of Copulation is not forbidden, but only that of lying with another mans wife; but the judgment which is another mans wife, belongs to the City, and is to be determined by the rules which the City prescribes: This precept therefore commands both male and female to keep that faith intire which they have mutually given, according to the statutes of the City. So also by the precept, Thou shalt not steal, all manner of invasion, or secret surreption is not forbidden, but of another mans only. The subject therefore is commanded this only, that he invade not, nor take away ought which the City prohibits to be invaded or taken away; and universally not to call any thing murder, adultery, or theft, but what is done contrary to the civill Lawes. Lastly, seeing CHRIST hath commanded us to honour our Parents, and hath not prescribed, with what Rites, what appellations, and what manner of obedience they are to be honoured, it is to be supposed that they are to be honoured with the will indeed, and inwardly, as Kings and Lords over their Children, but outwardly, not beyond the Cities permission, which shall assign to every man (as all things else, so also) his honour. But since the nature of justice consists in this, that every Man have his own given him, its manifest, that it also belongs to a Christian City to determin what is justice, what injustice, or a sinne against justice; Now what belongs to a City, that must be judg'd to belong to him or them who have the Soveraigne power of the City.

XI. Moreover, because our Saviour hath not shewed Subjects any other Lawes for the government of a City beside those of nature, that is to say, beside the Command of obedience, no Subject can privately determine who is a publique friend, who an enemy, when Warre, when Peace, when Truce is to be made; nor yet what Subjects, what authority, and of what men, are commodious, or prejudiciall to the safety of the Common-weale. These, and all like matters therefore are to be learned, if need be, from the City, that is to say, from the Soveraign powers.

XII. Furthermore, all these things, to build Castles, Houses, Temples; to move, carry, take away mighty weights; to send securely over Seas; to contrive engines, serving for all manner of uses; to be well acquainted with the face of the whole world, the Courses of the Starres, the seasons of the yeare, the accounts of the times, and the nature of all things; to understand perfectly all naturall and civill Rights; and all manner of Sciences, which (comprehended under the Title of Philosophy) are necessary partly to live, partly to live well; I say, the understanding of these (because CHRIST hath not delivered it) is to be learnt from reasoning, that is to say by making necessary consequences, having first taken the beginning from experience. But mens reasonings are sometimes right, sometimes wrong, and consequently that which is concluded, and held for a truth, is sometimes truth, sometimes errour. Now, errours even about these Philosophicall points doe sometimes publique hurt, and give occasions of great seditions, and injuries: It is needfull therefore, as oft as any controversie ariseth in these matters contrary to publique good, and common Peace, that there be some body to judge of the reasoning, that is to say, whether that which is inferred, be rightly inferred or not, that so the controversie may be ended. But there are no rules given by CHRIST to this purpose; neither came he into the world to teach Logick. It remaines therefore that the Judges of such controversies be the same with those whom God by nature had instituted before, namely those who in each City are constituted by the Soveraign. Moreover, if a controversie be raised of the accurate and proper signification (i.e.) the definition of those names or appellations which are commonly us'd, in so much as it is needfull for the peace of the City, or the distribution of right, to be determin'd, the determination will belong to the City; for men by reasoning doe search out such kind of definitions in their observation of diverse conceptions, for the signification whereof, those appellations were us'd at divers times, and for divers causes. But the decision of the question whether a man doe reason rightly, belongs to the City. For Example, if a woman bring forth a Child of an unwonted shape, and the Law forbid to kill a man, the question is, whether the Childe be a man. It is demanded therefore what a man is. No man doubts, but the City shall judge it, and that without taking an account of Aristotles definition, that man is a rationall Creature. And these things (namely Right, Politie, and naturall Sciences) are Subjects concerning which CHRIST denies that it belongs to his Office to give any Praecepts, or teach any thing, beside this onely, that in all Controversies about them, every single Subject should obey the Lawes, and determinations of his City. Yet must we remember this, that the same Christ as God could not onely have taught, but also commanded what he would.

XIII. The summe of our Saviours Office was to teach the way, and all the meanes of Salvation, and aeternall life; but justice and civill obedience, and observation of all the naturall Lawes is one of the meanes to

Salvation. Now these may be taught two wayes; one, as Theorems by the way of naturall reason, by drawing Right and the natural Lawes from humane Principles, and contracts; and this Doctrine thus deliver'd is subject to the censure of civill powers: The other, as Lawes, by divine authority, in shewing the will of God to be such; and thus to teach, belongs onely to him to whom the Will of God is supernaturally knowne, that is to say, to Christ. Secondly, it belong'd to the Office of Christ to forgive sinnes to the Penitent, for that was necessary for the Salvation of men who had already sinn'd; neither could it be done by any other; for remission of sinnes followes not Repentance naturally, (as a Debt) but it depends (as a free gift) on the will of God supernaturally to be reveal'd. Thirdly, it belongs to the Office of Christ to teach all those Commandements of God, whether concerning his worship, or those points of faith which cannot be understood by naturall reason, but onely by revelation; of which nature are those that he was the Christ; that his Kingdome was not terrestriall, but celestiall; that there are rewards, and punishments after this life; that the soule is immortall; that there should be such, and so many Sacraments, and the like.

XIV. From what hath beene sayed in the foregoing Chapter, it is not hard to distinguish betweene things Spirituall, and Temporall. For since by Spirituall, those things are understood which have their foundation on the authority, and Office of CHRIST, and unlesse CHRIST had taught them, could not have beene known; and all other things are temporall; it followes, that the definition, and determination of whats just, and unjust, the cognizance of all controversies about the meanes of Peace, and publique defence, and the Examination of doctrines, and books in all manner of rationall science, depends upon the temporall Right. But those which are mysteries of faith, depending on CHRIST his word, and authority onely, their judgements belong to spirituall Right. But it is reasons inquisition, and pertaines to temporall Right to define what is spirituall, and what temporall, because our Saviour hath not made that distinction; For although Saint Paul in many places distinguish betweene spirituall things, and carnall things, and calls those things spirituall, which are of the spirit, to wit, the word of wisdome, the word of knowledge, faith, the gift of healing, the working of miracles, Prophesie, divers kindes of tongues, interpretation of tongues, Rom. 8:5. 1 Cor. 12:8,9. All supernaturally inspired by the Holy Ghost, and such as the carnall man understands not, but he only who hath known the mind of CHRIST, 2. Cor. 2:14–16. And those things carnall which belong to worldly wealth, Rom. 15:27. And the men carnall men, 1 Cor. 3. vers. 1, 2, 3. yet hath he not defined, nor given us any rules whereby we may know what proceeds from naturall reason, what from supernaturall inspiration.

XV. Seeing therefore it is plain that our Saviour hath committed to, or rather not taken away from Princes, and those who in each City have obtained the Soveraignty, the supreme authority of judging determineing al manner of controversies about temporall matters, we must see henceforth to whom he hath left the same authority in matters spirituall. Which because it cannot bee known, except it be out of the word of God, and the Tradition of the Church, we must enquire in the next place what the word of God is, what to interpret it, what a Church is, and what the will and command of the Church. To omit that the word of God is in Scripture taken sometimes for the Sonne of God, it is used, three manner of wayes; First, most properly for that which God hath spoken; Thus whatsoever God spake unto Abraham, the Patriarchs, Moses, and the Prophets, our Saviour to his Disciples, or any others, is the word of God. Secondly, whatsoever hath been uttered by men on the motion, or by Command of the Holy Ghost; in which sense we acknowledge the Scriptures to be the word of God. Thirdly, in the New Testament indeed the word of God most frequently signifies the Doctrine of the Gospell, or the word concerning God, or the word of the Kingdome of God by CHRIST: as where it is said that CHRIST preach't the Gospell of the Kingdome, Mat. 4. vers. 23. Where the Apostles are said to preach the word of God, Acts 13. vers. 46. Where the word of God is called the word of life, Acts 5. vers. 20. The word of the Gospell, Acts 15. vers. 7. The word of faith, Rom. 10. vers. 8. The word of truth, that is to say, (adding an interpretation) The Gospel of salvation, Eph. 1:13. And where it is called the word of the Apostles; For Saint Paul sayes, If any man obey not our word, 2. Thess. 3. vers. 14. which places cannot be otherwise meant than of the doctrine Evangelicall. In like manner where the word of God is said to be sowen, to encrease, and to be multiplied, Acts 12. vers. 24. and Chap. 13. vers. 49. it is very hard to conceive this to be spoken of the voyce of God, or of his Apostles; but of their doctrine, easie. And in this third acception is all that doctrine of the Christian faith which at this day is preacht in Pulpits, and contained in the books of divines, the word of God.

XVI. Now the sacred Scripture is intirely the word of God in this second acception, as being that which we acknowledge to be inspired from God. And innumerable places of it, in the first. And seeing the greatest part of it is conversant either in the prediction of the Kingdome of Heaven, or in prefigurations before the incarnation of CHRIST, or in Evangelization, and explication after, The sacred Scripture is also the word of God, and therefore the Canon and Rule of all Evangelicall Doctrine, in this third signification, where the word of God is taken for the word concerning God, that is to say, for the Gospel. But because in the same Scriptures we read many things Politicall, Historicall, Morall, Physicall, and others which nothing at all concern the Mysteries of our faith, those places although they contain true doctrine, and are the Canon of such kind of doctrines, yet can they not be the Canon of the Mysteries of Christian Religion.

XVII. And truly it is not the dead voyce, or letter of the word of God, which is the Canon of Christian doctrine, but a true and genuine determination; For the minde is not governed by Scriptures, unlesse they be understood. There is need therefore of an Interpreter to make the Scriptures Canon. And hence followes one of these two things, that either the word of the Interpreter is the word of God, or that the Canon of Christian doctrin is not the word of God. The last of these must necessarily be false; for the rule of that doctrine which cannot be knowne by any humane reason, but by divine revelation only, cannot be lesse than divine; for whom we acknowledge not to be able to discern whether some doctrin be true or not, its impossible to account his opinion for a rule in the same doctrine. The first therefore is true, That the word of an Interpreter of Scriptures, is the word of God.

XVIII. Now that Interpreter whose determination hath the honour to be held for the word of God, is not every one that translates the Scriptures out of the Hebrew, and Greek tongue, to his Latine Auditors in Latine, to his French, in French, and to other Nations in their mother tongue; for this is not to interpret. For such is the nature of speech in generall, that although it deserve the chiefe place among those signes whereby we declare our conceptions to others, yet cannot it perform that office alone without the help of many circumstances; For the living voice hath its interpreters present, to wit, time, place, countenance, gesture, the Counsell of the Speaker, and himselfe unfolding his own meaning in other words as oft as need is. To recall these aids of interpretation, so much desired in the writings of old time, is neither the part of an ordinary wit, nor yet of the quaintest, without great learning, and very much skill in antiquity. It sufficeth not therefore for interpretation of Scriptures, that a man understand the language wherein they speak. Neither is every one an authentique Interpreter of Scriptures, who writes Comments upon them: For men may erre, they may also either bend them to serve their own ambition, or even resisting, draw them into bondage by their forestallings; whence it will follow that an erroneous sentence must be held for the word of God. But although this could not happen, yet as soon as these Commentators are departed, their Commentaries will need explications, and in processe of time, those explications, expositions; those expositions new Commentaries without any end: so as there cannot in any written Interpretation whatsoever be a Canon, or Rule of Christian doctrine, whereby the Controversies of Religion may be determined. It remains, that there must bee some Canonicall Interpreter whose legitimate Office it is to end Controversies begun, by explaining the word of God in the judgements themselves; and whose authority therefore must be no lesse obeyed, than theirs who first recommended the Scripture it selfe to us for a Canon of faith; and that one, and the same Person be an Interpreter of Scripture, and a supreme Judge of all manner of doctrines.

XIX. What concerns the word Ecclesia, or Church: originally it signifies the same thing that Concio, or a congregation does in Latin; even as Ecclesiastes, or Church man, the same that concionator, or Preacher, that is to say, He who speaks to the Congregation. In which sense wee read in the Acts of the Apostles, of a Church confused, and of a Lawfull Church, Acts 19. vers. 32, 39. that, taken for a Concourse of people meeting in way of tumult; this, for a convocated Assembly. But in holy writ by a Church of Christians, is sometimes understood the Assembly, and sometimes the Christians themselves, although not actually assembled, if they be permitted to enter into the Congregation, and to communicate with them. For example,

Tell it to the Church, Mat. 18. vers. 17. is meant of a Church assembled; for otherwise it is impossible to tell any thing to the Church: But, Hee laid waste the Church, Acts 8. vers. 3. is understood of a Church not assembled. Sometimes a Church is taken for those who are baptized, or for the professors of the Christian faith, whether they be Christians inwardly, or feignedly, as when we reade of somewhat said or written to the Church, or said or decreed, or done by the Church; sometimes for the Elect onely, as when it is called holy, and without blemish, Ephes. 5. vers. 27. But the Elect, as they are militant, are not properly called a Church; for they know not how to assemble, but they are a future Church, namely in that day when sever'd from the reprobate, they shall bee triumphant. Againe a Church may bee sometimes taken (for all Christians collectively,) as when Christ is called the head of his Church, and the head of his body the Church, Eph. 5. vers. 23. Colos. 1. vers. 18. sometimes for its parts, as the Church of Ephesus, The Church which is in his house, the seven Churches, Lastly, a Church as it is taken for a Company actually assembled, according to the divers ends of their meeting, signifies sometimes those who are met together to deliberate, and judge, in which sense it is also called a Councell, a Synod; sometimes those who meet together in the house of prayer to worship God, in which signification it is taken in the 1 Cor. 14. vers. 4, 5. 23. 28.

XX. Now a Church which hath personall Rights, and proper actions attributed to it, and of which that same must necessarily be understood, Tell it to the church, and, he that obeys not the church, and all such like formes of speech, is to be defin'd so, as by that word may be understood, A Multitude of men who have made a new Covenant with God in Christ, (that is to say, a multitude of them who have taken upon them the Sacrament of Baptisme) which multitude, may both lawfully be call'd together by some one into one place, and he so calling them, are bound to be present either in Person, or by others. For a multitude of men, if they cannot meet in assembly, when need requires, is not to be call'd a Person; For a Church can neither speak, nor discerne, nor heare, but as it is a congregation. Whatsoever is spoken by particular men, (to wit, as many opinions almost as heads) that's the speech of one man, not of the Church; farthermore, if an assembly be made, and it be unlawfull, it shall be considered as null. Not any one of these therefore who are present in a tumult shall be tyed to the decree of the rest, but specially if he dissent; and therefore neither can such a Church make any decree; for then a multitude is sayd to decree somewhat, when every man is oblig'd by the decree of the major part. We must therefore grant to the definition of a Church (to which we attribute things belonging to a Person) not onely a possibility of assembling, but also of doing it lawfully. Besides, although there be some one who may lawfully call the rest together, yet if they who are called may lawfully not appeare (which may happen among men who are not subject one to another) that same Church is not one Person. For by what Right they, who being call'd to a certaine time, and place, doe meet together, are one Church; by the same, others flocking to another place appointed by them, are another Church. And every number of men of one opinion is a Church, and by Consequence there will be as many Churches as there are divers opinions, that is to say, the same multitude of men will at once prove to be one, and many Churches. Wherefore a Church is not one, except there be a certaine, and known, that is to say, a lawfull power, by meanes whereof every man may be oblig'd to be present in the Congregation, either himselfe in person, or by Proxie. And that becomes One, and is capable of personall functions, by the union of a lawfull power of convocating Synods, and assemblies of Christians; not by uniformity of Doctrine: and otherwise, it is a multitude, and Persons in the plurall, howsoever agreeing in opinions.

XXI. It followes what hath beene already said by necessary connexion, that a City of Christian men, and a Church, is altogether the same thing, of the same men, term'd by two names, for two causes: For the matter of a City a Church is one, to wit the same Christian men. And the forme which consists in a Lawfull power of assembling them is the same too; for 'tis manifest that every Subject is oblig'd to come thither, whither he is summon'd by his City. Now that which is call'd a City, as it is made up of men, the same, as it consists of Christians, is styled a Church.

XXII. This too is very cohaerent with the same points, If there be many Christian Cities, they are not altogether personally one church. They may indeed by mutuall consent become one Church, but no otherwise, than as they must also become one City; For they cannot assemble but at some certaine time, and to some place appointed. But Persons, places, and times, belong to civill Right; neither can any Subject or stranger lawfully set his foot on any place, but by the permission of the City, which is Lord of the place. But the things which cannot lawfully be done but by the permission of the City, those, if they be lawfully done, are done by the Cities authority. The Universall church is indeed one mysticall body, whereof CHRIST is the head, but in the same manner, that all men together acknowledging God for the Ruler of the world, are one Kingdome, and one City, which notwithstanding is neither one Person, nor hath it one common action, or determination. Farthermore where it is said that CHRIST is the head of his body the Church, it manifestly appeares, that that was spoken by the Apostle of the Elect, who as long as they are in this world, are a Church onely in potentia, but shall not actually be so before they be separated from the reprobate, and gather'd together among themselves, in the day of Judgement. The Church of Rome of old was very great, but she went not beyond the bounds of her Empire; and therefore neither was she Universall, unlesse it were in that sense, wherein it was also said of the City of Rome, Orbem jam totum victor Romanus habebat, when as yet he had not the twentieth part of it. But after that the civill Empire was divided into parts, the single Cities thence arising were so many Churches; and that power which the Church of Rome had over them, might perhaps wholy depend on the authority of those Churches, who having cast off the Emperours were yet content to admit the Doctours of Rome.

XXIII. They may be called Church–men who exercise a publique office in the Church. But of offices there was one a Ministery, another a Maistery; The office of the Ministers was to serve Tables, to take care of the temporall goods of the Church, and to distribute (at that time when all propriety of riches being abolisht, they were fed in common) to each man his portion; The Maisters according to their order, were called some Apostles, some Bishops, some Presbyters, that is to say Elders; yet not so, as that by the name of Presbyter, the age, but the office might be distinguisht; For Timothy was a Presbyter although a young man; but because for the most part the Elders were receiv'd into the Maistership, the word, denoting age, was us'd to signifie the office. The same Maisters, according to the diversity of their employments were called some of them Apostles, some Prophets, some Evangelists, some Pastors or Teachers. And the Apostolicall worke indeed was universall; the Propheticall to declare their owne revelations in the Church; the Evangelicall to preach, or to be publishers of the Gospell among the infidels; that of the Pastors to teach, confirme, and rule the minds of those who already beleev'd.

XXIV. In the Election of Church–men two things are to be considered, the Election of the Persons, and their consecration, or institution, which also is called ordination. The first twelve Apostles CHRIST himselfe both elected, and ordain'd. After CHRISTS ascension Matthias was elected in the roome of Judas the Traitour, the Church (which at that time consisted of a Congregation of about one hundred and twenty men) choosing two men: And they appointed two, Joseph and Matthias; but God himselfe by lot approving of Mathias. And Saint Paul calls these twelve the first, and great Apostles, also the Apostles of the Circumcision. Afterward were added two other Apostles, Paul, and Barnabas; ordain'd indeed by the Doctours, and Prophets of the Church of Antioch, (which was a particular Church) by the imposition of hands, but elected by the command of the Holy Ghost. That they were both Apostles is manifest in the 13. of the Acts v. 2, 3. That they receiv'd their Apostleship from hence, namely because they were separated by command of the spirit for the work of God, from the rest of the Prophets, and Doctours of the Church of Antioch, Saint Paul himselfe shewes, who calls himselfe for distinctions sake an Apostle separated unto the Gospell of God, Rom. 1. ver. 1. But if it be demanded further; by what authority it came to passe that that was receiv'd for the command of the Holy Ghost, which those Prophets and Doctours did say proceeded from him, it must necessarily be answer'd; by the Authority of the church of Antioch. For the Prophets Doctours must be examined by the Church before they be admitted; For Saint John saith, Beleeve not every Spirit, but try the Spirits, whether they are of God, because many false Prophets are gone out into the world; but by what Church, but that to which that Epistle was written? In like manner Saint Paul reprooves the Churches of Galatia, because they Judaized, Gal. 2. v.

14. although they seemed to doe so by the Authority of Peter; for when he had told them that he had, reprehended Peter himselfe with these words, If thou being a Jew, livest after the manner of Gentiles, and not as doe the Jewes, why compellest thou the Gentiles to live as doe the Jewes? Not long after he questions them, saying, This onely would I learne of you: Received ye the Spirit by the works of the Law, or by the hearing of faith? Gal. 3. ver. 2. Where it is evident, that it was Judaisme which he reprehended the Galathians for, notwithstanding that the Apostle Peter compelled them to Judaize. Seeing therefore it belonged to the Church, and not to Peter, and therefore also not to any man, to determine what Doctors they should follow, it also pertained to the authority of the Church of Antioch to elect their Prophets and Doctors. Now because the Holy Ghost separated to himself the Apostles Paul Barnabas, by the imposition of hands from Doctors thus elected; its manifest, that imposition of hands, consecration, of the prime Doctors in each Church, belongs to the Doctors of the same Church. But Bishops, who were also called Presbyters, although all Presbyters were not Bishops, were ordain'd somtimes by Apostles (for Paul Barnabas when they had taught in Derbe, Lystra, and Iconium, ordained Elders in every Church, Acts 14. v. 23.) sometimes by other Bishops, for Titus was by Paul left in Crete, that he should ordain Elders in every City, Tit. 1. v. 5. And Timothy was advised not to neglect the gift that was in him, which was given him by Prophesy with the laying on of the hands of the Presbytery, 1. Tim. 4. v. 14. And he had rules given him concerning the Election of Presbyters. But that cannot be understood otherwise, than of the ordination of those who were elected by the Church; for no man could constitute a Doctor in the Church, but by the Churches permission. For the duty of the Apostles themselves was not to command, but to teach; and although they who were recommended by the Apostles, or Presbyters, were not rejected, for the esteem that was had of the recommenders, yet seeing they could not be elected without the will of the Church, they were also suppos'd elected by the authority of the Church. In like manner Ministers, who are called Deacons, were ordained by the Apostles; yet elected by the Church. For when the seven Deacons were to bee elected, and ordained, the Apostles elected them not, but look yee out, (say they) among you Brethren seven men of honest report, And they chose Stephen, And they set them before the Apostles, Acts 6. vers. 3, 5, 6. It is apparent therefore by the custome of the Primitive Church under the Apostles, that the ordination, or consecration of all Church—men, which is done by Prayer, and imposition of hands, belonged to the Apostles, and Doctors; but the Election of those who were to be consecrated, to the Church.

XXV. Concerning the power of binding, and loosing, that is to say of remitting, and retaining of sinnes, there is no doubt, but it was given by Christ to the Pastors then yet for to come, in the same manner as it was to the present Apostles. Now the Apostles had all the power of remitting of sins given them, which Christ himselfe had; As the Father hath sent me (sayes Christ) so send I you, John 20. vers. 21. and he addes, Whose soever sins yee remit, they are remitted, and whose soever sins ye retain, they are retained. vers. 23. But what binding and loosing, or remitting and retaining of sinnes, is, admits of some scruple. For first, to retain his sinnes who being baptized into remission of sins, is truly penitent, seems to be against the very

Covenant it selfe of the new Testament, and therefore could not be done by Christ himselfe, much lesse by his Pastors. And to remit the impenitent, seems to be against the will of God the Father, from whom Christ was sent to convert the world, and to reduce men unto obedience. Furthermore, if each Pastor had an authority granted him to remit and retain sinnes in this manner, all awe of Princes, and civill Magistrates, together with all kind of civill Government would be utterly destroyed. For Christ hath said it, nay even nature it selfe dictates, that we should not feare them who slay the body, but cannot kill the soule; but rather feare him who can cast both soule and body into hell, Mat. 10. vers. 28. Neither is any man so mad as not to choose to yeeld obedience rather to them who can remit, and retain their sinnes, than to the powerfullest Kings. Nor yet on the other side, it is to be imagined, that remission of sinnes is nothing else but an exemption from Ecclesiasticall punishments; for what evill hath excommunication in it, beside the eternall pains which are consequent to it? Or what benefit is it to be received into the Church if there were salvation out of it? We must therefore hold, That Pastors have Power, truly, and absolutely to forgive sinnes, but, to the penitent; and to retain them, but, of the impenitent. But while men think that to Repent, is nothing else but that every one condemn his Actions, and change those Counsels which to himselfe seem sinfull, and blameable, there is an opinion risen, that there may be repentance before any Confession of sinnes to men, and that repentance is not an effect, but a cause of Confession; and thence, the difficulty of those who say that the sins of the penitent are already forgiven in Baptisme, and theirs who repent not, cannot be forgiven at al, is against Scripture, and contrary to the words of Christ, Whose soever sins ye remit, We must therefore to resolve this difficulty know in the first place, that a true acknowledgement of sin is Repentance; for he that knows he hath sinned, knows he hath erred, but to will an errour is impossible; therefore he that knowes he hath sinned, wishes he had not done it, which is to repent. Farther, where it may be doubtfull, whether that which is done be a sin or not, we must consider, that repentance doth not precede confession of sins, but is subsequent to it: for there is no repentance but of sinnes acknowledged. The penitent therefore must both acknowledge the fact, and know it to be a sinne, that is to say, against the Law. If a man therefore think, that what he hath done, is not against the Law; its impossible he should repent of it. Before repentance therefore, its necessary there be an application of the facts unto the Law. But its in vain to apply the facts unto the Law without an Interpreter; for not the words of the Law, but the sentence of the Law−giver is the rule of mens actions; but surely either one man, or some men are the Interpreters of the Law, for every man is not judge of his own fact whether it be a sin or not; wherefore the fact of which we doubt whether it be a sinne or not, must be unfolded before some man or men, and the doing of this is confession. Now when the Interpreter of the Law hath judged the fact to bee a sinne, if the sinner submit to his judgement, and resolve with himselfe not to do so any more, tis repentance; and thus, either it is not true repentance, or else it is not antecedent, but subsequent to confession. These things being thus explained, it is not hard to understand what kinde of power that of binding and loosing is. For seeing in remission of sinnes there are two things considerable, one the Judgement or Condemnation whereby the fact is judged to be a sinne; the other, (when the Party condemned does acquiesce, and obey the sentence, that is to say, Repents) the remission of the sinne, or, (if he repent not) the Retention: The first of these, that is to say, the Judging whether it be a sinne or not, belongs to the Interpreter of the Law, that is, the Soveraign Judge; the second, namely Remission, or retention of the sinne, to the Pastor, and it is that concerning which the power of binding and loosing is conversant. And that this was the true meaning of our Saviour Christ in the institution of the same power, is apparent in the 18 of Mat. vers. 15, 16, 17, 18. thus, He there speaking to his Disciples, sayes, If thy Brother sinne against thee, goe, and tell him his fault betweene thee and him alone, (where we must observe by the way, that if thy Brother sinne against thee, is the same

130

with, if he doe thee injury; and therefore Christ spake of those matters which belonged to the civill Tribunall) he addes, if he heare thee not (that is to say, if he deny that he hath done it, or if having confest the fact, he denies it to be unjustly done) take with thee yet one or two, and if he refuse to heare them, tell it the Church. But why to the Church, except that she might judge whether it were a sinne or not? But if he refuse to hear the Church, that is, if he doe not submit to the Churches sentence, but shall maintain that to be no sin, which She Judges to be a sinne, that is to say, if he repent not (for certain it is that no man repents himselfe of that action which She conceives not to be a sinne) he saith not, Tell it to the Apostles, that we might know that the definitive sentence in the question, whether it were a sin or not, was not left unto them, but to the Church; but let him be unto thee (sayes he) as an Heathen, or Publican, that is, as one out of the Church, as one that is not baptized, that is to say, as one whose sinnes are retained. For all Christians were baptized into remission of sinnes. But because it might have been demanded who it was that had so great a power, as that of withholding the benefit of Baptisme from the impenitent, Christ shewes that the same Persons to whom he had given authority to baptize the penitent into the remission of sinns, and to make them of heathen men, Christians, had also authority to retain their sins who by the Church should be adjudged to be impenitent, and to make them of Christian men Heathens; and therefore presently subjoynes, Verily I say unto you, Whose soever sinnes yee shall binde upon Earth, they shall bee bound also in Heaven, and whose soever sins yee shall loose upon Earth, they shall be loosed also in Heaven. Whence we may understand, that the power of binding, and loosing, or of remitting, and retaining of sinnes, which is called in another place, the power of the keyes, is not different from the power given in another place in these words, Goe, and teach all Nations, Baptizing them in the Name of the Father, and of the Sonne, and of the Holy Ghost, Mat. 28. ver.

19. And even as the Pastours cannot refuse to Baptize him whom the Church judges worthy, so neither can they retaine his sinnes whom the Church holds fitting to be absolv'd, nor yet remit his sinnes whom the Church pronounceth disobedient. And it is the Churches part to judge of the sinne, the Pastours, to cast out, or to receive into the Church those that are judg'd. Thus Saint Paul to the Church of Corinth (1 Cor. v. 12): Do not ye judge, saith he, of those that are within? Yet he himself pronounc't the sentence of Excommunication against the incestuous Person, I indeed (saith he, verse 3) as absent in body, but present in Spirit,

XXVI. The act of retaining sinnes is that which is called by the Church Excommunication, and by Saint Paul, delivering over to Satan. The word Excommunication, sounding the same with aposunagogon poiein, casting out of the Synagogue, seems to be borrowed from the Mosaicall Law, wherein they who were by the Priest adjudged leprous, were commanded to be kept apart out of the Camp, untill by the judgement of the Priest they were againe pronounc't cleane, and by certaine rights (among which the washing of the body was one) were purified, Levit. 13. ver. 46. From hence in processe of time it became a custome of the Jewes, not to receive those who passed from Gentilisme to Judaisme, (supposing them to be uncleane) unlesse they were first washed; and those who dissented from the Doctrine of the Synagogue, they cast out of the Synagogue. By resemblance of this custome, those that came to Christianity, (whether they were Jewes, or Gentiles) were not receiv'd into the Church without Baptisme; and those that dissented from the Church were depriv'd of the Churches Communion. Now, they were therefore said to be deliver'd over to Satan, because all that was out of the Church, was comprehended within his Kingdome. The end of this kind of Discipline was, that being destitute for a time of the grace and spirituall priviledges of the Church, they might be humbled to salvation. But the effect in regard to secular matters, that being excommunicated, they should not onely be prohibited all Congregations, or Churches, and the participation of the mysteries, but as being contagious they should be avoided by all other Christians, even more than Heathen: for the Apostle allowed to accompany with Heathen, but with these not so much as to eate, 1 Cor. 5. ver. 10, 11. Seeing then the effect of Excommunication is such, it is manifest in the first place, that a Christian city cannot be excommunicated. For a Christian City is a Christian Church, as hath been declar'd above in the 21. Art. and of the same extension. But a Church cannot be excommunicated; For either she must excommunicate her selfe, which is impossible; or she must be excommunicated by some other Church, and this, either universall, or particular. But seeing an Universall Church is no Person, (as hath been prov'd in the 22. Artic.) and therefore neither acts, nor does any thing, it cannot excommunicate any man. And a particular church by excommunicating another Church doth nothing; for where there is not one common Congregation, there cannot be any Excommunication. Neither if some one Church (suppose that of Jerusalem) should have excommunicated an other (suppose that of Rome) would it any more have excommunicated this, than her selfe: for he that deprives another of his Communion, deprives himselfe also of the Communion of that other. Secondly, No man can excommunicate the subjects of any absolute government all at once, or forbid them the use of their Temples, or their publique worship of God. For they cannot be excommunicated by a Church which themselves doe constitute; for if they could, there would not onely not remain a Church, but not so much as a common–weale, and they would be dissolved of themselves; and this were not to be excommunicated, or prohibited. But if they be excommunicated by some other Church, that church is to esteem them as Heathen. But no christian Church by the doctrine of Christ, can forbid the Heathen to gather together, and Communicate among themselves, as it shall seem good to their Cities, especially if they meet to worship Christ, although it be done in a singular custome, and manner: therefore also not the excommunicated, who are to be dealt with as Heathen. Thirdly, a Prince who hath the Soveraign Power, cannot be excommunicated. For by the doctrine of Christ, neither one, nor many subjects together can interdict their Prince any publique, or private places, or deny him entrance into any Assembly whatsoever, or prohibit him the doing of what hee will within his own jurisdiction. For it is Treason among all Cities, for any one, or many subjects joyntly to arrogate to themselves any authority over the whole City; but they who arrogate to themselves an authority over him who hath the supreme power of the City, doe arrogate the same authority over the City it selfe. Besides, a Soveraign Prince, if he be a Christian, hath this farther advantage, that the City whose Will is contained in His, is that very thing which we call a Church; the Church therefore excommunicates no man, but whom it excommunicates by the authority of the Prince: but the Prince excommunicates not himselfe, his subjects therefore cannot doe it. It may be indeed that an Assembly of rebellious Citizens or Traytors, may pronounce the sentence of excommunication against their Prince, but not by Right. Much lesse can one Prince be excommunicated by another, for this would prove not an excommunication, but a provocation to Warre by the way of affront. For since that is not one church which is made up of Citizens belonging to two absolute Cities, for want of power of lawfully assembling them, (as hath been declar'd before in the 22. Art.) they who are of one Church are not bound to obey an other, and therefore cannot be excommunicated for their disobedience. Now, what some may say, that Princes, being they are members of the Universall church, may also by the authority of the Universall church be excommunicated, signifies nothing: because the Universall church (as hath beene shewed in the 22. Art.) is not one Person, of whom it may be said that shee acted, decreed, determin'd, excommunicated, absolv'd, and the like personall attributes; neither hath she any Governour upon Earth at whose command she may assemble, and deliberate: For to be guide of the Universall church, and to have the power of assembling her, is the same thing as to be Governour, and Lord over all the Christians in the world, which is granted to none, but God onely.

XXVII. It hath beene shewed above in the 18. Art. that the authority of interpreting the Holy Scriptures consisted not in this, that the interpreter might without punishment, expound, and explicate his sentence opinion taken thence, unto others, either by writing, or by his owne voice; but, that others have not a Right to doe, or teach ought contrary to his sentence; insomuch as the interpretation we speak of is the same with the power of defining in all manner of controversies to be determined by sacred Scriptures. Now we must shew that that power belongs to each Church, and depends on his, or their authority who have the Supreme command, provided that they be Christians. For if it depend not on the civill authority, it must either depend on the opinion of each private Subject, or some forraigne authority. But among other reasons, the inconveniencies that must follow private opinions cannot suffer its dependance on them; of which this is the chiefe, that not onely all civill obedience would be taken away (contrary to Christ his praecept) but all humane society and peace would be dissolved (contrary to the Lawes of nature;) for seeing every man is his owne interpreter of Scripture, that is to say, since every man makes himselfe judge of what is pleasing and displeasing unto God, they cannot obey their Princes before that they have judg'd whether their commands be conformable to the Word of God, or not. And thus either they obey not, or they obey for their owne opinions sake, that is to say, they obey themselves, not their Soveraigne; civill obedience therefore is lost. Againe, when every man followes his owne opinion, it's necessary that the controversies which rise among them will become innumerable, and indeterminable; whence there will breed among men (who by their own naturall inclinations doe account all dissention an affront) first hatred, then brawles and warres, and thus all manner of peace and society would vanish. We have farthermore for an example, that which God under the old Law required to be observed concerning the book of the Law, namely, that it should be transcrib'd, and publiquely us'd, and he would have it to be the Canon of Divine doctrine: but the controversies about it not to be determined by private Persons, but onely by the Priests. Lastly, it is our Saviours Precept, that if there be any matter of offence between private Persons, they should hear the Church. Wherefore it is the Churches duty to define controversies; it therefore belongs not to private men, but to the Church, to interpret Scriptures. But that we may know that the authority of interpreting Gods Word, that is to say, of determining all questions concerning God, and Religion, belongs not to any forraign Person whatsoever, we must consider first what esteem such a power carries in the mindes of the subjects, and their civill actions. For no man can be ignorant that the voluntary actions of men by a naturall necessity, doe follow those opinions which they have concerning good, and evill, Reward, and Punishment; whence it happens that necessarily they would chuse rather to obey those by whose judgement they beleeve that they shall be eternally happy, or miserable. Now, by whose judgement it is appointed what Doctrines are necessary to salvation, by their judgement doe men expect their eternall blisse, or perdition; they will therefore yeeld them obedience in all things. Which being thus, most manifest it is, that those subjects who believe themselves bound to acquiesce to a forraign authority in those Doctrines which are necessary to salvation, doe not per se constitute a City, but are the subjects of that forraign power. Nor therefore although some Soveraign Prince should by writing grant such an authority to any other, yet so, as he would be understood to have retained the civill power in his own hands, shall such a Writing be valid, or transferre ought necessary for the retaining, or good administration of his command. For by the 2. Chap. 4. artic. no man is said to transferre his Right, unlesse he give some proper sign, declaring his Will to transferre it; but he who hath openly declared his will to keep his Soveraignty, cannot have given a sufficient sign of transferring the means necessary for the keeping it. This kinde of Writing therefore will not be a sign of Will, but of Ignorance in the contractors. We must consider next how absurd it is for a City, or Soveraign, to commit the ruling of his Subjects consciences to an enemy. For they are, as hath been shewed above in the

5. Chap. 6. artic. in an hostile state, whosoever have not joyn'd themselves into the unity of one Person. Nor contradicts it this truth that they doe not alwayes fight: (for

truces are made between enemies) it is sufficient for an hostile minde, that there is suspition, that the Frontiers of Cities, Kingdomes, Empires, strengthned with Garisons, doe with a fighting posture and countenance, though they strike not, yet as enemies mutually behold each other. Lastly, how unequall is it to demand that, which by the very reason of your demand, you confesse belongs to anothers Right? I am the Interpreter of Scriptures to you who are the Subject of anothers Realme: Why? By what Covenants past between you and me? By Divine authority. Whence knowne? Out of holy Scripture. Behold the Book, read it. In vain, unlesse I may also interpret the same for my self; That interpretation therefore doth by Right belong to me, and the rest of my private fellow—subjects; which we both deny. It remains therefore that in all christian Churches, that is to say, in all christian Cities, the interpretation of sacred Scripture depend on, and derive from the authority of that man, or Councell, which hath the Soveraign power of the City.

XXVIII. Now because there are two kindes of controversies, the one about spirituall matters, that is to say, questions of faith, the truth whereof cannot be searcht into by naturall reason; such are the questions concerning the nature, and office of Christ, of rewards and punishments to come, of the Sacraments, of outward worship, and the like: the other, about questions of humane science, whose truth is sought out by naturall reason, and Syllogismes, drawne from the Covenants of men, and definitions (that is to say, significations received by use, and common consent of words) such as are all questions of Right, and Philosophy. For example, when in matter of Right its questioned whether there be a Promise, and Covenant, or not? That is nothing else, but to demand, whether such words spoken in such a manner be by common use, and consent of the Subjects, a Promise or Covenant; which if they be so called, then it is true that a Contract is made, if not, then it is false: that truth therefore depends on the compacts, and consents of men. In like manner when it is demanded in Philosophy whether the same thing may entirely be in divers places at once; the determination of the question depends on the knowledge of the common consent of men about the signification of the word entire: for if men when they say a thing is entirely somewhere doe signifie by common consent that they understand nothing of the same to be elsewhere, it is false that the same thing is in divers places at once: that truth therefore depends on the consents of men, and by the same reason in all other questions concerning Right, and Philosophy. And they who doe judge that any thing can be determin'd, (contrary to this common consent of men concerning the appellations of things) out of obscure places of Scripture, doe also judge that the use of speech, and at once all humane society, is to be taken away; for he who hath sold an whole field, will say, he meant one whole ridge, and will retaine the rest as unsold; nay, they take away reason it selfe, which is nothing else but a searching out of the truth made by such consent. These kinde of questions therefore need not be determin'd by the City by way of interpretation of Scriptures; for they belong not to Gods Word, in that sense wherein the Word of God is taken for the Word concerning God, that is to say, for the Doctrine of the Gospell; neither is he who hath the Soveraigne Power in the Church, oblig'd to employ any Ecclesiasticall Doctours for the judging of any such kind of matters as these. But for the deciding of questions of Faith, that is to say, concerning God, which transcend humane capacity, we stand in need of a divine blessing (that we may not be deceiv'd at least in necessary points) to be deriv'd from CHRIST himselfe by the imposition of hands. For, seeing to the end we may attaine to aeternal Salvation, we are oblig'd to a supernatural Doctrine, which therefore it is impossible for us to understand; to be left so destitute, as that we can be deceiv'd in necessary points, is repugnant to aequity. This infallibility our Saviour Christ promis'd (in those things which are necessary to Salvation) to his Apostles untill the day of judgement; that is to say, to the Apostles, and Pastors succeeding the Apostles who were to be consecrated by the imposition of hands. He therefore who hath the Soveraigne power in the City, is oblig'd as a Christian, where there is any question concerning the Mysteries of Faith, to interpret the Holy Scriptures by Clergy—men lawfully ordain'd. And thus in Christian Cities the judgement both of spirituall and temporall matters belongs unto the civill authority. And that man, or councell who hath the Supreme power, is head both of the City, and of the Church; for a Church, and a Christian City is but one thing.

CHAPTER XVIII. CONCERNING THOSE THINGS WHICH ARE NECESSARY FOR OUR ENTRANCE INTO THE KINGDOME OF HEAVEN

I. It was ever granted that all authority in secular matters deriv'd from him who had the Soveraigne power, whether he were one Man, or an Assembly of Men. That the same in spirituall matters depended on the authority of the Church, is manifest by the next foregoing proofs; and besides this, that all Christian Cities are Churches endued with this kind of authority From whence a man though but dull of apprehension may collect, that in a Christian City, (that is to say, in a City whose Soveraignty belongs to a Christian Prince, or Councell) all Power, as well spiritual, as secular, is united under Christ; and therefore it is to be obey'd in all things. But on the other side, because we must rather obey God than Men, there is a difficulty risen, how obedience may safely be yeelded to them, if at any time somewhat should be commanded by them to be done which CHRIST hath prohibited. The reason of this difficulty is, that seeing God no longer speakes to us by CHRIST, and his Prophets in open voice, but by the holy Scriptures, which by divers men are diversly understood, they know indeed what Princes, and a congregated Church doe command; but whether that which they doe command be contrary to the word of God, or not, this they know not, but with a wavering obedience between the punishments of temporall, and spirituall death, as it were sailing betweene Scilla and Carybdis, they often run themselves upon both. But they who rightly distinguish betweene the things necessary to Salvation, and those which are not necessary, can have none of this kind of doubt. For if the command of the Prince, or City be such, that he can obey it without hazard of his aeternall Salvation, it is unjust not to obey them, and the Apostles praecepts take place: Servants in all things obey your Masters according to the flesh. Children obey your Parents in all things. Col. 3. v. 20, 22. And the command of CHRIST, The Scribes and Pharisees sit in Moyses chair, all things therefore whatsoever they command you, that observe, and doe. Mat.

23. v. 2. On the contrary, if they command us to doe those things which are punisht with aeternall death, it were madnesse not rather to chuse to dye a naturall death, than by obeying, to dye eternally; and then comes in that which CHRIST sayes, Feare not them who kill the body, but cannot kill the Soule. Mat. 10. v. 28. We must see therefore what all those things are, which are necessary to Salvation.

II. Now all things necessary to Salvation are comprehended in two vertues, Faith, and Obedience. The latter of these if it could be perfect would alone suffice to preserve us from damnation; but because we have all of us beene long since guilty of disobedience against God in Adam, and besides we our selves have since actually sinned, Obedience is not sufficient without remission of sinnes. But this, together with our entrance into the Kingdome of Heaven is the reward of Faith. Nothing else is requisite to Salvation; for the Kingdome of Heaven is shut to none but sinners, that is to say, those who have not perform'd due Obedience to the Lawes; and not to those neither, if they beleeve the necessary articles of the Christian Faith. Now, if we shall know in what points Obedience doth consist, and which are the necessary articles of the Christian Faith, it will at once be manifest what we must doe, and what abstaine from, at the commands of Cities, and of Princes.

III. But by Obedience in this place is signified not the fact, but the Will and desire wherewith we purpose, and endeavour as much as we can to obey for the future: in which sense the word Obedience is aequivalent to Repentance. For the vertue of repentance consists not in the sorrow which accompanies the remembrance of sinne; but in our conversion to the way, and full purpose to sinne no more, without which that sorrow is said to be the sorrow not of a Penitent but a desperate person. But because they who love God cannot but desire to obey the divine Law, and they who love their Neighbours cannot but desire to obey the morall Law, which consists as hath beene shewed above in the 3. Chapter, in the prohibition of Pride, ingratitude, contumely, inhumanity, cruelty, injury, and the like offences, whereby our Neighbours are prejudic't, therefore also Love or charity are aequivalent to Obedience. Justice also (which is a constant will of giving to every man his due) is aequivalent with it. But that Faith and Repentance are sufficient for Salvation, is manifest by the Covenant it selfe of Baptisme; for they who were by Peter converted on the day of Pentecost, demanding him what they should do? He answered, Repent, and be Baptiz'd every one of you in the name of Jesus for the remission of your Sins. Act. 2. v. 38. There was nothing therefore to be done for the obtaining of Baptisme, that is to say, for to enter into the Kingdome of God, but to Repent, and beleeve in the Name of JESUS. For the Kingdome of Heaven is promis'd by the Covenant which is made in Baptisme; farthermore, by the words of CHRIST answering the Lawyer who askt him what he should doe to inherit eternall life, Thou knowest the Commandements, Thou shalt not Kill, Thou shalt not commit Adultery, which refer to Obedience; and, Sell all that thou hast, and come, and follow me, which relates to faith, Luke 18. ver. 20. Mar. 10. ver. 18. And by that which is said, The just shall live by Faith, (not every man, but the just) for justice is the same disposition of Will which Repentance and Obedience are; And by the words of Saint Mark, The time is fulfilled, and the Kingdome of God is at hand, Repent yee, and beleeve the Gospell, by which words is not obscurely signified that there is no need of other Vertues, for our entrance into the Kingdome of God, excepting those of Repentance and Faith. The Obedience therefore which is necessarily requir'd to Salvation is nothing else but the Will, or endeavour to obey, that is to say, of doing according to the Lawes of God, that is the morall Lawes, which are the same to all men; and the civill Lawes, that is to say, the commands of Soveraignes in temporall matters, and the Ecclesiasticall Lawes in spirituall; which two kinds of Lawes are divers in divers Cities, and Churches, and are knowne by their promulgation, and publique sentences.

IV. That we may understand what the Christian Faith is, we must define Faith in generall, and distinguish it from those other acts of the minde wherewith commonly it is confounded. The object of Faith universally taken, namely for that which is beleev'd, is evermore a proposition, (that is to say a speech affirmative, or negative) which we grant to be true. But because Propositions are granted for divers causes, it falls out, that these kind of concessions are diversly called: But we grant Propositions sometimes which notwithstanding we receive not into our mindes; and this either for a time, to wit, so long, till by consideration of the consequencies, we have well examin'd the truth of them, which we call supposing; or also simply, as through feare of the Lawes, which is to professe, or confesse by outward tokens; or for a voluntary compliance sake, which men use out of civility to those whom they respect, and for love of Peace to others, which is absolute yeelding. Now the Propositions which we receive for truth, we alwaies grant for some reasons of our owne, and these are deriv'd either from the Proposition it selfe, or from the Person propounding. They are deriv'd from the Proposition it selfe, by calling to minde what things those words which make up the Proposition doe by common consent usually signifie: if so, then the assent which we give is called knowledge, or Science. But if we cannot remember what is certainly understood by those words, but sometimes one thing, sometimes another seeme to be apprehended by us, then we are said to thinke. For example, if it be propounded that two and three makes five; and by calling to minde the order of those numerall words, that it is so appointed by the common consent of them who are of the same language with us, (as it were by a certaine contract necessary for humane society) that five shall be the name of so many unities as are contain'd in two and three taken together, a man assents, that this is therefore true because two and three together, are the same with five. This assent shall be called knowledge, and to know this truth is nothing else but to acknowledge that it is made by our selves; For by whose will and rules of speaking the number | | is called two, | | | is called three, | | | | | is called five, by their will also it comes to passe, that this Proposition is true, Two and three taken together makes five. In like manner if we remember what it is that is called theft, and what injury, we shall understand by the words themselves, whether it be true that theft is an injury, or not. Truth is the same with a true Proposition; but the Proposition is true in which the word consequent, which by Logicians is called the praedicate, embraceth the word antecedent in its amplitude, which they call the Subject; and to know truth is the same thing as to remember that it was made by our selves in the common use of words. Neither was it rashly, or unadvisedly said by Plato of old, that knowledge was memory. But it happens sometimes that words although they have a certaine, and defin'd signification by constitution, yet by vulgar use either to adorne, or deceive, they are so wrested from their owne significations, that to remember the conceptions for which they were first impos'd on things is very hard, and not to be maistered but by a sharpe judgement, and very great diligence. It happens too, that there are many words which have no proper, determin'd, and every where the same signification; and are understood not by their owne, but by vertue of other signes us'd together with them. Thirdly, there are some words of things unconceivable; of those things therefore whereof they are the words, there is no conception; and therefore in vaine doe we seeke for the truth of those Propositions, which they make out of the words themselves. In these cases, while by considering the definitions of words we search out the truth of some proposition, according to the hope we have of finding it, we thinke it sometimes true, and sometimes false; either of which apart is called thinking, and also beleeving; both together, doubting. But when our reasons for which we assent to some Proposition, derive not from the Proposition it selfe, but from the Person Propounding, whom we esteeme so learned that he is not deceiv'd, and we see no reason why he should deceive us; our assent, because it growes not from any confidence of our owne, but from another mans knowledge, is called Faith: And by the confidence of whom, we doe beleeve, we are said to trust them, or to trust in them. By what hath been said, the difference appeares first betweene Faith, and Profession; for that is alwaies joyn'd with inward assent, this not alwayes; That is an inward perswasion of the minde, this an outward obedience. Next, betweene Faith, and Opinion; for this depends on our owne reason, that on the good esteeme we have of another. Lastly betweene Faith and Knowledge; for this deliberately takes a proposition broken, and chewed; that swallowes downe whole and entire. The explication of words, whereby the matter enquir'd after is propounded, is conducible to knowledge; nay, the onely way to know, is by definition. But this is prejudiciall to Faith; for those things which exceede humane capacity, and are propounded to be beleev'd, are never more evident by explication, but on the contrary more obscure, and harder to be credited. And the same thing befalls a man who endeavours to demonstrate the mysteries of Faith by naturall reason, which happens to a sick man, who will needs chew before he will swallow his wholsome, but bitter Pills; whence it comes to passe, that he presently brings them up againe, which perhaps would otherwise, if he had taken them well downe, have prov'd his remedy.

V. We have seene therefore what it is to beleeve. But what is it to beleeve in CHRIST? Or what Proposition is that which is the object of our Faith in CHRIST? For when we say, I beleeve in CHRIST, we signifie indeed Whom, but not What we beleeve. Now, to beleeve in

CHRIST is nothing else but to beleeve that JESUS IS THE CHRIST, namely Hee, who according to the Prophesies of Moyses, and the Prophets of Israel, was to come into this world to institute the Kingdome of God. And this sufficiently appeares out of the words of CHRIST himselfe to Martha: I am (saith he) the Resurrection and the life, HE THAT BELEEVETH IN ME, though he were dead, yet he shall live, and WHOSOEVER LIVETH, AND BELEEVETH IN ME, shall never dye. Beleevest thou this? She saith unto him, Yea Lord, I beleeve that THOU ART THE CHRIST the Son of God, which should come into the world. John 11. ver. 25, 26, 27. In which words we see that the question BELEEVEST THOU IN ME? is expounded by the answer, THOU ART THE CHRIST. To beleeve in CHRIST therefore is nothing else but to beleeve JESUS HIMSELFE saying that he is THE CHRIST.

VI. Faith and Obedience both necessarily concurring to Salvation, what kinde of Obedience that same is, and to whom due, hath beene shewed above in the 3. Article. But now we must enquire what articles of Faith are requisite: And I say, that to a Christian [1] there is no other article of Faith requisite as necessary to Salvation, but only this, THAT JESUS IS THE CHRIST. But we must distinguish (as we have already done before in the 4. Article) betweene Faith, and Profession. A Profession therefore of more articles (if they be commanded) may be necessary; for it is a part of our obedience due to the Lawes; but we enquire not now what Obedience, but what Faith is necessary to salvation. And this is prov'd first out of the scope of the Evangelists which was by the description of our Saviours life to establish this one Article. And we shall know that such was the scope, and counsell of the Evangelists, if we observe but the History it selfe. Saint Matthew beginning at his Genealogy shewes that JESUS was of the linage of David, borne of a Virgin, Chap. 1. that He was adored by the Wise men as King of the Jewes; that Herod for the same cause sought to slay him, Chap. 2. That his Kingdome was Preacht both by john the Baptist, and Himselfe, Chap. 3, 4. That He taught the Lawes, not as the Scribes, but as one having authority, Chap. 5, 6, 7. That he cur'd diseases miraculously, Chap. 8, 9. That He sent his Apostles the Preachers of his Kingdome throughout all the parts of judea, to proclame his Kingdome, Chap. 10. That He commanded the Messengers sent from john to enquire whether he were the CHRIST or not, to tell him what they had seene, namely the miracles which were onely competible with CHRIST, Chap. 11. That he prov'd and declar'd his Kingdome to the Pharisees, and others by arguments, parables and signes, Chap: 12. and the following Chapters to the 21. That He maintain'd himselfe to be the Christ against the Pharisees, That He was saluted with the title of King, when he entred into Jerusalem, Chap. 21. That he forewarn'd others of false Christs, and That He shewed in Parables what manner of Kingdome his should be, Chap. 22, 23, 24, 25. That He was taken, and accused for this reason, because He said He was a King; and that a Title was written on his Crosse, THIS IS JESUS, THE KING OF THE JEWES, Chap. 26, 27. Lastly, that after his resurrection, He told his Apostles that all power was given unto Him both in Heaven, and in Earth, Chap. 28. All which tends to this end, That we should beleeve Jesus to be the Christ. Such therefore was the Scope of Saint Matthew in describing his Gospell; but such as his was, such also was the rest of the Evangelists; which Saint John sets down expresly in the end of his Gospel, These things (saith He) are written, that ye may know that Jesus is the Christ, the Sonne of the living God.

John 20. vers. 31.

VII. Secondly, this is proved by the preaching of the Apostles. For they were the Proclamers of his Kingdome, neither did Christ send them to preach ought but the Kingdome of God, Luke 9. vers. 2. Act. 15. vers. 6. And what they did after Christ his Ascension may be understood by the accusation which was brought against them, They drew Jason (saith Saint

Luke) and certain Brethren unto the Rulers of the City, crying, These are the men that have turned the world upside down, and are come hither also, whom Jason hath received; and these all do contrary to the decrees of Caesar, saying that there is another King, one Jesus. Acts 17. vers. 6, 7. It appears also what the subject of the Apostles Sermons was, out of these words: Opening, and alleadging out of the Scriptures (to wit, of the old Testament) that Christ must needs have suffered, and risen again from the dead, and that THIS JESUS IS THE CHRIST. Acts 17. vers. 2, 3.

VIII. Thirdly, By the places in which the easinesse of those things which are required by Christ to the attaining of salvation, is declared. For if an internall assent of the minde were necessarily required to the truth of all and each Proposition which this day is controverted about the Christian Faith, or by divers Churches is diversly defined, there would be nothing more difficult than the Christian Religion. And how then would that be true, My yoke is easie, and my burthen light? Mat. 11. vers. 30. and that litle ones doe beleeve in Him? Mat. 18. vers. 6. and that it pleased God by the foolishnesse of Preaching, to save those that beleeve? 1 Cor.

1. vers. 21. or how was the thiefe hanging on the Crosse sufficiently instructed to salvation, the confession of whose Faith was contained in these words, Lord remember me when thou comest into thy Kingdome; or how could Saint Paul himselfe, from an enemy, so soon become a Doctor of Christians?

IX. Fourthly, by this, that that Article is the foundation of Faith, neither rests it on any other foundation. If any man shall say unto you, Loe here is Christ, or He is there, beleeve it not, for there shall arise false Christs, and false Prophets, and shall shew great signes, and wonders, Mat. 24. vers. 23. Whence it followes, that for the Faiths sake which we have in this Article, we must not beleeve any signes, and wonders. Although we, or an Angell from Heaven (saith the Apostle) should preach to you any other Gospel, than what we have preacht, let him be accursed. Gal. 1:8. By reason of this Article therefore we might not trust the very Apostles, and Angels themselves (and therefore I conceive not the Church neither) if they should teach the contrary. Beloved, beleeve not every spirit, but try the spirits whether they are of God, because many false Prophets are gone out into the world, hereby know yee the spirit of God, every spirit that confesseth Jesus Christ is come in the flesh, is of God, 1 John 4. vers. 1, 2. That Article therefore is the measure of the Spirits whereby the authority of the Doctors, is either received, or rejected. It cannot be denied indeed, but that all who at this day are Christians, did learn from the Doctors, that it was Jesus who did all those things whereby he might be acknowledged to be the Christ; yet it followes not that the same Persons beleeved that Article for the Doctors, or the Churches, but for Jesus his own sake. For that Article was before the Christian Church, although all the rest were after it, and the Church was founded upon it, not it upon the Church. Mat. 16. vers.

18. Besides, this Article, that Jesus is the Christ, is so fundamentall, that all the rest are by Saint Paul said to be built upon it, For other foundation can no man lay, than that which is layd, which is Jesus Christ (that is to say, that Jesus is the Christ). Now if any man build upon this foundation, gold, silver, precious stone, wood, hay, stubble; every mans work shall be made manifest: If any mans work abide which he hath built thereupon, he shall receive a reward; if any mans work shall be burnt, he shall suffer losse, but he himselfe shall be saved. 1 Cor. 3. vers. 11, 12, 13. From whence it plainly appears, that by foundation is understood this Article, THAT JESUS IS THE CHRIST. For gold, and silver, precious stones, wood, hay, stubble (whereby the Doctrines are signified) are not built upon the Person of Christ; and also, that false Doctrines

may be raised upon this foundation, yet not so, as they must necessarily be damned who teach them.

X. Lastly, that this Article alone is needfull to be inwardly beleeved, may be most evidently proved out of many places of holy Scriptures, let who will be the Interpreter: Search the Scriptures, for in them yee think yee have eternall life; and they are they which testify of me. John 5:39. But Christ meant the Scriptures of the old Testament only: for the new was then not yet written. Now, there is no other testimony concerning Christ in the old Testament, but that an eternall King was to come in such a place, that He was to be born of such Parents, that He was to teach, and doe such things; whereby, as by certain signes, he was to be knowne: All which testify this one thing, that JESUS who was so born, and did teach, and doe such things, was THE CHRIST. Other Faith then was not required to attain eternall life, besides this Article. Whosoever liveth and beleeveth in me, shall never dye. John 11. vers. 25. But to beleeve in Jesus (as is there exprest) is the same with beleeving that JESUS WAS THE CHRIST. He therefore that beleeves that, shall never dye, and by consequence, that Article alone is necessary to salvation. These are written that yee might beleeve that JESUS IS THE CHRIST the Sonne of God, and that beleeving yee might have life through his name. Jo. 20. vers. 31. Wherefore he that beleeves thus, shall have eternall life, and therefore needs no other Faith. Every spirit that confesseth that Jesus Christ is come in the flesh, is of God. 1 Jo. 4. v. 2. And, Whosoever beleeveth that JESUS IS THE CHRIST, is born of God. 1 Jo. 5. vers. 1. And, Who is he that overcometh the world, but he that beleeveth that JESUS is the Son of God? 1 Jo. 5. v. 5. If therefore there be no need to beleeve any thing else, to the end a man may be of God, born of God, and overcome the world, than that JESUS IS THE CHRIST. that one Article then is sufficient to salvation. See, here is water, what doth hinder me to be baptized? And Philip said, If thou beleevest with all thine heart, thou maist. And he answered and said, I beleeve that JESUS CHRIST is the Sonne of God. Acts 8. vers. 36, 37. If then this Article being beleeved with the whole heart, (that is to say, with inward Faith) was sufficient for Baptisme, it is also sufficient for salvation. Besides these places there are innumerable others which doe clearly, and expresly affirm the same thing. Nay, wheresoever wee read that our Saviour commended the Faith of any one, or that he said, Thy Faith hath saved thee, or that he healed any one for his Faiths sake, there the Proposition beleeved was no other but this, JESUS IS THE CHRIST, either directly, or consequently.

XI. But because no man can beleeve JESUS TO BE THE CHRIST, who, when he knowes that by Christ is understood that same King who was promised from God by Moyses, and the Prophets, for to be the King, and Saviour of the world, doth not also beleeve Moyses, and the Prophets, neither can he beleeve these, who beleeves not that God is, and that he governs the world; it is necessary that the Faith of God, and of the old Testament be contained in this Faith of the new. Seeing therefore that Atheisme, and the deniall of the Divine Providence, were the only treason against the Divine Majesty in the Kingdome of God by Nature; but Idolatry also in the Kingdome of God by the Old Covenant; now in this Kingdome wherein God rules by way of a new Covenant, apostasie is also added, or the renunciation of this article once receiv'd, that JESUS IS THE CHRIST. Truly other Doctrines, provided they have their determination from a lawfull Church, are not to be contradicted; for that is the sinne of disobedience; but it hath been fully declar'd before that they are not needfull to be beleev'd with an inward Faith.

XII. Faith and Obedience have divers parts in accomplishing the salvation of a Christian; for this contributes the power, or capacity; that the Act. And either is said to justifie in its kinde.

For Christ forgives not the sins of all men, but of the Penitent, or the Obedient, that is to say the just, I say not the guiltlesse, but the just; for justice is a Will of obeying the Lawes, and may be consistent with a sinner, and with Christ the Will to obey is Obedience; for not every man, but the just shall live by Faith. Obedience therefore justifies because it maketh just in the same manner as temperance maketh temperate, Prudence Prudent, Chastity chaste, namely essentially; and puts a man in such a state, as makes him capable of pardon. Againe, Christ hath not promis'd forgivenesse of sinnes to all just men, but only those of them who beleeve Him to be the Christ. Faith therefore justifies in such a sense as a judge may be said to justifie who absolves; namely by the sentence which actually saves a man. And in this acception of justification (for it is an aequivocall terme) Faith alone justifies, but in the other, Obedience onely: but neither Obedience alone nor Faith alone doe save us, but both together.

XIII. By what hath been said hitherto, it will be easy to discerne what the duty of Christian Subjects is towards their Soveraignes, who as long as they professe themselves Christians cannot command their Subjects to deny Christ, or to offer him any contumely; for if they should command this, they would professe themselves to be no Christians. For seeing we have shewed both by naturall reason, and out of holy Scriptures, that Subjects ought in all things to obey their Princes and Governours, excepting those which are contrary to the command of God; and that the commands of God in a Christian City concerning temporall affairs, (that is to say, those which are to be discust by humane reason) are the Lawes and sentence of the City deliver'd from those who have receiv'd authority from the City to make Laws, and judge of controversies; but concerning spirituall matters; (that is to, say those which are to be defin'd by the holy Scripture) are the Lawes, and sentences of the City, that is to say the Church (for a Christian City, and a Church, as hath beene shewed in the foregoing Chapter in the 20. Art. are the same thing) deliv'rd by Pastors lawfully ordain'd, and who have to that end authority given them by the City; it manifestly followes, that in a Christian Common weale, Obedience is due to the Soveraign in all things, as well Spirituall, as Temporall. And that the same obedience even from a Christian subject is due in all temporall matters to those Princes who are no Christians, is without any controversie; but in matters spirituall, that is to say, those things which concern Gods worship, some christian Church is to be followed. For it is an hypothesis of the Christian Faith, that God speaks not in things supernaturall, but by the way of Christian Interpreters of holy Scriptures. But what? Must we resist Princes when we cannot obey them? Truly no; for this is contrary to our civill Covenant. What must we doe then? Goe to Christ by Martyrdome. Which if it seem to any man to be an hard saying, most certain it is that he beleeves not with his whole heart THAT JESUS IS THE CHRIST the Sonne of the living God, (for he would then desire to be dissolved, and to be with Christ) but he would by a feigned Christian Faith elude that obedience which he hath contracted to yeeld up unto the City.

XIV. But some men perhaps will wonder, if, (excepting this one Article, that JESUS IS THE CHRIST, which only is necessary to salvation in relation to internall faith) all the rest belong to obedience, which may be performed, although a man doe not inwardly beleeve, (so he doe but desire to beleeve, and make an outward profession, as oft as need requires, of whatsoever is propounded by the Church); how it comes about that there are so many Tenets which are all held so to concern our Faith, that except a man doe inwardly beleeve them, He cannot enter into the Kingdome of Heaven. But if he consider that in most controversies the contention is about humane Soveraignty; in some, matter of gain, and profit; in others, the glory of Wits; he will surely wonder the lesse. The question about the propriety of the Church, is a question about the Right of Soveraignty; for, it being known what a Church is, it is known at once to whom the Rule over Christians doth belong. For if every Christian City be that Church which Christ

142

himselfe hath commanded every Christian subject to that city, to hear, then every subject is bound to obey his City, that is to say, Him, or them who have the supreme power, not only in temporall but also in spirituall matters. But if every Christian City be not that Church, then is there some other Church more universall, which must be obeyed. All Christians therefore must obey that Church just as they would obey Christ if He came upon Earth. She will therfore rule either by the way of Monarchy, or by some Assembly: This question then concerns the Right of ruling. To the same end belongs the question concerning infallibility; for whosoever were truly, and internally beleeved by all mankinde, that he could not erre, would be sure of all Dominion, as well temporall as spirituall, over all mankinde, unlesse himselfe would refuse it; for if he say that he must be obeyed in temporalls, because it is supposed he cannot erre, that Right of Dominion is immediately granted him. Hither also tends the priviledge of interpreting Scriptures. For he to whom it belongs to interpret the controversies arising from the divers interpretations of Scriptures, hath authority also simply and absolutely to determine all manner of controversies whatsoever. But he who hath this, hath also the command over all men who acknowledge the Scriptures to be the Word of God. To this end drive all the disputes about the Power of remitting, and retaining sinnes; or the authority of excommunication. For every man, if he be in his wits, will in all things yeeld that man an absolute obedience, by vertue of whose sentence he beleeves himselfe to be either saved, or damned. Hither also tends the power of instituting societies; for they depend on him by whom they subsist, who hath as many subjects as Monks, although living in an Enemies City. To this end also refers the question concerning the Judge of lawfull Matrimony; for he to whom that judicature belongs, to him also pertains the knowledge of all those cases which concern the inheritance, and succession to all the goods, and Rights, not of private men onely, but also of Soveraign Princes. And hither also in some respect tends the Virgin—life of Ecclesiasticall Persons; for unmarried men have lesse coherence than others with civill society: and besides, it is an inconvenience not to be slighted, that Princes must either necessarily forgoe the Priesthood (which is a great bond of civill obedience) or have no hereditary Kingdome. To this end also tends the canonization of Saints which the Heathen called Apotheosis; for he that can allure forraign subjects with so great a reward, may bring those who are greedy of such glory to dare, and doe any thing. For what was it but an honourable Name with posterity which the Decii and other Romans sought after, and a thousand others who cast themselves upon incredible perils? The controversies about Purgatory, and indulgencies, are matter of gain.

The questions of Free—will, Justification, and the manner of receiving Christ in the Sacrament, are Philosophicall. There are also questions concerning some Rites not introduced, but left in the Church not sufficiently purged from gentilisme; but we need reckon no more. All the world knows that such is the nature of men, that dissenting in questions which concern their Power, or profit, or preeminence of Wit, they slander, and curse each other. It is not therefore to be wondred at, if almost all tenets (after men grew hot with disputings) are held forth by some or other to be necessary to salvation, and for our entrance into the Kingdome of Heaven; insomuch as they who hold them not, are not only condemned as guilty of disobedience (which in truth they are after the Church hath once defined them) but of Infidelity, which I have declared above to be wrong out of many evident places of Scripture; to which I adde this one of Saint Pauls, Let not him that eateth, despise him that eateth not; and let not him that eateth not, judge him that eateth; for God hath received him. One man esteemeth one day above another, another esteemeth every day alike. Let every man be fully perswaded in his own mind, Rom. 14. v. 3, 5.

1. I say, that to a Christian. Although I conceive this assertion to be sufficiently proved by the following reasons, yet I thought it worth my labour to make a more ample explication of

143

it, because I perceive that being somewhat new, it may possibly be distastfull to many Divines. First therefore when I say this Article, That Jesus is the Christ, is necessary to salvation; I say not that Faith onely is necessary, but I require justice also, or that Obedience which is due to the Lawes of God, that is to say, a Will to live righteously. Secondly, I deny not but the profession of many Articles, (provided that that profession be commanded by the Church) is also necessary to salvation; but seeing Faith is internall, Profession externall, I say that the former onely is properly Faith; the latter a part of Obedience; insomuch as that Article alone sufficeth for inward beleefe, but is not sufficient for the outward profession of a Christian. Lastly, even as if I had said that true and inward Repentance of sinnes was onely necessary to salvation, yet were it not to be held for a Paradox, because we suppose justice, Obedience, and a mind reformed in all manner of vertues to be contained in it: so when I say that the Faith of one Article is sufficient to salvation, it may well be lesse wondred at, seeing that in it so many other Articles are contained. For these words, Jesus is the Christ, do signifie that Jesus was that Person whom God had promised by his Prophets should come into the world to establish his Kingdom, that is to say, that Jesus is the Sonne of God, the Creatour of Heaven and Earth, born of a Virgin, dying for the sinnes of them who should beleeve in Him; that Hee was Christ, that is to say a King; that He reviv'd (for else He were not like to reign) to judge the world, and to reward every one according to his works, for otherwise he cannot be a King; also that men shall rise again, for otherwise they are not like to come to judgement. The whole Symbol of the Apostles is therefore contained in this one Article; which notwithstanding I thought reasonable to contract thus, because I found that many men for this alone, without the rest, were admitted into the Kingdome of God, both by Christ, and his Apostles; as the Thief on the Crosse, the Eunuch baptized by Philip, the two thousand men converted to the Church at once by Saint Peter. But if any man be displeased that I doe not judge all those eternally damned, who doe not inwardly assent to every Article defined by the

Church (and yet doe not contradict, but if they be commanded, doe submit) I know not what I shall say to them; for the most evident Testimonies of Holy Writ which doe follow, doe withhold me from altering my opinion.

END

CONTENIDOS

CPSIA information can be obtained
at www.ICGtesting.com
Printed in the USA
LVHW051827111222
735004LV00001B/33